Sufis in Western Society

In recent years Sufism has undergone something of a revival as a spiritual alternative to other manifestations of Islam. This book investigates the development of Sufism in Western societies, with a regional focus on North America and Europe. Exploring a number of issues relating to the dynamic tensions between religious globalization processes and specific sacred localities, this book looks at the formation of Sufi movements that have migrated from their place of origin to become global religious networks.

Sufi groups are highly differentiated and often inaccessible, so the origins and development of Sufism in the West have not been widely studied. Employing a comparative approach based on regional fieldwork and case studies, this book addresses theoretical issues and gives a comprehensive analysis of distinct communities and the development of regional branches of Sufi orders, providing an international perspective on Sufism in the West. With contributions from well-known international experts on the topic, the book addresses Sufi orders in the context of the transnational networks in which they are operating and the constraints of the localities in which they live.

This book will be of interest to scholars and students of religion, Islam and Sufism in particular.

Ron Geaves is Professor of the Comparative Study of Religion at Liverpool Hope University. He has been researching Muslims in Britain since 1988 and is the current Chair of the Muslims in Britain Research Network.

Markus Dressler teaches Religious and Islamic Studies at Hofstra University. His research focuses on the religious history of modern Turkey, religion and secularism theory, and formations of contemporary Sufism in Western societies.

Gritt Klinkhammer is Professor of the Study of Religion at Bremen University, Germany. Her research focuses on diverse facets of Islam in Germany, on theory of secularization and modernity and contemporary forms of religion in Western societies.

Routledge Sufi series
General Editor: Ian Richard Netton
Professor of Islamic Studies, University of Exeter

The Routledge Sufi series provides short introductions to a variety of facets of the subject, which are accessible both to the general reader and the student and scholar in the field. Each book will be either a synthesis of existing knowledge or a distinct contribution to, and extension of, knowledge of the particular topic. The two major underlying principles of the series are sound scholarship and readability.

Previously published by Curzon
Al-Hallaj
Herbert I.W. Mason

Beyond Faith and Infidelity
The Sufi poetry and teaching of Mahmud Shabistari
Leonard Lewisham

Ruzbihan Baqli
Mysticism and the rhetoric of Sainthood in Persian Sufism
Carl W. Ernst

Abdullah Ansari of Herat
An early Sufi master
A.G. Ravan Farhadi

The Concept of Sainthood in Early Islamic Mysticism
Bernd Radtke and John O'Kane

Suhrawardi and the School of Illumination
Mehdi Amin Razavi

Persian Sufi Poetry
An introduction to the mystical use of classical poems
J.T.P. de Bruijn

Aziz Nasafi
Lloyd Ridgeon

Sufis and Anti-Sufis
The defence, rethinking and rejection of Sufism in the modern world
Elizabeth Sirriyeh

Sufi Ritual
The parallel universe
Ian Richard Netton

Divine Love in Islamic Mysticism
The teachings of al-Ghâzalî and al-Dabbâgh
Binyamin Abrahamov

Striving for Divine Union
Spiritual exercises for Suhrawardi Sufis
Qamar-ul Huda

Revelation, Intellectual Intuition and Reason in the Philosophy of Mulla Sadra
An analysis of the al-hikmah al-'arshiyyah
Zailan Moris

Published by Routledge
1   **Muslim Saints of South Asia**
    The eleventh to fifteenth centuries
    Anna Suvorova

2   **A Psychology of Early Sufi Sama**
    Listening and altered states
    Kenneth S. Avery

3   **Sufi Visionary of Ottoman Damascus**
    'Abd al-Ghani al-Nabulusi, 1941–1731
    Elizabeth Sirriyeh

4   **Early Mystics in Early Mystics in Turkish Literature**
    Mehmed Fuad Koprulu
    Translated, edited and with an Introduction by Gary Leiser and Robert Dankoff

Sufis in Western Society

Global networking and locality

**Edited by Ron Geaves,
Markus Dressler and
Gritt Klinkhammer**

LONDON AND NEW YORK

First published 2009
by Routledge
2 Park Square, Milton Park, Abingdon, Oxon OX14 4RN

Simultaneously published in the USA and Canada
by Routledge
270 Madison Ave, New York, NY 10016

Routledge is an imprint of the Taylor & Francis Group, an informa business

© 2009 Selection and editorial matter, Ron Geaves, Markus Dressler and
Gritt Klinkhammer; individual chapters, the contributors

Typeset in Times by Wearset Ltd, Boldon, Tyne and Wear
Printed and bound in Great Britain by TJI Digital, Padstow, Cornwall

British Library Cataloguing in Publication Data
A catalogue record for this book is available from the British Library

Library of Congress Cataloging in Publication Data
Sufis in Western society: global networking and locality/edited by Ron
Geaves, Markus Dressler, and Gritt Klinkhammer.
p. cm. – (Routledge Sufi series)
Includes bibliographical references and index.

1. Sufism–Europe. 2. Sufism–North America. I. Geaves, Ron. II. Dressler,
Markus. III. Klinkhammer, Gritt Maria.

BP188.8.E9S83 2008
297.409182'1–dc22   2008030177

ISBN10: 0-415-45711-4 (hbk)
ISBN10: 0-203-88364-0 (ebk)

ISBN13: 978-0-415-45711-8 (hbk)
ISBN13: 978-0-203-88364-8 (ebk)

Contents

Illustrations

Figures

Table

Acknowledgements

The original idea for this volume came after a panel session entitled "Sufis in Western Societies" held at the annual convention of the American Academy of Religion in Atlanta in November 2003, in which all three editors participated. Building upon the panel, the editors organized a three-day seminar at Bremen University in the winter of 2005, where most of the contributors to this volume attended and gave papers. Our thanks and acknowledgements go to Deutsche Forschungsgemeinschaft for providing the funding which made the seminar possible. We also acknowledge Ian Netton and the editorial staff at Routledge for providing the opportunity for publication. Long-suffering partners need to be remembered for their patience and special thanks to Catherine for her editing work.

1 Introduction

*Markus Dressler, Ron Geaves and
Gritt Klinkhammer*

Islamic mysticism has always played an important role in the development and spread of the Islamic faith. In the Western orientalist tradition, however, Islamic mysticism has often been perceived as distinct from Islam. This understanding is expressed in the concept of "Sufism", which suggests that Islamic mysticism would differ significantly from "orthodox" Islamic practice and belief. From the perspective of the founders of European Islamic Studies (e.g. I. Goldziher, C.H. Becker, S. Hougronje), Sufism served the function of closing the gap between Islamic law, theology and individual piety and was labelled as being secondary to the development of the Islamic mainstream.

In the context of Western colonial prejudices and the racial theories of nineteenth-century Europe, Islam was categorized as a "Semitic" religion like Judaism and both were considered anti-spiritual. Accordingly, Sufism was understood as an "orgiastic collectivistic fanaticism" (M. Weber), or as a "primitive aimless spirituality" in comparison to Christian mysticism (F.A.G. Tholuck). Until the beginning of the twentieth century, only a few Western scholars of Islam viewed Sufism in a positive light, at least insofar as it could be constructed as an antipode to orthodox Islam. However, it was not until the middle of the twentieth century that Sufism came to be understood as an integral part of the Islamic tradition.

The Western categorization of Sufism had been complicated in the nineteenth century when Muslims began to invoke the sacred symbols of the past to resist colonialism. In their quest for a return to an authentic Islamic society, Islamic revivalists targeted not only the colonial West, but also the local Sufi traditions. Muslim reform movements like the Wahhabis claimed to be the only true Muslims and often rejected Sufis as unbelievers. In Saudi Arabia and Iran, Sufi movements face severe restrictions in their activities and are often forced to operate secretly. In Turkey, Sufi Orders have been officially banned since 1925 as a consequence of Mustafa Kemal's attempts to secularize the new republic from above, even if today they are usually tolerated as long as they are not perceived to threaten Turkey's form of secularization. In Egypt, the government exerts control over Sufi Orders through their integration into the state bureaucracy.

Following twentieth-century Muslim migration to Europe and North America, thriving Sufi communities have been developing, originating from outside the

Arabic-speaking world. Muslims from places with vibrant traditions of Islamic mysticism like India, Pakistan, Bangladesh, South-East Asia, Algeria, the Maghreb and South-East Africa have settled in North America and Western Europe. They have brought with them their religious traditions – Sufi or not – and adopted them to their new environments. Often they also brought along the political and social debates of their homelands. The Muslim migration to Europe and the US has offered new prospects for Sufi practice and forms of organization, given the often difficult conditions for Sufism to flourish in many parts of the Muslim world.

The phenomenon of Sufism in the West, however, is not only a product of immigration. A number of Western Sufi Orders have to be understood in terms of processes of "resacralization" in Western societies since the 1960s. At a time when secularization was widely taken for granted as an irreversible process, many from the younger generations of the apparently secularized Western world showed an increasing interest in the spiritual traditions of non-Christian traditions. However, Western curiosity about the spiritual traditions of the East was not totally new. Some Western intellectuals had been fascinated by the ideas of Sufism at the end of the nineteenth and the beginning of the twentieth century and absorbed it into Western esotericism and the ideas of a perennial philosophy. In this context, Sufism in its Western universalist forms formulated a new antimodern and alternative discourse that competed with and critiqued Western modernity[1] whilst Islamic Sufism was simultaneously seen as backward and superstitious by both new Islamic revival movements and Muslim modernists.

The practice of Sufism had been introduced to the West by Western oriental travellers who had come into contact with Islamic mysticism during their journeys in the East, as well as by Eastern travellers to the West, most prominently Hazrat Inayat Khan, who had already in the 1910s founded the Sufi Order in the West with local groups in the United States and in Europe. However, the main Western reception of Sufism began in the second half of the twentieth century when an interesting shift of perception occurred. New Western interest in the East turned colonial stereotypes on their head by proclaiming the East the home of spirituality and mysticism and the West the abode of soulless materialism. Such ideas echoed early attempts by Indian religious figures such as Swami Vivekananda, Paramahansa Yogananda and others to move away from apologia in response to nineteenth-century criticism of their respective religions and to begin to proselytize and market Eastern spiritualities in Europe and North America. This position maintained some appeal to the present day and has influenced the "Easternization" of Western spirituality. Thus, the beliefs and practices of Sufism have been assigned a role as bridge between Eastern and Western spiritual or mystical philosophy. Today this is also manifested in everyday life in the commodification of Sufism in the West, expressed in a thriving Sufi market – especially Sufi music and poetry, but also Sufi rituals used as therapy.

Any study of Sufism in Western societies will have to deal with the problem of how to define its subject. The question of Sufism's relationship to Islam is not only of importance for a critical reassessment of Orientalist scholarship, but much more importantly, one of the most contested issues within contemporary Islamic discourse itself.[2] In the debate on Sufi belief and practice, questions of global and local power politics and Muslim identity are strongly entangled. Given the fact that a comprehensive and systematic study of Islam in Western societies is itself a rather new field of interest and research, it is barely surprising that Sufism in the West, already located at the very margins of Islam from a discursive point of view, has so far been widely neglected despite the pioneering studies of Sufism by scholars in the Orientalist tradition such as Browne, Arberry and Nicholson. The origins, development and consolidation of Sufism in Western Europe and North America continue to constitute a hardly documented and rarely investigated field of research. Scholars are still busy obtaining an overview of the highly differentiated and often barely visible Sufi groups. Therefore, most of the studies on Sufism in the West are not much more than introductions, trying to present a general outline of the history of the best-known Sufi communities in a particular country. Comprehensive work on distinct Sufi traditions is almost nonexistent. Such studies, however, which are based on fieldwork, are of crucial importance for a broader picture.

The emergent study of Sufism in the West should be perceived as part of a shift towards researching Sufism as a lived religion, a vital part of popular or vernacular Islam as well as its significance in the study of diasporic Muslim communities. In 1997 David Westerlund and Eva Rosander alerted scholars to the encounters between Sufis and Islamists in the struggles between Muslims in Africa in their edited work *African Islam and Islam in Africa.* This was followed in 1999 by Elizabeth Sirriyeh's *Sufis and Anti-Sufism.* Both these texts increased awareness of Sufism as a vibrant player in the contemporary Muslim world. Ron Geaves and Pnina Werbner began their interest in British South Asian forms of Sufism in the 1990s. Geaves published his *Sufis of Britain: An Exploration of Muslim Identity* in 2000. In 2002 and 2003 Werbner published her *Manchester Migration Trilogy* which included *Imagined Diasporas among Manchester Muslims* (2002) and *Pilgrims of Love* (2003). In the former she demonstrated the involvement of Sufis in local diaspora politics, and in the latter she documented the global and local manifestations of a Naqshbandi Sufi movement. During the same timeframe Marcia Hermansen was beginning to document both diaspora and American Sufi movements. During the early years of the twenty-first century, a number of scholars in Western Europe and Scandinavia began to research Sufi movements in their respective nations or in the places of origin. The first anthology of Western Sufi movements, *Sufism in the West,* edited by Jamal Malik and John Hinnells, appeared in 2006 with articles by several of the above-mentioned scholars, and more recently, in 2009, *Exile and Tradition: Transnational Contemporary Sufism,* edited by Catharina Raudvere. Many of the same pioneer authors that appear in these works also feature in our work, along with a number of younger scholars drawn to the area. Perhaps *Sufism and the Modern in Islam* should also be mentioned, edited by Martin van Bruinessen and Julia Day Howell and published in 2007. This excellent anthology concentrates principally on Sufism in Muslim majority countries but offers some very good methodological insights and two or three contributions on Sufism in the West. We are beginning to build a literature of case studies that document the transmission of and transition of Sufism to the West and we hope that our endeavour will be welcomed to the pool.

All the above literature focuses on Sufism as a lived religion, unlike traditional scholarship which has often reduced Sufism to certain philosophical ideas, psychological techniques or mystical experiences. The equation of Sufism with its great medieval poets, whose works are translated into various European languages, is an example of a narrow reduction of Sufism. As a consequence of this literary approach and its focus on mystical poems and treatises, Sufism was turned into an extinct tradition represented by exceptional men and women of special mystical consciousness.[3] It is hoped that the present work will help to challenge such Orientalist perspectives with their romantic and literary biases.

The study of Sufism transcends the strict boundaries of the regional and disciplinary compartmentalized field of Islamic study. The research on Sufism has rather uncovered new questions and demands for future approaches, which are connected to the process of globalization. In this regard the following developments and questions are of particular importance: traditional centre–periphery models are losing their viability in the wake of migration and globalization. New Sufi leaders that have emerged in the West, and marginalized groups in the countries of origin can move into a more central position in the country of migration; a prominent example is the Naqshbandi branch led by the Turkish Cypriot Shaikh Nazim al-Haqqani. Thus we have to ask about the impact of the development of Sufi Orders in the West on the transfer of traditions from the places of origin to the countries of migration and vice versa. In some examples, Sufism seems to adopt American and European cultural practices, e.g. strict gender hierarchies are being questioned, although this may not always be the case. Perhaps more significantly, the meaning of East and West starts to lose its geographical significance, for example, when tombs of Sufi masters who died in the West become sacred Muslim spaces and pilgrimage centres.[4]

The process of globalization not only opens the door for the worldwide exchange of social and cultural ideas and practices but also has an impact on transformations of traditional social and cultural behaviour. It creates new bricolage-style, hybrid forms. In the context of post-colonial studies, scholars have not only tried to discover such hybrid identities but understand them as the necessary empowerment of de-colonized people. In this volume we put emphasis on the influence of globalization upon new forms of Sufi identity in the Western world and the impact of the encounter of different cultures upon each other. The underlying assumption is that cultural and sociological theories of identity, which are based on the hypothesis that political, social and cultural encounters produced new discourses of differentiation, hold true.[5] Thus, it is expected that Western perceptions of Sufism as well as the organization of Sufism in the West will evoke new forms of Islamic tradition. Both self-identifications and perceptions of the "other" are challenged in the cultural setting of the non-Muslim West.

For Sufis that have arrived in the West, questions of identity politics and how to cope with the new cultural context whilst re-evaluating their relationships with their respective places of origin are of great importance. One option is to keep contact with the Sufi Order in the place of origin, and to seek reaffirmation of their difference drawing on notions of tradition and authenticity. An alternative is to draw upon new cultural resources originating in the migration process to legitimate innovative practices.

The question of authenticity particularly concerns Western converts to Sufism. They will need to resolve tensions that arise from creating new hybrid forms of Western spirituality or to convert fully to Islam. Sufism has oftentimes attracted Westerners because of its psychological, spiritual and physical techniques for transformation of the self. To some extent, these techniques can be compared to practices of Western human potential psychology, which are sold in the marketplace of new spiritualities.[6] Authenticity, in this context is understood as a technique to embody religion.[7] While the Western process of secularization has made belief in God and in the truth of sacred texts increasingly implausible, the experience of the body is perceived to carry truth more directly. Daniel Gold traces the attraction of Indian religions for Westerners back to their focus on body techniques: the Jewish–Christian intellectualizing process of dealing with religious scriptures has supported a general scepticism towards the written word. Hence, the more practical teachings of Gurus such as meditating, chanting and dancing generate a new "pragmatic" truth for Westerners, which is more bodily marked and immediately plausible and less intellectually comprehensible.[8] Therefore we have to ask questions concerning the significance of the embodiment of rituals in Sufism and their specific attraction for Westerners. Authenticity is also concerned with the religious identity of Sufis as understood by the dominant discourse of practitioners in the place of origin which is perceived as primordial. In some cases, like the Sudanese Burhaniya or the Egyptian Shadhiliya, this means that continuous negotiation is required between close cultural contact with the place of origin and the new cultural context of the West. Orders which are highly hierarchical and/or centralized possibly show dynamics like that. The order's place of origin creates an aura of authenticity. The acknowledgement of the shaikh as authentic is also connected with his ethnic Muslim background. Moreover, it is interesting to see what happens in the reverse situation: a Western shaikh with adherents mostly from the Muslim world or among Westerners of Muslim origin.[9]

As mentioned previously, there is an apparent power struggle between more Shari'a-oriented attempts to create an Islamic orthodoxy and Sufism. This is apparent both in Muslim nations as well as in the Western diaspora. Western converts to Sufism often argue that Islamic mysticism would be more compatible to modernity than other forms of Islam since it is more spiritual and less dogmatic. The assumption that Sufi-Muslims are more likely to adjust to Western societies needs to be questioned. It would appear that traditionally Sufism has been based on charismatic hierarchies and thus one could argue along with Weber that it might have the creative and imaginative potential to overcome rigid social structures. Charismatic rule has the authority to change norms and rules and appears to accommodate flexibility, but on the other hand it is also unpredictable regarding the direction it might take. However, the picture changes when charisma is formalized as a consequence of adjustment to pragmatic concerns. This development can be understood as part of the rationalization or routinization of authority. In the context of Sufi brotherhoods, the question would be how far processes of rationalization are encouraged within Western contexts, or, more broadly, how does charismatic leadership respond to secularized, pluralist Western societies? To which extent will implicit notions of charisma change in the new environments that demand both authenticity and innovation? Will Sufi brotherhoods tend to formalize charismatic structures, or might charismatic leadership undergo democratization? In some communities, for example, the Sudanese Burhaniya in Europe, such a tendency appears to be taking place. The question has been raised as to whether the attraction of charismatic groups in the West might even challenge the democratic principles of Western societies.

Peter Beyer is interested in the impact of globalization on religion and, more precisely, its consequences on questions of authority and authenticity. From there, he addresses one of the major issues of this volume, that is, the question of how particular religious traditions negotiate and legitimize universalized religious norms in the face of their particular local contestations. He argues that one of the consequences of the globalized situation is that religious authority is increasingly becoming de-localized, and multi-centred. Global religion, he holds, "is globalised only in and as particular variations". To capture this semantic, he introduces the notion of the "(g)localization of religion", which allows going beyond constructions of the global and the local as dichotomous antipodes and rather emphasizes their dialectic relationship, i.e. the "(g)local" dimension of religion in the globalized world. The following case studies from North America and Europe provide ample evidence for the centrality of his arguments.

In his attempt to determine how religions with strong exclusivist truth claims deal with the fact of internal variety and dissent, Beyer takes a comparative approach. The case of Islam is instructive in this regard since, as Beyer concludes from comparison with other monotheistic world religions such as Christianity and Judaism, Muslims are relatively less bound to religious institutions that channel and formalize difference. In the case of Islam, the lack of representative organizations, for example churches, is intrinsically connected with the traditional Islamic understanding that religious authority rests in the Qur'an and Sunna, not in hierarchical forms of human authority. As Beyer shows, in Chapter 2, through a comparison of two Canadian female Muslim students, subjective concepts of Islam leave the individual Muslim with a lot of space to individually choose whom to recognize as a religious authority and to individually assert chosen Islamic lifestyles with relatively low pressure. This is especially true for Muslims who follow reformist interpretations of Islam, which are highly critical of culturally specific Islamic practices and traditional authorities (such as ulama, Sufi shaikhs and political leaders), emphasizing instead the normativity of the Qur'an and Sunna as emancipative tools against such authorities. Individualized reformist formulations of Islam go hand-in-hand with strong assertions of the universality of Islam and rejection of the idea of heterogeneity, which is seen as contrary to the premise of Islamic unity. As other contributions in this volume show, this anti-cultural stance often contrasts with Sufism, where authority is located in the Sufi tradition, the Sufi community and the charisma of the shaikh.

The situation of Islam in the US with the large-scale conversion of African-Americans, the melting-pot ideal and the particular immigration history of Muslims in the twentieth century, creates a very singular Islamoscape. In Chapter 3 Marcia Hermansen aims for an approach to Sufism that transgresses static constructs of "global" and "local" by drawing on network theory models. She does so by mapping North-American Sufi movements, with a focus on Shadhili groups, against a scheme of "theirs" and "ours" – categories which she conceptualizes as dynamically transgressing geographic locations. Hermansen exemplifies how cultural locations can be fluid and shifting at times, affected by modes of globalization such as migration, extended use of media – especially the Internet – and travelling. All these processes can foster conversion and encourage the development of hybrid identities and practices. Hermansen demonstrates with particular examples how Sufi groups compete in their adaptation to and negotiation of Western contexts. She reflects on the differences in Sufi approaches to Islamic law (shari'a and fiqh), and in the degree to which they reject (following some of the rhetoric of Islamic revivalists) or integrate local cultural idioms (as, for example, the South Asian Barelwi and the Turkish Fethullah Gulen movement). More specifically and importantly, she questions stereotypes that juxtapose Sufism and revivalist Islamic groups (for example, the Wahhabi) by showing how Sufi groups vary in their rhetoric against Wahhabism, with some rejecting it as their very other, while others align with some of its major tenets such as the call for revivalism, purity and authenticity.

Michael Frishkopf's highly instructive contribution in Chapter 4 draws on his own experience with local Muslim communities of Edmonton, Canada when inviting a famous Egyptian Sufi-Muslim artist, a Qur'an reciter and chanter of traditional religious songs with strong Sufi connotations. He uses the mixed reaction and controversies the visit evoked among the Muslim communities of Edmonton as a matrix for a discussion of how Muslim sonal sensibilities and normativities were transformed through globalization and migration. Frishkopf shows how second- and third-generation Canadian Muslims, accustomed to the comparatively silent, textual and rational forms of Islam, as espoused by revivalist and Islamist currents, become uneasy when confronted with the rich traditional "soundworlds" of a Muslim majority country such as Egypt and have problems integrating Muslim music and song into their more narrowly defined sense of what is considered licit within Islam. Skilfully combining his musicologist and Islamicist training, Frishkopf uses his case to sketch out the impact of modern developments such as the medialization of culture, the success of rational/textual and sound-critical interpretations of Islam, and the impacts of globalization on Islamic soundworlds. He argues that the disruptions and shifts thus created lead to new Islamic "soundscapes", a term used to convey the sense

of dislocation, disruption and hybridity caused by the globalizing forces of capitalism and migration and their impact on consumer tastes and new reifications of
religion and culture.

Based on research in the New York City area, Markus Dressler explores the
discursive and practical negotiation of Sufi-Muslim identities in a North American metropolitan context in Chapter 5. He focuses on how religious boundaries
between Muslims are formulated and contested within a pluralist framework.
The chapter gives examples of how Sufi groups adapt to pluralist situations in
non-Muslim majority countries. Reflecting the heterogeneity of Sufism in the
West, Sufi communities in New York represent not only different orientations of
Sufism but also position themselves in a variety of ways towards American
culture and society. These positions range from a very critical stance towards
American society in general and a strongly integrative position that tries to amal-
gamate Sufi-Muslim and American values and identities. Dressler then draws out
some of the ways in which Sufi-Muslim groups adjust to the pluralist situation,
showing how Sufis use the new opportunity spaces to negotiate their particular
Sufi identities in the light of a rather competitive Sufi scene. His contribution
makes clear that the particular ethnic, cultural and social backgrounds of Sufis
have an impact on how Sufism is re-formulated in the West. Despite these cen-
trifugal forces, however, Dressler argues that it is precisely the secular pluralist
environment that creates possibilities to bridge differences by emphasizing
common Sufi traditions allowing for Sufis to join forces in their attempt to prove
their legitimacy within Islam, in addition to improving the perception of Islam to
the non-Muslim public.

The next two contributions shift the geographical location to Britain. Ron
Geaves discusses the transformations traditional Muslims in Britain with roots in
Sufism have undergone in the last decades in Chapter 6. Based on his extensive
research on Sufism in England, he argues that after a long phase in which Sufi-
inclined Muslims tended to simply reproduce the religion and culture of their –
mainly South Asian – homelands, a mode which he terms "Cultural Binary
Fission", there are recently developments which reflect increasing willingness to
engage more constructively with the socio-cultural realities of the new homeland
and the need to transform but continue historic strategies for legitimacy in the
face of reformist rhetoric. There are the needs of the British-born generations,
which are gradually moving away from the cultural norms and ethnic identities
offered by their parents and grandparents. These younger generations are more
likely to seek refuge in culturally and ethnically less exclusive, universalist ren-
ditions of Islam such as those conceptions offered by Salafi and Wahhabi movements. This trend naturally moves them away from the Sufi-inspired
interpretations of Islam of their parents so deeply embedded in South-Asian
Muslim culture. However, as Geaves shows, there are increasingly more
attempts to counter the anti-Sufi criticism of the revivalists. Thus, on a national
and transnational scale, traditional Muslims attempt to strengthen the legitimacy
of the Sufi tradition and focus on spirituality. This brings up the important question as to whether the reassertion of Sufi elements within a less culturally and

ethnically specific framework will lead to new forms of Sufism, more transglobal in nature, and less bound to traditional tariqa structures of allegiance, but still focused on traditional Sufi values and practices, reified as "traditional Islam".

Pnina Werbner's contribution in Chapter 7 discusses the case of a Sufi circle in Manchester and the ways in which its leader, Shaikh Abidi, establishes his authority. She argues that in the diasporic situation the Muslim community is not only created through traditional allegiances such as kinship and politically driven agendas as in the many reformist movements, but that the new environment "opens up new worlds of association and trust within the modern nation-state". In the case of Shaikh Abidi's circle, community is created through the shared belief in the shaikh's charisma and a relationship of intimacy shared by him and his adherents. Shaikh Abidi is a true esoteric, deeply embedded in traditional Muslim numerological studies and practices through which he aims to penetrate the divine mystery. While the sources of his authority are rather traditional – he claims to descend from Ali, is a recognized healer, interpreter and author of mystical texts and admired for his ability as a seer – he also transgresses traditional boundaries, for example, when he dismisses questions of his tariqa affiliation, or when he publicly takes issues with Islamic norms and beliefs such as the prohibition on music, or the idea of beautiful virgins awaiting the male Muslims in paradise. In his numerological endeavours he employs modern tools such as computers for his mystical speculations, rendering modern technology as just another means of proving the mystery of God and for the numerological interpretation of sacred texts. Shaikh Abidi and his small circle are a fascinating example for the diverse ways in which modern diaspora Muslims establish authority, authenticity and legitimacy. Examples like this are important since they complicate broad sociological schemes such as the tradition–modernity dichotomy and bring our intention to more subtle categories such as intimacy and charismatic evidence.

The next two studies focus on Sufism in Germany. In Chapter 8 Gritt Klinkhammer charts how Sufism began to be studied in the classical tradition of German Orientalism with its focus on mystical writings. She shows that the German view of Islam, and Sufism in particular, is in some respects different to that of the classical European Orientalist countries, such as Great Britain and France, because of its lack of colonial engagement in the Orient. In Germany, an aesthetic turn to the Orient, imagining the Orient as positive and ethical, could be observed during the eighteenth and early nineteenth century. This, in turn, influenced the development of a more experience-based form of Sufism introduced in Germany in the 1960s and 1970s by people who did not seek a new religion, but were searching for a spiritual self. Consequently, the spread of mainstream Sufism was only minimally related to the immigration of labourers in the 1960s. The presence of trans-ethnic Sufism in Germany must be identified and investigated as a phenomenon within the scope of the "re-sacralization" of Western society, which began in the early 1970s.

In Chapter 9, however, Søren Lassen explores a Burhaniya tariqa originating in the Sudan that has transmigrated into Germany through the processes described by Klinkhammer. He explores the arrival of the second-generation Burhanis who are born both Muslim and Burhani. However, in recent years Germany has received migrant Sudanese, and the spiritual seekers of the first generation have become more under the orthodox influence of the Sudanese shaikhs. A recent development has seen the new leader of the order marry a second-generation German murid and move to Germany, thus merging the two types of follower but also relocating the centre of the order from Sudan to Western Europe. This will have a major impact on the reproduction of Sudanese culture and its relationship with German culture in future years.

In the example of Gaši and Raudvere, in Chapter 10, it is, however, precisely the possibility to reproduce Bosnian culture in Sweden, made possible by the size of the Bosnian community and state support for ethno-culturally specific spaces, that enables the Bosnian community of Malmö to stick to its Sufi-entrenched practices. The concentration of Muslims from a particular back-ground and the amount of time passed since the migration, as well as long-term prospects in the host country, obviously play an important role. In the US, where immigration has largely focused on attracting well-educated, highly skilled immigrants, Muslims are socially positioned very differently compared to a place like Sweden, where Muslim immigration is dominated by labour immigra-tion and civil-war refugees.

It is interesting to compare Frishkopf's analysis of diasporic Islam in Canada with Gaši and Raudvere's discussion of a Bosnian immigrant community in Sweden. While both host countries espouse forms of multicultural politics, the specific consequences thereof for the more traditional Sufi forms of Islam within the particular Swedish and Canadian "Islamoscapes" are rather different. As Frishkopf argues, multiculturalism can increase the pressure on Muslim com-munities to represent themselves as a homogeneous unit towards the non-Muslim public, thus discouraging the display and continuation of culturally specific prac-tices; Sufism, in its diverse forms embedded in particular Muslim cultures, is disadvantaged in such a situation.

Ašk Gaši and Catharina Raudvere provide an interesting example of how the multicultural Swedish politics of "strategic pluralism" support Bosnian institution-building in the Swedish diaspora. The authors describe how Sufi lan-guage and practices help a Bosnian immigrant community in Malmö "to define heritage in times of national awakening and also to cope with life in new circum-stances". The case of the featured community shows how Bosnian Islam, com-paratively less influenced by reformist objectifications of Islam as a universal doctrine, draws successfully on locally specific, i.e. Bosnian, idioms and prac-tices, which are permeated by Sufism and simultaneously support both religious and national identities – a double function which universalist reformist rendi-tions of Islam are unable to offer due to their attitude towards local cultural spe-cifics, which they tend to regard with suspicion, if not rejection. In the portrayed community, Sufi practices are packaged in Bosnian vernacular idioms more so than in explicitly Sufi language. This is an important observation since it points to the relatively low degree of objectification of Sufism in a context where it is still a broadly unquestioned part of Islamic lifestyle and worldview and where Islam and Sufism have accordingly not yet been divided into potentially competing entities. On top of this, Gaši and Raudvere show how Bosnian Sufi practitioners, which are organized in more or less institutionalized forms of Sufi practice, draw on local idioms to defend their Islamic lifestyles and reject Wahhabi-style universalism.

In the final chapter, Mark Sedgwick examines the extent, origins and nature of the popularity of Sufi literature. He confirms that Sufi literature is now read in the West by millions, traces this phenomenon back to 1812, and argues that Sufi literature in the West is mostly read in distinctively Western ways. He concludes that the popularity of Sufi and neo-Sufi texts must be seen in the context of contemporary Western spirituality, as well as of contemporary Western tastes in poetry. He contends that these two contexts are a more appropriate way of understanding the popularity of Sufi and neo-Sufi literature in the West than any analysis that supposes a revolt against rationality or a crisis of liberalism. He concludes that the phenomena can be understood in terms of globalization. Globalization also implies "localization", however, as any of today's global businesses know well. A global product must be adapted for local circumstances and tastes. Sufism became a global product in the nineteenth century, and during the twentieth century was localized for Western consumption by the neo-Sufis his article discusses.

Notes

1 Sedgwick (2004).
2 Sirriyeh (2001).
3 The work of Annemarie Schimmel has often been criticized in this regard.
4 Ernst (1997).
5 See, for example, Luhmann (1993: 243). For corresponding criticism on Edward Said see Al-Azm (2000).
6 See Carrette and King (2005: Chapter 2).
7 See also Csordas (2002) and Werbner and Basu (1998).
8 Gold (1988: 121).
9 Stauth (1999) and Robertson (1995: 25–44). You can describe these processes as the "Glocalization" and "Fragmentation" of identities which are countered by the emphasis of regional styles of origin and authentic experiences of "the Self".

References

Al-Azm, S.J. (2000) "Orientalism and Orientalism in Reverse", in Macfie, A.L. (ed.) *Orientalism: a Reader*, New York: New York University Press, 217–238.
Carrette, J. and King, R. (2005) *Selling Spirituality. The Silent Takeover of Religion*, London: Routledge.
Csordas, Th. (2002) *Body/Meaning/Healing*, New York: Palgrave Macmillan.
Ernst, C.W. (1997) *The Shambala Guide of Sufism. An Essential Introduction to the Philosophy and Practice of the Mystical Tradition of Islam*, Boston and London: Shambala.
Gold, D. (1988) *Comprehending the Guru. Towards a Grammar of Religious Perception*, Atlanta: Scholars Press.

Luhmann, N. (1993) *Soziale Systeme. Grundriss einer allgemeinen Theorie*, Frankfurt am Main: Suhrkamp.

Robertson, R. (1995) "Glocalization: Time-Space and Homogeneity and Heterogeneity", in Featherstone, M., Lash, S. and Robertson, R. (eds) *Global Modernities*, London: Sage, 25–44.

Sedgwick, M. (2004) *Against the Modern World. Traditionalism and the Secret Intellectual History of the Twentieth Century*, New York: Oxford University Press.

Sirriyeh, E. (2001) *Sufis and Anti-Sufis: the Defence, Rethinking and Rejection of Sufism in the Modern World*, Richmond: Curzon Press.

Stauth, G. (1999) *Authentizität und kulturelle Globalisierung*, Bielefeld: transcript.

Werbner, P. and Basu, H. (eds) (1998) *Embodying Charisma: Modernity, Locality and the Performance in Sufi Cults*, London: Routledge.

2 Glocalization of religions

Plural authenticities at the centres and at the margins

Peter Beyer

Among the more remarkable features of religions in our contemporary world are the following: first, virtually in all regions of global society, we find a similar idea of what counts as religion and what are to be recognized as religions. Second, what counts and what is recognized is nonetheless highly contested, principally along two lines, between religion and non-religion and between one religion and another. Third, every religion exhibits a high degree of internal variety, often to such an extent that one may legitimately wonder what it is that nonetheless makes for the unity of any one of them. These three features are, of course, interconnected. Contestation around what should count as one of the religions often takes the form of declaring a particular religion as a non-religion, for instance, Scientology in some countries; or of disagreeing about whether a certain manifestation is within the fold or outside of it. For example, are Jehovah's Witnesses or Mormons Christians? Is Baha'i a separate religion or a heretical movement within Islam? Are Sikhs a variety of Hindus?

In what follows, I want to concentrate on the question of how religions manage and understand internal variety, and how that management has an effect on how a religion is perceived both among its adherents and among outside observers. My fundamental hypothesis in this regard is that this question is very much related to the globalized social context in which we all find ourselves. Today's religions are to a significant extent modern and increasingly global (re) constructions, meaning not that they have been necessarily recently invented, but rather that the modern globalized context has brought about re-formation (and only in that context reformation) of religions in particular ways. Above all, as globalized structures, religions are no longer (to the extent that in any particular case they ever were) regional affairs which can be understood primarily with reference to a particular core region, a region that serves as the centre of authenticity and authority and with respect to which all else is peripheral, marginal and comparatively inauthentic. Rather, in the process of their globalization, they have become (even more) multi-centred such that the claim to authenticity and authority of any particular variation is no longer nearly as much dependent on geographic location, concentration of adherents or longevity of existence. The variation that can successfully claim legitimacy as a version of that religion need not be located in a particular place or even any particular place at all; it can have very few adherents and still be highly influential; it can also be of very recent provenance. What is more, that situation is fluid, subject to change in relatively short order. Another way of putting this is that the global or globalized religion is not by itself already a clear universal against which all particular versions can be measured. Rather the global religion, say Islam or Christianity or Buddhism, is globalized only in and as particular variations. It is both global and local at the same time; any variation can be global only as a series of localized forms. Hence the globalization of religion has taken the form of the *glocalization* of religions; the authentic variations are not only plural, they are located both at the centres and at the margins or at neither, irrespective of how one conceives these.[1]

Rather than elaborate this argument in such an abstract fashion, I want to take and then develop a specific and reasonably concrete example, that of Islam in today's world, and to do so from a Canadian point of departure. My central aim is to show how the concrete management of unity and diversity in Islam affects the image and the reality of that religion. Unity and diversity in religions are not just facts; they have to be constructed and understood in particular ways and these ways are themselves subject to variation, which is to say that they are contingent.

Corresponding to this aim, I turn first to a story of two young Canadian Muslim women, let us call them Noor and Maryam (not their real names).[2] They attend the same university in Toronto, Canada; they are ambitious, self-confident and have high expectations of themselves. They are the children of relatively recent immigrants, but they grew up in Canada, are at home there and lead comfortable, middle-class lives. They look and sound like a great many other Canadians in the large urban agglomerations they inhabit, especially in the Toronto region with its rich mixture of people with origins in all parts of the world. Moreover, they are both highly practising Muslims; Islam is a very important part, from some aspects the most important part, of their lives and certainly a key part of their sense of themselves.

Their visions of what is most important about being a Muslim are in many senses quite similar. For instance, they both insist on the absolute centrality of the Qur'an and the Traditions of the Prophet Muhammad, on the five pillars of Islam as the core of Islamic practice, and on a common series of moral prescripts, including halal dietary regulations, scrupulous modesty and the eschewing of all sexual relations before heterosexual marriage to another Muslim. Other similarities are no less significant. Both are involved in Muslim organizations, specifically the Muslim Student Association (MSA) on their respective campuses. Beside these associations, their main source of inspiration and knowledge about Islam is through personal study, sometimes through talking to other Muslims in whom they have some confidence, but mostly through direct consultation of sources, especially the Qur'an and the Sunna of the Prophet, as well as secondary print and Internet sources that they have come to regard as reliable. This individualistic, non-mediated style of deciding on authentic Islam is fairly critical. It means, among other things, that they do not place imams, ulama, their parents, MSA leaders or other authority figures in the centre of their sense of correct belief and practice. They trust in the ability of each Muslim to have direct access to what is true in Islam and what therefore is not part of Islam or at least a matter of interpretation and variation. Corresponding to this individualism, they share a relative distrust of the leadership in the Muslim world, and are not hesitant to criticize, where they feel it is warranted, their fellow Muslims for themselves being ignorant about what Islam is all about. In this context, they both draw a clear distinction between Islamic religion and the cultures in which it is embedded, feeling that too often other Muslims confuse cultural styles with authentic Islam. It is on this basis, for instance, that they not infrequently disagree with their parents on various issues, although it must also be said that they both hold their parents in the highest regard – another Islamic value – even if they do not also feel obliged to do what they say and believe as they believe.

In the light of this congruence, the differences are potentially just as significant. For Maryam, Islam is above all about how to lead the correct, God-willed life. Her search takes the form of trying to decide what she must do as a Muslim and what she must avoid, what is necessary and what is optional. For her, part of being a Muslim is an ongoing personal search for what is correct or incorrect; she changes her behaviour and attitudes as this search reveals new things to her. Thus, over the past few years, she has become progressively more stringent about what sort of contact she has with men; she now takes care not to socialize with men on a one-on-one basis, but has no problem working with men in the context of her studies and other public activities. Moreover, recently she has begun to wear hijab on a regular basis, in each case having come to these conclusions after researching what Islam truly required. Her attitude to other religions and the secular world around her is tolerant in that she accepts that other people act and believe differently; but she is convinced that Islam is the only really true path and describes what she has been doing over the past few years as a process of "minoritizing" herself, of making herself a member of a minority that looks, believes and acts differently from the majority. Her Islam, in sum, is very rule and obedience oriented; it separates her from the world around her and is thereby slightly but not extremely sectarian; and it, as opposed to a national or ethnic identity, is the centre of her identity.

Noor, in contrast, places value questions at the centre of her Islam. She considers honesty along with humility and modesty to be the cardinal virtues enjoined by Islam. Rules are to be understood in that light. This differing emphasis has different outcomes when compared to Maryam. Noor is more positively oriented to people of other faiths; Islam is the correct path for her, but she accepts that this is not the case for others. Mutual toleration of religions on an equal footing is important to her. In addition, she admits to having difficulty with certain teachings of Islam, for instance the insistence on male/female segregation. Her interpretation of the possibility of polygamy in Islam effectively eliminates it, saying that a second wife can only be had if the first wife gives her express consent. She makes a distinction between culture and religion when it comes to dating members of the opposite sex: the blanket proscription of such dating is cultural; Islam forbids pre-marital sexual relations. And yet she does not date. What is more, Noor does not wear hijab. Yet she admires Muslim women who do, not because, as Maryam would have it, this is in the final analysis what Islam enjoins, but because such women must have such a strong and confident sense of themselves as Muslims that they can do this. It is what it says about the integrity of the person that makes it important, not because it is a rule. Finally, Noor is a dancer. She considers this merely a phase of her life and says that, once she stops, perhaps in the context of raising a family, she may come to the point where she too will wear hijab. Interestingly enough, whereas Maryam feels that she is a stronger Muslim than a great many of her fellows, Noor feels she is less religious than many others, but without condemning herself for it. This difference again points to the common core that the two women share, albeit indirectly in this case.

On one level, these introductory vignettes simply tell the story of two young Canadian Muslim women, how they understand their religion and their place in the world. There are hundreds of millions of other Muslim women and men in Canada and elsewhere who could also tell their stories and relate their understandings of Islam. The same observation could be made with respect to the billions of both women and men who follow other religious paths or none at all. On a different level, however, these two examples point to a much broader problematic in that they indicate something significant about the place and structure of religion in our contemporary world, and most particularly about Islam as one of two religions in that world which can claim something close to the status of a religious "superpower". The other such religion is, of course, Christianity.

One can begin with the idea, quite clear in the minds of both Noor and Maryam, that Islam is something distinct and systematic, with definite structure that identifies it and separates it from all that which is not Islam, whether it is another religion or just the secular world. Our two subjects are entirely aware of this religious and secular world around them. That said, Islam is also for them something encompassing, a system of living that touches on all areas of life. While Maryam is perhaps a little less charitable as concerns the validity of the other ways of living that surround her, both are reasonably tolerant of these, by contrast, other religious and secular life paths. Islam is only one (albeit, for them, the best) religion among at least several and there are non-religious people in the world and, indeed, among one's friends and relations.

While that much may seem pretty obvious, it also almost goes without saying that there are other Muslims in the world, and indeed among Noor and Maryam's fellow Muslim women in Canada, who reject this view of Islam, either as concerns the validity and tolerance of other paths and the secular world, or with respect to the centrality of Islam that these two women espouse. I could have chosen such contrasting opinions from among the research participants of which Maryam and Noor are but two. Some would declare the falseness of any other religion and deny the legitimacy of a secularized world in which Islam is but one possibility among many. Others would reject the idea that Islam as religion and as way of life should be all that central and all-encompassing. What the two young women therefore point to indirectly is not only the systematic identity of

Islam as religion, but also difference both within and outside the Islamic fold. That brings us to a second point concerning where these differences and this identity are located.

Maryam and Noor are the children of immigrants (Maryam is actually of mixed Pakistani and Quebec parentage), meaning that each of them has relations, with which they are often still in regular contact, in other parts of the world. While these two and many other Muslims live in Canada and are also Canadians, most Muslims live in other regions of global society. Many of them, we can safely assume, have similar attitudes towards Islam; many and probably most have different ones. In other words, the variation that we could detect among Canadian Muslims such as Noor, Maryam and a host of others, repeat themselves among Muslims everywhere, albeit undoubtedly not in the same proportions. We must therefore distinguish between the Islam of Canadian Muslims and the possibility of a "Canadian Islam", or more broadly an "immigrant" or "diaspora" Islam. *Mutatis mutandis*, the same would also go for Muslims in Belgium and Europe more broadly (cf. Nielsen 1999; Ramadan 2004; Roy 1999). One cannot straightforwardly map variations within Islam on regions, however styled. Yet this then raises the question of how one *can* understand the variations, not only between Noor and Maryam, but among Muslims and therefore within Islam worldwide.

Further indications of the potential difficulty in this regard is how these two Canadian women have "constructed" their visions of Islam. Their sources are varied, including their parents and family, imams and other leaders at their local mosque, friends and associations like the Muslim Student Associations on their university campuses, but most importantly personal searches in literature – including most especially the Qur'an itself and often on the Internet. Although their sense of religious belonging and practice definitely has a communal component, it is not strongly local. Correspondingly, the way that they have come to understand their Islam is also significantly personal and individualistic. Their sense of who or what has authority in Islam and what constitutes authentic Islam has a strong individualistic component, even if they do not arrogate authority to themselves for deciding these matters. This style of "doing Islam", of course, has significant precedent in Islamic history. This individualism also manifests itself in the distinction that Noor and Maryam both make between culture and religion, specifically between their parents' cultures and Islam as religion. What their personal searches have shown not to be authentic Islam in their parents' practices or beliefs, they reserve the right to discard or render optional.[3] To the degree that cultures express different regions of origin, this is another manifestation of how one cannot reliably use region to understand variation in Islam.

While these features may seem to indicate that Islam is largely amorphous, subject to the varied interpretations of each individual Muslim, this is of course also not the case. The consistency in what both women consider to be the core of Islam in fact points in the opposite direction: if they are to be taken as representative, then Islam is in these core features quite uniform both as concerns beliefs and practices. The individualism does not contradict convergence of an authentic

Islamic core; that core is rather the terms in which the individualism is expressed. Another way of saying this is that it is not centralized authority structures like an organization, a hierarchy, virtuoso institutions (e.g. religious orders or lineages), or a state that assure Islamic orthodoxy, but rather the agreement among such a large number of Muslims that authority lies in the basic sources and that these basic sources will by themselves be effective in preventing the dissipation of Islam into myriad local and personal directions. That unity, however, still raises the question of how Islam, and by extension any of the world's religions, manages its variations, and how the image and reality of Islam are affected by them. This brings us to some further considerations of how the Islam of "diasporic migrants" like Noor and Maryam impinges upon that question.

Noor and Maryam are the children of migrants. They practice their Islam in a Western country where, even today, Muslims form a small minority of the population. Yet their minority and diasporic status does not mean that their Islam is thereby necessarily atypical, isolated or unrepresentative. It may be particular, a reflection of the fact that they live and grew up in a particular social context in a particular country. Yet the translocal and transnational way in which their two versions are constructed, and the strong awareness of that fact on their part, is symptomatic of how these versions are tied into a larger, indeed global, Islam and are expressive of that globalized religious system. Local as it is from one perspective, therefore, it is also at the same time a global Islam. It is, as I indicated, glocal. Among the implications of this status is that their versions can also claim to be authentic Islam, especially since that is the way that they have consciously arrived at them: they have researched, they have consulted the core sources, and they have accepted or rejected elements precisely on the basis of whether or not they consider them to be authentic to the Islamic system. That, however, says little about a related question, namely how much authority their particular versions carry in the wider Islamic world.

Above I noted that neither Noor nor Maryam orient their Islam to any even locally or regionally centralized authority structure, much less a global one. It is the core sources that carry authority for them, not those sources as incarnated in specific organizations, movements, lineages, orders, leadership positions or Islamic states. I also pointed out that this way of doing Islam is not unusual in Islamic history or among Muslims today. One might, on the contrary, say that it is rather enjoined by a great many Muslims (Esposito and Voll 2001; Rahman 1982; Ramadan 2004). This does not mean that such potentially centralized authority structures do not exist. There is after all, the local imam in a Western mosque, one's parents and elder relatives, organizations like the Muslim Student Association to which Noor and Maryam belong, transnational movement organizations like the Tablighi Jamaat, traditional authority centres like Al-Azhar University in Cairo, various Sufi lineages like the Naqshbandiyya or the Murid, particular authority figures ranging from Tariq Ramadan to Osama bin Laden, and Islamicized states like Saudi Arabia or Iran with their representative religious authorities. It also does not mean that no one pays attention to these potential sources of Islamic authority; many people do, many Muslims do indeed belong or follow. It is even more than likely that Noor or Maryam have used one or more of these structures in their personal searches. Yet it is precisely in this "one or more" that the salient point lies. Our two women do not refer to any of these structures predominantly, let alone exclusively. They do not belong to these organizational, movement or network units, but at best only refer to them. It is the implications of this feature on which I wish to focus.

The diaspora Islam of Noor and Maryam as such carries no authority outside themselves. They do claim authenticity for their versions, however, and it would not be going too far to suggest that they would be recognized as such by a great many other Muslims, or at least they could as easily find supporters as detractors in this regard. Other versions of doing Islam, such as the ones just mentioned, may well have more authority in that they have a fair number of explicit and self-identified followers. Yet in terms of authenticity, none of these is really all that different, except perhaps the abstract core Islamic system to which Noor and Maryam also subscribe. Other than the core programme itself, there is no single clear centre or even set of centres that authoritatively represent dominant versions of Islam. That amorphousness contrasts with the situation in other prominent, globally structured and recognized religions.

Let us take the contrasting examples of Christianity, Judaism, Hinduism and Sikhism. The first of these has in the modern era adopted a highly organizational strategy for managing difference within identity. Beside the major organizational distinction between Roman Catholic, Eastern Orthodox and Protestant branches of Christianity, there are numerous internal and likewise organizational subdivisions, especially within the latter two. Many are the Protestant subdivisions ranging from the American Assemblies of God to the Church of England or Sweden. Not as numerous but still significant are the organized Orthodox churches from the Russian and the Ukranian to the Coptic, Armenian and the Orthodox Church of America. While there is only one significant Roman Catholic Church, it practically represents the religious organization par excellence on the global scale. Such an organizational strategy not only has deep roots in the history of this religious tradition, it is also used to structure the relative authenticity and authority of more recent versions of Christianity, such as Latin American Pentecostal, Korean Full Gospel or African Instituted Churches. Most, if by no means all, those people who practice Christian religion or who consider themselves to be Christians expressly belong to or identify with one of these organizations, something that of course does not exclude the occasional switching or conversion from one church to another.

Thus does Christianity portray and do outsiders recognize the differences that structure the Christian religion, but this does not detract from both the outside observation and the internal conviction that at root Christianity is a single religion with a core programme parallel to the Islamic one that Noor and Maryam share. Indeed, one might even go so far as to say that this organizational way of structuring difference within Christianity allows a greater range of variation without thereby losing the real sense of a common enterprise and identity.

Moreover, and of critical importance in the present context, the difference among the differences is thereby rendered clear in the sense that the common core can be identified as its different versions: Catholics are Catholics and not some species of Protestant or Orthodox Christian in spite of all that they religiously have in common. Both outsiders and insiders can be relatively clear about which is which and that one is not another. And this in spite of the fact that at the individual level there is just as much variation among Catholics or among Protestants as there is among the organizations or among Muslims with respect to Islam. *The organizations represent the differences primarily, not the individual Christians.* The glocal in the form of these organizations is primary; the global and the local are abstractions from them.

We can conduct a similar analysis for Judaism, another virtually globally recognized and structured religion that has, in the modern era, availed itself substantially of organized forms to express internal differences. In Europe and then North America from the nineteenth century, there developed three main and organized expressions in the form of Reform, Conservative and Orthodox synagogues and Jewish religious organizations. Within the Orthodox segment there was also a fair amount of internal variation. Since the founding of the State of Israel in 1948, there has been the complicating factor of a self-identified Jewish state, where Judaism receives very controversial political and state expression, and the two other main diaspora Judaic organizations are poorly represented. The variations on Judaism that prevail in Israel, however, are on a global scale just that: more variations, albeit important ones. The organizational form and strength of the other possibilities that are more dominant in diaspora regions are not thereby rendered invisible or irrelevant. Within the Jewish world and outside it they still count and prevent an identification of Judaism with the more Orthodox Israeli versions.

As with Christianity, the organizations translate and simplify a wide variation among individual Jews themselves into a relatively few concrete manifestations through which the differences that constitute the programmatic unity of Judaism can be and are recognized. As with Christianity, Judaism cannot simply be identified with these organizations; it is much more a core (also contested) set of beliefs and practices that accomplishes this identification. The organizations translate the differences from the abstract and amorphous into the concrete and clearly formed.

A significantly less clear picture emerges in the case of Hinduism. Perhaps foremost among the differences is that this religion *as a unity* is of historically rather recent construction as argued by Dalmia and von Stietencron (1995) or Frykenberg (1989).[4] This would coincide with the eighteenth- and nineteenth-century transformations of Christianity and Judaism into their currently much more extensively organized forms. The challenge for a wide array of Hindu movements and organizations from the early nineteenth-century Brahmo Samaj and Dharma Sabhas, the later nineteenth-century Sanatana Dharma and Arya Samaj movements, to twentieth-century manifestations like the Rashtriya Swayamsevak Sangh/Vishwa Hindu Parishad and the Swami Narayan movement has been to fashion the unity of Hinduism in a convincing fashion. Today's Hinduism is not nearly as highly organized as are Christianity and Judaism, and yet features at least as much – if not frankly more – internal variation in what counts as Hinduism as do other religions, the former two and Islam included. What is far more contested in the case of Hinduism is the programmatic core of beliefs and practices upon which the professed adherents of this religion for the most part agree. The variations, while only somewhat organized, refer far less easily to such a programmatic core. What this means concretely is that the representatives of the different variations, whether organized, individual or in the form of religious movements, are far less easily seen to be "saying the same thing". Difference in Hinduism takes practical precedence over identity. Correspondingly, the entire category of Hinduism is itself significantly more contested among both insiders and outsiders than are the corresponding names for the other religions.

The case of Sikhism provides a sort of bridge back to the case of Islam. This religion has since the ninetenth century taken on a much clearer internal and external identity, especially as regards its separation and distinction from the parallel-forming Hinduism.[5] Although, as with the other religions, there is today a great amount of internal variation, it would not be going too far to say that one particular version, associated with the Khalsa orientation that has its roots in the very early eighteenth century, has come to be accepted as the standard of Sikh orthodoxy and orthopraxy to the detriment of those versions that, perhaps, "looked too much like Hinduism".

During this development, this increasingly unified (or orthodoxified) Sikhism received typical organizational expression, some of it, like the governing SGPC in Punjab and the World Sikh Federation in the diaspora, of relatively recent origin, others, like the Akal Takht in Amritsar with deeper historical roots but with renewed authority today. What this means is that variation within Sikhism, while important, is not expressed using an organizational strategy parallel to other religions like Judaism and Christianity, and yet there is a strong sense of a programmatic core which represents core or orthodox Sikhism. It is this situation that is similar to the contemporary structure of Islam as a religion. There are, however, also very important differences, beside the obvious differences in the religions themselves. One of these is sheer size: there are fewer than 20 million Sikhs in the world; there are around one billion professed Muslims. Another is that, in spite of the persistently accompanying Sikh nationalism that again received very clear recent expression in the Khalistan movement, Sikhism is not manifested in addition in particular sovereign states as are not only Islam, but also Judaism, Hinduism and, historically if less clearly today, Christianity.

This comparative look at the situation of a few other religions in today's world highlights the peculiarity of Islam as one of those religions. Islam is one of the two religious "superpowers", as noted. It features a relatively clear programmatic core upon which individual Muslims and groups of Muslims construct significant variations. Our two representative Canadian Muslim women demonstrate a couple of the many possibilities. The lack of clear, especially organized, centres that can successfully claim to represent the main possibilities for variation, such as one finds in many other religions and the other religious "superpower" in particular, raises the question of how that variation will be perceived by outsiders and insiders alike.

One of the constants of Islamic reform movements since the eighteenth century has been a triple stress on four elements of an Islamic system: the oneness of God and the oneness of God's creation under the heading of "tawhid"; the singularity of the worldwide Islamic community under the title of "umma"; the necessity of going back behind received tradition to the original sources of Islam ("salafism"), namely Qur'an and Sunna; and the need for the application of Islam to bring about the socio-moral reconstruction of all aspects of human life.[6] In conjunction with the fact that the vast majority of Muslims are Sunni, we have some of the basic building blocks of the current situation, one that is well exemplified in the Islam of our two Canadian women.

They are both Sunni Muslims, they wish to recognize no divisions among Muslims and feel any that exist are tragic, they reserve the right to construct their Islam only on what the core sources dictate or enjoin, and they stress the way in which their Islam is a total way of life. Therefore, just by the way they understand and approach Islam, there is little room for building anything like a sectarian Islam, a confessional or denominational Islam. Even such main historic divisions as between Sunni and Shi'a are decried and denied legitimacy. Certainly there is much criticism of other Muslims and thereby an awareness of internal differences, but that is about as far as the recognition of variation goes. Accordingly, still taking Noor and Maryam as in some fashion representative, contemporary or modern Islam tends to present itself and conceive of itself as a seamless whole; or at least the voices that would have it otherwise are very much in the minority and hardly ever heard. Differences such as, for example, Sunni/ Shi'a, Middle Eastern Arab/Indonesian, heartland/diaspora, Sufi/scriptural, all point to salient lines of difference of which most insiders and a good number of outsiders are aware. But these do not translate themselves into ready social form differences and they are not used theologically/discursively by Muslims to structure variation in Islam. Rather, one far more frequently hears exactly the opposite: Islam is one and internal differences should as such be accorded no legitimacy.[7]

Given, however, that there are serious differences among Muslims about what constitutes proper Islam, differences that even manifest themselves between Noor and Maryam who in many respects have very similar visions, who, then, speaks for Islam? Whoever it is, the structural situation of Islam, with its theological stress on seamless unity and resistance against giving difference easily recognizable socio-structural form, will have the effect of making it difficult for insiders and outsiders alike to identify the differences with any certainty: one knows there are differences, but beyond individuals, it is difficult to locate them with any precision. And on the individual level, the differences are located everywhere and nowhere. One can find Noors and Maryams in Canada, in Belgium, in Germany, in Indonesia and even, although not perhaps "in public", in Saudi

Arabia. One can similarly find in all these places variations of Tariq Ramadan and even Osama bin Ladens.[8] Therefore, those voices that manage to get heard the best will have a tendency to "bleed over" onto Muslims everywhere because one can safely assume that they will at least have some followers everywhere; and because there is no solid alternative for making alternate distinctions.

Under current circumstances, unfortunately for us all, but especially for Muslims and Islam as one of the world religions, the Islamic voices that are being heard – at least to the outside – are more often than not the extreme voices, the ones that, for instance, very unlike Noor and Maryam, see the world in a very Manichean vision that pits the West against Islam, the Crusaders against the Jihadists, or, in Sayyid Qutb's formulation, Muslims against Jahiliyyah (Qutb n.d.). "Everyone knows" that these people are but a tiny minority, but the fact that they clearly have sympathizers among Muslims all over the world has the effect of "tarring all Muslims with the same extremist brush", and this precisely because no other readily available ways of knowing the difference on something other than an individual basis can be pressed into service. Moreover, to return to the beginning, this situation is reflected in the wider sample of second-generation Canadian Muslims who formed part of the study in which Noor and Maryam also participated: there are a very few among them whom one might well consider to be extremists, but the vast majority exhibit an astounding variation around several common characteristics that make them all Muslim. On the other extreme, of course, there are those Muslims who reject their religious tradition entirely, but they are also a small minority and certainly exceedingly unlikely to be heard as the voices of Islam.

It would, of course, be absurd to suggest that Muslims of the modern era have done something "wrong" in eschewing easily recognizable ways of expressing their variations in socio-structural forms. And that is not in the least what I wish to suggest with this analysis. More critical for my purposes is the whole question of the multiply variant reconstruction or glocalization of religions that seems to be such a clear aspect of modern and increasingly global society. The Islamic example not only shows that such reconstruction has occurred, it not only demonstrates by way of contrast how this reconstruction can happen and has happened in different ways in different religions; it also establishes how these different ways can have serious consequences in how that religion is perceived and therefore how it operates in the lives of its adherents. All religions are multi-centred. As a result of global migration and the ever complexifying network of global communications, a great many religions, Islam included, are now global religions in every sense of that term. Yet it makes a difference how that multi-centredness is given expression in social forms, how that glocalization is carried out. One cannot easily rely on geography, region or even territorial states to serve as proxies for these multiple centres as we often do when trying to understand cultural differences in our world. In the world of religions, other means must be found, and these means have different implications. The example I have outlined here is one of them.

Notes

1 Beyer (2003) and Robertson (1995).
2 "Noor" and "Maryam" are two participants in a research project conducted by the author and a team of collaborators among second-generation immigrants in three Canadian cities. The project examines how Canadian-born/raised youth from 18 to 27 years old and from Muslim, Hindu and Buddhist family backgrounds relate to, reconstruct and practice these religious traditions. For a preliminary report on some of the findings, see Beyer *et al.* (2005).
3 For similar conclusions regarding second-generation Muslims in Europe, see Khosrokhavar (1997) and Vertovec and Rogers (1998).
4 Dalmia and von Stietencron (1995) and Frykenberg (1989).
5 Oberoi (1994).
6 Voll (1982).
7 See, for various perspectives, Donohue and Esposito (1982), Esposito (1983), Esposito and Voll (2001) and Kurzman (2002).
8 See Ramadan (2004), Manji (2003), Abdolkarim Soroush in Kurzman (1998), and Anwar Ibrahim in Esposito and Voll (2001).

References

Beyer, P. (2003) "De-Centring Religious Singularity; The Globalization of Christianity as a Case in Point", *Numen*, 50, 357–386.
Beyer, P., Ramji, R. and Saha, S. (2005) "Religion among Second Generation Immigrant Youth in Canada: Muslims and Buddhists", Paper presented at the annual conference of the Society for the Scientific Study of Religion, Rochester, NY.
Dalmia, V. and von Stietencron, H. (eds) (1995) *Representing Hinduism: The Construction of Religious Traditions and National Identity*, New Delhi: Sage.
Donohue, J.J. and Esposito, J.L. (eds) (1982) *Islam in Transition: Muslim Perspectives*, New York: Oxford University Press.
Esposito, J.L. (ed.) (1983) *Voices of Resurgent Islam*, New York: Oxford University Press.
Esposito, J.L. and Voll, J.O. (eds) (2001) *Makers of Contemporary Islam*, Oxford: Oxford University Press.
Frykenberg, R.E. (1989) "The Emergence of Modern 'Hinduism' as a Concept and as an Institution: A Reappraisal with Special Reference to South India", in G.D. Sontheimer and H. Kulke (eds) *Hinduism Reconsidered*, Delhi: Manohar, pp. 29–49.
Khosrokhavar, F. (1997) *L'islam des jeunes*, Paris: Flammarion.
Kurzman, C. (ed.) (1998) *Liberal Islam: A Sourcebook*, New York and Oxford: Oxford University Press.
—— (ed.) (2002) *Modernist Islam, 1840–1940*, Oxford: Oxford University Press.
Manji, I. (2003) *The Trouble with Islam: A Wake-Up Call for Honesty and Change*, Toronto: Random House.
Nielsen, J. (1999) *Towards a European Islam*, Basingstoke: Macmillan.
Oberoi, H. (1994) *The Construction of Religious Boundaries: Culture, Identity, and Diversity in the Sikh Tradition*, Chicago: University of Chicago Press.
Qutb, S. (n.d.) *Milestones*, Cedar Rapids: Unity Publishing.
Rahman, F. (1982) *Islam and Modernity: Transformation of an Intellectual Tradition*, Chicago: University of Chicago Press.
Ramadan, T. (2004) *Western Muslims and the Future of Islam*, Oxford: Oxford University Press.

Robertson, R. (1995) "Glocalization: Time-Space and Homogeneity-Heterogeneity", in M. Featherstone, S. Lash and R. Robertson (eds) *Global Modernities*, London: Sage, pp. 25–44.

Roy, O. (1999) *Vers un islam européen*, Paris: Éditions Esprit.

Vertovec, S. and Rogers, A. (eds) (1998) *Muslim European Youth: Reproducing Ethnicity, Religion, Cutlure*, Aldershot: Ashgate.

Voll, J.O. (1982) *Islam: Continuity and Change in the Modern World*, Boulder: Westview Press.

3 Global Sufism

"Theirs and ours"

Marcia Hermansen

The title, "Global Sufism: 'Theirs and Ours'" highlights transformations of Sufi organizations and styles occurring both in the West and in the Muslim world and how these complicate the "global" and "local" as constructs. For example, the construct "ours" could indicate how Westerners have reinterpreted and institutionalized Sufism, and perhaps re-exported some elements back to Muslim societies. "Theirs", on the other hand, would consider how Sufi movements originally based in Muslim societies have modified elements of the classical Sufi Orders (tariqas) in the face of modernization and globalization and subsequently attempted to export these new forms of Sufism to the West.

Some specific effects of globalization are mobility, rapid dissemination of information through print, video and the Internet, and encounters of Eastern (Muslim) and Western (European and American) individuals and cultural elements in ways that, while they do not entirely eliminate power discrepancies, have the potential for more equal contributions in shaping interactions and ultimately constituting networks. In fact "theirs" and "ours" ultimately converge in an age of globalization. At the same time, we may inquire whether the differences that exist among today's global Sufi movements arise due to the persistence of cultural concepts and practices of networking developed in pre-modernity. One theoretical problem is the tendency to conflate the Western and the modern. The inevitable adoption of technologies such as print or the Internet by groups certainly occasions shifts in strategies, discourse and outreach – but are these shifts to the West, to the modern or to the global?

Networking in theory and practice

Network theory is employed at various levels of sophistication and disciplinary specificity. For example, some social scientists approach network analysis by studying links among individuals that are then mapped in terms of nodes and ties. The concept of network may function as a metaphor used to understand organizational behaviours in terms of relationships rather than the characteristics and propensities of individual actors. Therefore, network theory is a way to understand the role that interconnectedness and relationships play within social movements, avoiding explanations geared only to individual choices.

While networks as wholes have been characterized as either more "closed" or "open", hierarchical or egalitarian, individual actors in networks have been classified based on their positioning as being stars, gatekeepers, bridges and so on. Explaining how networks converge and coalesce combines both idealist and materialist theorizing, for example, through explanations grounded in world systems and the economic factors (rational choice, material circumstances) or by stressing the network as a community of discourse.[1]

Muslim styles of networking

Sufism may be considered a major example of classical networking in Muslim societies.[2] These networks are often conceived in term of links of genealogy such as silsilas (chains) and shajaras (trees) incorporating precedence whether through blood/kin relations, the exchange of privileged information and charisma, or both. Sufi networks were usually hierarchical and involved ritualized and informal exchanges. They often spread among ethnically related persons sharing the same space or having social relations in other contexts, although they might also draw together persons of vastly differing social strata through common loyalty to an Order or to a specific shaikh.

At the same time Sufis have historically been among the most prominent agents of Islamic expansion through networks of preaching, trade, and clientage, and in particular are known for being adaptable to local linguistic and cultural conditions. In terms of movement through space, a notable example of network expansion or relocation would be the cases of Sufi deputies (khalifas) being instructed by their shaikh to move to new cities or regions in order to establish further branches of an existing order.

In terms of network theory as developed in the field of sociology, traditional Sufi Orders overlapped with other webs of relationships in Muslim societies of the pre-modern period. Primarily these networks might consist of family, tribal and ethnic affiliations, contacts developed in the proximate urban or rural location (guild or futuwwa associations), ties developed through madrasa education and links forged within the same madhhab (legal school). I would characterize these sorts of networks as being more horizontal, linking members possessing similar "social capital" of status, wealth and education.

Vertical aspects of Sufi networks would empower those attaining the highest levels of charismatic status and leadership to extend horizontal linkages to other power networks of the wealthy and noble classes through patronage and clientship relationships, and in many cases through exchange of females in order to create kinship relations through marriage.

In terms of the local, the sites of traditional Sufi Orders were the lodge (khanqah) or the shrine. Globalized Sufism, however, due to the lack of such places in the West, adapts to other spaces such as mosques, clubs and secular meeting halls as well as to the virtual space of the Internet.[3]

In describing culturally distinct styles of networking in the traditionally defined Muslim world, one may consider the ideas of clientage and patronage networks that are not specifically Islamic but rather Mediterranean.[4] In this regard, Clifford Geertz and Lawrence Rosen have elaborated the idea of a specifically Arabo-Islamic understanding of relationality in personal networks as represented by the use of the nisba naming suffix that marks the connection to place, tribe or genealogy.[5] Thus an individual, depending on his or her context or positioning, might be referred to by the nisba (name suffix) indicating variously the home city, region or country.[6] In Sufism "nisba" was also used as a technical term to indicate affiliation to an Order as well as to suggest spiritual affinity to a particular prophet, saint or spiritual state.[7]

From 1000–1800 the Muslim world incorporated diverse systems of networks based on mystical brotherhoods, a standard educational curriculum, pilgrimage and travelling in search of knowledge that established interpersonal links fostering transregional connections. The period post-1500 is marked by the rise of regionally and linguistically discrete empires, although the pilgrimage, the use of Arabic in the high religious tradition, and Sufism, still allowed transregional networks and transmission of ideas to persist.[8]

The coming of modernity to Muslim societies (overlooking for the sake of clarity transitional eighteenth- and nineteenth-century developments) is characterized by shifts such as the nation state replacing the old nobility (often interrupted by periods of colonial rule), altered or ruptured clientage and patronage patterns, and contestations in understandings of Sufism including what a disciple (murid) would gain through affiliating with a Sufi order. In addition, in Muslim societies the entire concept of authoritative knowledge in modernity is displaced from charismatic religious authority to professions such as medicine and engineering,[9] and even within religious circles from the "hikmat" synthesis of theology, mysticism and the textual sciences[10] to jurisprudential expertise or reformist zeal.[11]

In his prospectus for the conference on "Sufism and the Modern" convened in Indonesia in 2003, Martin van Bruinessen construed the continued vitality of globalized Sufism as one indication that the decline of the Sufi orders had been prematurely pronounced by Orientalist scholars such as A.J. Arberry who stated that, "Sufi orders continue to attract the ignorant masses but no man of education would care to speak in their favor".[12] According to van Bruinessen, even Clifford Geertz and Ernest Gellner had erred in their predictions that rural miracle-working saints and mystics would be soon replaced by the dry scripturalism of urban scholars.[13]

While many Sufi orders even in the pre-nation-state era were "transnational", if such as term can be used,[14] modern communications and the diaspora (Arjun Appadurai's scapesand flows of media, finance, techology, ideas and people)[15] have introduced new modalities into the global context of Sufi networking. In particular, we find the continued existence of vibrant "urban" Sufi networks in many regions that retain social capital in terms of status, literacy and religious knowledge. Some of these movements have enabled the revitalization of Sufism in the Muslim World and inspired some of the notable examples of global Sufism reaching the West through travel, migration and media.

Global Sufi networks may be bi-local or multinational but what now attracts our attention as unique is their ability to range across transcultural "world-systems" from the West to Asia and Africa and even beyond the bonds of Muslim communities of discourse.[16]

"Global" Sufi networking: "theirs"

In this section, I interrogate how several "post-tariqa" Sufi movements originating from the Muslim world decide to gain influence or interact with constituencies in the West – and with which constituencies? This necessarily complicates the category of Sufi – because I'd like to start with a South Asian Barelvi Sufi coalition and with the Turkish Fethullah Gulen movement, both of which are primarily twentieth-century movements that depart strikingly from classical Sufi norms such as direct initiation, teaching shaikhs and so on.

South Asian Barelvi-ism could be understood as a movement that provides a doctrinal and institutional context for popular Sufi practices.[17] It is therefore now centred in mosques and madrasas, no longer exclusively in shrines and khanqahs. Rather than functioning as an initiatory Sufi order, adherents and sympathizers may come together in multiple contexts and may or may not be formal initiates of various Sufi orders. The Barelvi/Ahl-i Sunnat interpretation of Islam stresses the role of charismatic saints, devotionalism and the supernatural powers of the prophet and saints meditated through Sufis and ulama.

Both the Turkish Gulen and the South Asian Barelvi movements have thus far been ethnically restricted, rarely trying to attract members from outside of the same group. However, each movement has attempted over the past decade or so to engage the goodwill of broader constituencies in the West whether among co-ethnics, likeminded Muslims of other ethnicities or, in the case of the Gulen movement, non-Muslims with an interest in inter-faith dialogue. Drawing from the American context with which I am most familiar two recent examples come to my mind.

Sufi Barelvis: the Naqshbandiyya Foundation for Islamic Education

In one case (1990s) the Naqshbandi Foundation for Islamic Education, founded by Barelvi-oriented Sufis from Pakistan, specifically murids of Jamaat Ali Shah (d. 1955), a Naqshbandi, studied by Arthur Buehler,[18] tried to have an impact in the United States by organizing "Milad" conferences (celebrations of the birth of the Prophet Muhammad), and at one point gathering ulama of the Ahl-e Sunna wa l-Jama'at (Barelvi) orientation to try to form some kind of North American umbrella organization. The group envisioned a broad Sufi–Barelvi consensus as is evident from their website which links both Western and Muslim world Sufi Orders and the sites of Ahl-e Sunnat associations in various countries.[19] Here a form of contemporary South Asian Sufism – Barelvi-ism was being exported to the US through immigrant networks and attempts were made to cooperate with three local groups – American (Muslim) academics sympathetic to Sufism, American Sufi Orders, including at one point the Herlveti-Jerrahis, Naqshbandi-Haqqanis, the Guru Bawa Fellowship, and others, as well as Barelvi ulama (immigrants). Several Milad conferences held in Chicago (1993–1995) attempted to combine all three constituencies[20] and branches in several other American cities hosted smaller events.[21]

I would characterize this effort as one based on the efforts of a handful of immigrant Muslim professionals, and one that did not take strong hold. The main target of this initiative was to influence the Muslim community in North America towards more inclusion of the Barelvi element. However, most Muslim institutions, mosques, ISNA (the Islamic Society of North America) and so on, rejected these manifestations of Sufism – and the Barelvis were not ultimately able to organize in the United States at the national level.[22] The ulama didn't achieve consensus among themselves, while the Sufi groups often were not very Barelvi in style, and had different concerns. For example, the divergent interests of American convert Sufis included a focus on Sufism as a source of personal development, promoting their respective charismatic shaikhs,[23] identifying with classical "high" tradition Sufism, and nostalgia for the great Sufi past.

At the same time in Pakistan, India and even in Britain, one finds successful Barelvi institutions and networks, in some cases even political parties – but these of course have emerged in ethnically more homogenous "local" settings.[24] Therefore we may question whether the problem with organized Barelvi-ism taking hold in the United States is the paucity of a certain "class" of South Asian immigrants? We may also view it as attributable to elements in the wider American culture. Alternatively its failure may have occurred as a result of factors specific to the Muslim sub-culture in the United States; for example, the fact that most community organizations were already controlled by anti-Sufi Islamists?

The Gulen movement

The Fethullah Gulen group, like the Nursi movement from which it derives, has been categorized as a tradition transmitted through print and study.[25] I will briefly consider the recent (post-2000) activities of the Fethullah Gulen movement in the United States. In this case we have a local form of networking based on patterns of Turkish Anatolian Sufism[26] trying to make organized inroads into the American/global scene. It may be objected that this movement is not explicitly "Sufi" and in fact eschews features of Sufi organizations such as initiation. I prefer to consider it as a variety of "post-tariqa" Sufism, a development emerging in the modern period that represents a new articulation of Sufi networking.

Successful exportation of some activities of the Gulen movement has occurred in the ex-Soviet republics since 1994 due to the establishment of schools and consequent outreach in the Turkish language.[27] Due to its original and continued emphasis on education as a vehicle for inculcating moral values in the modern world while promoting a scientific outlook, one may characterize the Gulen movement as building on a network model based on the school, especially of the madrasa type. In this type of network the links between student and teacher are life-long and in some cases close to the master–disciple ties of Sufism.[28] "Exemplary" figures, Gulen, the Aghabeys (older brothers), and the other teachers facilitate Islamic learning and morally edifying discussions and dispense hospitality and service to the members and clients who in turn are supported in sharing this with ever-widening circles.

Hakan Yavuz divides the activities of Gulen's movement into two phases:

1   The first period consists of religious community building 1966–1982 in which Gulen (b. 1938), a state-appointed religious teacher and preacher (hoca), tutored a spiritually oriented and intellectually motivated core group of followers to build a religious community in Izmir. Gradually the circle of supporters expanded beyond local students and businessmen to include outreach to many Turkish cities. Institutions were founded that would focus on the needs of an upcoming generation by providing dormitory facilities and ultimately an extensive network of primary and secondary schools.

2   During the second phase (1983–1997) the Gulen movement expanded into the public sphere and loosened some of its boundaries.[29] Increasing outreach involved a middle segment of Turkish society amenable to Islamization or moral rectification as subtly encouraged through television, radio, news, publishing, educational, and other support aspects of the movement.

During this time Gulen's "inclusive and liberal interpretation of Islam as a religion of love, peace and social responsibility helped him build bridges and add new circles to the movement".[30] The movement judiciously positioned itself in mainstream Turkish society by developing important holdings in the media, financial and educational sectors. With the collapse of the Soviet empire in the 1990s the Gulen movement expanded its outreach, internationalizing by founding schools in Central Asia, especially in Turkish speaking areas.

The year 1997 marked a new phase after Gulen left Turkey to reside in the United States at a time of severe government pressure on what were perceived to be Islamizing currents threatening the secular Turkish state. His movement, now some six million strong in Turkey, continues to expand its outreach globally through schools and, more recently, through activities in the United States. The main outreach in the US is currently not to fellow Muslims – but rather to the academic and inter-faith communities. Outreach efforts have included sponsoring fast-breaking dinners (Iftars), conferences, the promotion of Turkish culture through events such as Mevlevi performances, as well as the founding of charter schools. Increasingly, American business and political networks are tapped for participation and mutual support. These initiatives resonate with Fethullah Gulen's stated objectives of encouraging a tolerant Islam engaged with the modern world through scientific education and tolerance while cooperating with those of diverse religions and backgrounds.

Activities of this group engage this chapter's theme of global and local because one thrust of Gulen's outreach is that Turkish Islam can model on a global scale a moderate and tolerant expression of the religion – a combination of Sufi Islam and Turkish culture. In addition, Gulen turns from the Arab world to the West – evidenced by a focus on English rather than Arabic in the movement's schools. In what sense could we say that this Turkish movement is either similar to, or unlike, classical practices of Sufism? In fact, the writings of both Nursi and Gulen[31] critique traditional forms of Sufi organization and suggest that the scope of Sufism for these times should be compatible with modern knowledge (science) and social formations. Baya (initiation)[32] and tariqa identification are not practiced in any of the Nur movements despite their Naqshbandis roots.[33] A remaining question is – if this movement represents a new style of modern global Sufi networking that could be more easily communicated across cultures – how is the local/Turkish cultural element going to be negotiated in the future?

This question of Turkish cultural identity among Sufis in the West has already arisen in the case of the Mevlevi and Jerrahi Sufi movements in the United States. The American Mevlevi Sufis (under Jelaluddin Loras,[34] or Kabir Helminski,[35] for example) seem to have moved more towards the New Age attitude of eclecticism and gender equality, allowing women to perform the sema turning ritual, for example.[36] The American Helveti-Jerrahis have internally differentiated themselves into sub-branches, both regionally and according to the extent to which adherence to the shari'a is emphasized and traditional gender norms maintained, thereby negotiating Turkish Muslim and American New Age norms in various permutations.[37]

Clearly the Gulen movement in the United States is less interested in direct recruitment, which in Turkey takes place through social networks such as family, education and religious meetings. Broader creation of a "community of discourse" occurs as associates become committed through "moral obligation" to work for a better society through reforming the private sphere. This message is transmitted in Turkey through media (newspapers, television, radio) and publications (300 bookstores) and small study circles that support and propagate the movement's philosophy. Most Gulen followers in Turkey are young people who, while at high school or university, adopted a more "Islamic" and service-oriented philosophy that at least for a time may alienate them from secularized relatives.

The objectives of the movement in the West are therefore somewhat ambiguous. Is the goal an expansion of the project of "moral reform" and "tolerance" to the entire world (globalism) or it is a means to gaining credibility in the Turkish homeland?

Global Sufism: "ours"

By "ours" I wish to indicate any mode of Sufism that is primarily centred in the West, although it must at some level invoke Eastern roots, unless one changes the definition of Sufi to mean "mystic" in the most general and all-embracing sense. This is in fact a position taken by some New Age Sufis and some from the Islamic world who see in Sufism a re-emergence of mystical elements derived from pre-Islamic practices of indigenous cultures.

While there may be quite a number of ways of categorizing types of "Western" Sufi movements,[38] for the purpose of the present analysis I will discuss three types:

1 eclectic Sufi movements;
2 those with a Western convert as shaikh and, finally;
3 movements headed by charismatic shaikhs from the Muslim world.

1 Eclectic Sufi movements. Two movements that seem to be based in the West with only residual links to a Muslim homeland are:
  a the Sufi Order in the West (Inayat Khan) and;
  b the International Association of Sufism.

Comparatively speaking, each movement traces its origins to a Sufi who came to the West from a Muslim country. Each features leadership based on family or hereditary connections and has experienced rivalries concerning succession to the original teacher among his descendents.[39] Each gives more equitable treatment and leadership roles to females. Each primarily recruits Westerners who may not convert to Islam. Each stresses Sufism as a path of personal transformation and employs Western psychological/scientific knowledge along with mysticism and Sufi terminology, in order to validate its mission and teachings.[40]

2 Convert Shadhili shaikhs. As a second case of "ours" Sufi movements I would like to look at several Shadhili movements in which a Western convert has become the shaikh or the central node in the network.
  They are:
  a the Maryamiyya of Frithjof Schuon (d. 1997);
  b the Murabitum of Abdalqadir as-Sufi;
  c the Hashimi Darqawi of Nuh Ha Mim Keller.

In each of these cases, I would argue, the Sufi movement is largely driven by its opposition to something – in the case of Shadhiliyya Sufi movements in the West this has often been the "modern". In terms of networking styles, the tightest bonds are among convert shaikhs and their (largely) Western followers due to the element of world-denying orientation and protest. It may be noted that in the instances where the convert shaikh resided in the West, a pattern of encouraging communal living emerges at least for a time. This signals the fact that those who join the network are often lacking other sets of relationships and social capital and have been amenable to locating their entire web of links within the movement.[41] However in terms of wealth, race and education many followers of these two movements of Frithjof Schuon (Maryamiyya) and Abdalqadir as-Sufi (Murabitun) have generally been advantaged Europeans and Euro-American converts.

However, these two movements differ in that Schuon stressed the idea of traditionalism derived from the philosophy of Rene Guenon and seems to have attracted disciples from disparate networks: New Age eclectic, Islamically oriented Westerners and intellectuals, and elite Muslims from the Muslim world. The Murabitun, on the other hand, initially recruited upper-class dropouts in London but in more recent years has developed some following among disaffected Muslim youth in the diaspora and in the Muslim world, as well as some populations attracted by its radical political and spiritual critique of the modern West.[42] The Hashmimi Darqawi of Keller arose a generation later and finds its membership largely among Muslim youth in the Western diaspora.

Shadhiliyya-Maryamiyya

This group had been headed by Frithjof Schuon (d. 1998), more privately known as Shaikh Isa Nur al-Din.[43] Schuon, who was originally from Switzerland, moved to Bloomington, Indiana in the 1970s.[44] He was connected with the Shadhiliyya-Alawiyya tariqa of Algeria through Shaikh al-Alawi (d. 1934). Many prominent academic scholars of Islam living in the West including Seyyed Hossein Nasr, Martin Lings, Titus Burckhardt, Victor Danner[45] and William Stoddart[46] have been associated with Schuon's teaching. As Mark Sedgwick has demonstrated, the academic influence of this movement in terms of traditionalist philosophy in the lineage of Rene Guenon has been more important than its specifically Islamic Shadhili teachings.[47]

After briefly studying with Shaikh Ahmad al-Alawi[48] whom he met in 1932, Schuon seems to have had his own visionary inspiration to connect with Mary and Jesus in his spiritual practices. His movement has been known as the "Tariqa Maryamiyya", or the path of Mary. While the practices of the tariqa are Islamic, there is also a certain eclecticism featuring terminology and practices from Christian, Hindu and Native American traditions[49] on which Schuon had also written. Schuon chose not to lecture publicly and to remain personally secluded,[50] but taught a closed circle of followers in Bloomington.

Since Schuon's death in 1998 the leader of the American branch of the movement has been Professor Seyyed Hossein Nasr. The tariqa's focus has been characterized as discernment and gnosis, and elite, rather than popular or devotional, Sufism.[51] The mode resonated with the project of resacralizing the West or at least swimming against the tide of secularization, modernity and the disenchantment of the world.

In addition to the formal initiates of the Order, it has had a broader influence on educated readers both in the West and the Muslim world interested in Islamic mysticism and comparative religion through the writings of Schuon and of his prominent disciples who as scholars of religion articulate a "traditionalist" or perennial perspective.

Shadhili-Darqawi Order (also known as the Darqawi, Habibiya and Murabitun order)

The Darqawiyya-Habibiyya movement is led by Abdalqadir al-Murabit also known as Abdalqadir as-Sufi, who publishes at times under the name, Ian Dallas

(b. *circa* 1931). Dallas was at one time editor of *The International Times*, a socialist paper.[52] He also worked as a scriptwriter and played the part of the magician in Fellini's movie *8 1/2*. A frequent traveller to North Africa, Dallas was initiated by a Moroccan Sufi, Shaikh Muhammad ibn al-Habib al-Darqawi (d. 1971) in 1967.[53] He claimed to be appointed a deputy (*muqaddam*) by the Shaikh and his followers would visit the centre near Meknes.

In 1976 in England Abdalqadir declared himself to be a shaikh in the Habibiyya Order and his movement began to attract followers who were mainly young British and American converts to Islam. For some time he and his murids lived in flats donated by South Asian immigrant businessmen or in squatter houses in Bristol Gardens, West London.[54] The decline in modern knowledge and education is a recurring theme in Abdalqadir's writings, appearing again in his preface to *The Meaning of Man*, a translation of Darqawi writings.[55] By 1976 Abdalqadir had enough followers to establish a Sufi community in Norwich, England. His leadership became more and more autocratic. At one point he commanded all his followers to sell their cars, at another to divorce their wives. He later began to promote the study of the Muwatta' of Imam Malik as basis for an ideal social and legal system, and thereafter gave less emphasis to esoteric Sufism as he developed more of a strict and militant Islamic position. Ali Kose distinguishes two phases in Abdalqadir's teachings, beginning with an earlier esoteric Sufi period favouring isolation from society and later entering an activist political phase.[56]

Although Abdalqadir seems to have initially attracted mainly Western converts to Islam as immediate disciples, his aggressively anti-modern and anti-Western ideology gained him support and hearings from Islamist networks in the Muslim world.

The concerns of the movement began to align with tenets of Islamist movements, becoming increasingly activist and global. Noteworthy is the Murabitun project of rejecting paper currency in favor of minting gold and silver coinage, and ultimately establishing an e-dinar (Internet) monetary system to displace Western economic interests.[57] Internet photos and news items indicate the project being enthusiastically received and the gold dinar being endorsed by Islamist political leaders such as Malaysia's Muhathir and Turkey's Erbakan.[58] The Murabitun movement has also involved itself in ethnic and revolutionary unrest and promoted conversions to Islam in areas such as South Africa and Chiapas, Mexico.[59]

Followers of 'Abdal Qadir have also been instrumental in organizing, with assistance from other Spanish Muslims and foreign donors, the construction of a mosque in Granada on the hill right across from the Alhambra, inaugurated to worldwide attention on 10 July 2003.[60]

Many of the early Murabitun were highly motivated and intelligent convert intellectuals who now occupy high places in academia or more significantly have become what I term "public intellectual convert Sufis" (PICS). This model of the "alim as cultural critic" appeals to the Muslim community, especially among diaspora Muslim youth, maintaining strong Internet presences, and offering sophisticated cultural critique of both Western culture and decadent tendencies in the global Muslim scene. Abdalqadir's books are carried by a variety of Islamic bookstores and Internet sites.

In his study, *Sufis of Britain*, Ron Geaves notes the fact that Abdalqadir's movement has little appeal to immigrant Muslims within Britain although it has received worldwide support and publicity in the Muslim world at large, either due to its dawa activities[61] or its political stance.[62] Abdalqadir himself seems to maintain some connections with political Islamic movements, such as the Ikhwan al-Muslimin,[63] despite his criticism of its philosophy. His works have been translated into Turkish[64] and other languages of the Muslim world and have attracted the attention of Turkish immigrants in Europe,[65] also Spanish[66] and Indonesian Muslim youth.[67]

In addition, Murabitun/Darqawiyya followers have published many translations of classical Shadhili works, Islamic law, hadith, etc. and some pursue academic careers in Western universities.

Shaikh Nuh Ha Mim Keller of the Hashimi-Darqawi Order

As the final example of "ours" Sufi movements led by convert shaikhs we take the Hashimi-Darqawi of Nuh Ha Mim Keller (b. 1954), an American Shadhili who has lived in Jordan for the past 20 years but has a large (several thousands) following composed primarily of young immigrant Muslims in the United States and Britain. Keller visits the United States where he has a number of American disciples once or twice a year, offering three-day sessions in various key locations. His American followers are mainly young Muslims born of immigrant parents and raised in the West who are seeking a return to Islamic authenticity, although he also has a following among American converts to Islam. This phenomenon of the young Western Muslims going for training in a madrasa to absorb both the intricacies of fiqh and Sufi learning emerged in the 1990s and continues unabated at the time of writing.

Keller is a direct disciple of 'Abd al-Rahman al-Shaghuri (d. 2004),[68] a Damascene Shadhili Shaikh in the line of both Shaikh Muhammad Sa'id Kurdi[69] and Shaikh Hashimi (d. 1961) who was a disciple of Shaikh al-'Alawi. al-Kurdi was born in Jordan and studied the traditional Islamic sciences in Damascus.

Keller is an example of the first generation of Western Sufis who have studied Islamic and Arabic sources extensively and have their own followings of shari'a-oriented Muslims, including some from South Asia and the Middle East. He has become somewhat of a public intellectual since the terrorist attacks of 9/11 where a number of Internet websites reproduce his interviews and commentaries on this as well as other topics.[70] His approach to Sufism has been characterized as "techno-fiqh" or "ultra orthodoxy" by other American Sufis. On the other hand, his followers perceive his style as being the most authentic and legitimate.[71]

Keller's main publications to date have been translations of classical Shafi'i legal manuals, such as the *Reliance of the Traveller* or *Maqasid* of al-Nawawi.[72]

Members of his tariqa can access audio files of the shaikh's lessons on a private website. Keller's following in the West is growing rapidly and may attract further notice in the future.[73] Reports are that hundreds attend his lectures in Europe, Canada and the United States, representing a significant development among Western Sufi movements.

3   Charismatic shaikhs. The third category of "ours" Sufi movements to be considered here are those led by charismatic shaikhs from the Muslim world. Among such groups the Naqshbandiyya-Haqqaniyya and the Helveti Jerrahis are examples of Sufi movements that span more than one country and maintain a presence in the Muslim world. Generally, compliance to the shari'a and Muslim identity is maintained by members although within each movement there have been factions that drift towards more eclectic "New Age" practices.

In fact, these movements over time have tended to split along ethnic lines and in terms of practice. In the case of the Helvetis and Haqqanis this has occurred both in England and the United States. In these instances some members, especially converts to Islam, have drifted away or adopt a more eclectic "New Age" form of Sufism deviating from formal Islamic norms and shari'a compliant practice.

Thus, I would argue that in order to network broadly in Western societies and to persist over time, Islamic Sufi movements based on the charisma of particular shaikhs (Helveti, Naqshbandi-Haqqani) either have had to develop tiers or splits between Muslim and non-Muslim elements or they have to become more oriented towards inner development (psychology) and New Age concerns.

Conclusions

Scholars of networks in the diaspora have recognized the need to distinguish between forms that are essentially composed of bi-local linkages between the home country and the site of migration, and movements that are transnational and transcultural. In the case of Sufi movements, the truly global ones are those that network their Sufi activities in some meaningful way in multiple and culturally diverse societies.

One conclusion derived through comparing these various Sufi groups in terms of networking patterns and styles is that two dimensions of the networks themselves should be noted.

The first is the "vectoring" of such movements, their goals and mission, will determine their relationship to persons, ideas and other movements outside the group, helping to determine how much they are able to spread and interact across diverse populations. It seems on the basis of comparative work on global Sufism that the mission of the movement is important in the style of networking and possible affinities and conflicts among individuals and across networks.

The second is the nature of what circulates within the network, binding the individual members together. This provides important indications regarding a movement's identity, style of networking and possible affinities and conflicts both among its members and to other movements.

In order to illustrate the issue of vectoring and mission I would like to cite the case of tension between Murabitun and the Naqshbandi Haqqani intellectuals on questions of doctrine. I would state that both movements potentially appeal to the same cohort of youth disaffected with life in the West.

The Murabitun critique centres on the style of the Naqshbandi-Haqqanis in promoting their shaikh and his controversial millennial teachings.[74] Its author, Umar Vadillo (deputy of Abdalqadir), promotes the political and economic ventures of the Murabitun while taking aim at Sufi perennialist movements (Schuon and Nasr's Maryamiyya) and the Naqshbandi lineages of the Syrian shaikh Ahmad Koftaru and the Haqqani Shaikh Nazim.[75]

In brief the Murabitun, who stress fiqh and anti-Western discourse, oppose the Haqqanis, who stress the charisma of their shaikh and to an extent, Sufi esotericism. At the same time, this mission has enabled the Haqqanis to network with other Sufis self-defined as "traditionalists" who are opposed to Wahhabis, including perennialist and Barelvi groups.

In terms of the second feature, i.e. what circulates within Sufi networks:

a   one may contrast an emphasis on the personal charisma (of the shaikh and others) vs.
b   a focus on some specific content or information (such as fiqh, ideology, psychology, methods for personal transformation, etc.) that were not discussed in these terms in classical Sufism.

For example, most Sufi eclectic groups discussed above incorporate "Sufi psychology" as something that is cultivated and even practiced professionally, in some cases, by members.

The concept of global Sufism also helps us theorize debates about Islam and the role of culture in which Sufism is usually seen as being "culture friendly"[76] as opposed to the deterritorialized, "pure Islam" discourse of the Islamists. As I noted in a previous article, "deterritorialized" Islam appeals to diaspora youth who are disadvantaged in terms of the cultural capital of adult immigrants.[77] Since the Murabitun and Keller focus on "fiqh as the answer", these latter are correspondingly more successful with such diaspora Muslim youth.

The nature of what circulates within a Sufi network (fiqh, esoteric lore, psychology) also shapes its structures in ways that mimic other sorts of economic and social networks–franchises, multi-level marketing schemes, trade fairs or clubs. It may also predict the other networks in the society with which a Sufi movement may establish affinities and relationships, for example with holistic healing circles in the case of the Sufi Order, or Neo-Con lobbies in the case of the American Naqshbandi-Haqqanis, or at least their leader, Shaikh Hisham.

Modernity is marked by increased rationality and bureaucratic procedures leading to the disenchantment of the world and the emergence of civil religion. In general, global Sufism may be viewed as resistance to this trend of modernity in western terms. The recruitment issue for Sufi movements in the West is that they do not draw on the indigenous symbols, language and identities that generally facilitate social and religious mobilization. At the same time, they conform to definitions of a species of "new [Islamic] social movements" that are driven more by issues of identity, culture and post-materialism rather than class, economic or narrow political interests.[78]

In this sense many global Sufi movements are like "new" Islamic movements in being driven by identity, culture etc. However, in Western societies such causes are likely to appeal only to a narrow field of indigenous protestors against a spiritual or moral deficiency in the West.[79]

The concern with identity and culture therefore gives such global Sufi movements a certain affinity with moderate Islamist movements as vehicles for moral protest and personal rectification. However, the Western Sufi movements are likely to be less interested in political activity, and will be more inward looking. When exported back to the Muslim world, however, the anti-modern and quest for authenticity expressed through perennialist movements, fiqh expertise, or critique of the West may circulate among broader Muslim constituencies where they may take on a political valance and recruit a certain cohort of Muslim youth.

"Global" Sufi movements of various sorts inevitably must adapt to local environments. For example take the cases of the Barelvi group I cited (NFIE), the Gulen movement, and even the Naqshbandi Haqqanis. Each of these groups has some Naqshbandi Sufi background. Each has had to adapt according to local environments. For example the Gulen activities in Germany differ from those in the United States and those in Central Asia.

Other global Sufi movements such as the Naqshbandi Haqqanis are known to attract different types of members in the various countries where they operate: Malaysia, Germany, Britain and the United States, and Egypt, for example in terms of the class background and Islamic interpretation.

Therefore we observe that in terms of Sufi networking, the traditional mode of tariqa or brotherhood has come under pressure in the modern global context. New forms of networks include multi-tariqa Sufi conferences, post-tariqa Sufi movements and many individual articulations of Sufi practice and identity.

Notes

1 Loimeier (2000: 64). John Voll's work on ulama networks is an example of the "community of discourse approach".
2 Ibid.
3 Schmidt (2004).
4 Gellner and Waterbury (1977).
5 The anthropologists Clifford Geertz and Lawrence Rosen have commented on the importance of nisba as a concept within the Islamic, in particular, Moroccan system. See, for example, Geertz (1976: 234f.) and Rosen (1984).
6 Geertz, 1976 and Rosen, 1984.
7 Hermansen (1992).
8 Reichmuth (2000: 64ff.).

9   For example, as cited in Eickelman, 1992.
10 Muhsin Mahdi, "Islamic Theology and Philosophy" entry in *Encyclopedia Britannica* 9 (1974):1012–25.
11 Fusfeld (1984).
12 Arberry (1950: 122).
13 Martin van Bruinessen, "Sufism and the 'Modern' in Islam". Online, available at: www.let.uu.nl/~martin.vanbruinessen/personal/conferences/sufism_and_the_modern. html (accessed 16 September 2005).
14 Ibid.
15 Appadurai (1996: 45ff.).
16 Reichmuth (2000: 55–56).
17 Sanyal (1996).
18 Buehler (1998).
19 Online, available at: www.nfie.com/links.htm, although the site seems to have been dormant since 2002.
20 Publications arising from these conferences are the two issues called *Sufi Illuminations*.
21 While NFIE continues sporadically only at the local level, an offshoot Islamic Studies and Research Association (ISRA) has a similar style of networking, and host several annual conferences with a regional appeal. Online, available at: www.israinternational.com (accessed 24 September 2005).
22 In fact a later organization, ISRA, tries to draw on many of the same networks. While localized in the South-East of the United States, the movement recently tried to enter the Chicago area through a network of Pakistani Punjabi businesmen. This seems to have met with little enthusiasm from the persons who were initially gathered from the Chicago businessman's contacts in the Pakistani business association (ethnic and professional networks) but who have less interest in Barelvi spirituality or American Sufism, although sympathetic to Islamic activities in a more general sense.
23 In particular Naqshbandi-Haqqanis who at one point threatened to pull out of the event if their Shaikh Hisham was not given top billing.
24 See Geaves (2002), on Barelvis.
25 Yavuz (2003: 297–316) and Bekim Agai, "Zwischen Netzwerk und Diskurs: Die Bildungnetzwerk um Fethullah Gulen". Online, available at: www.ruhr-uni-bochum.de/orient/Agai.pdf (accessed 24 September 2005), also Agai's longer dissertation.
26 Yavuz (2003: 116, passim).
27 Agai (2001); Balci (2003).
28 Motahhedeh (1985).
29 Yavuz and Esposito (2003: 183).
30 Ibid. Yavuz (1999: 125–142).
31 Nursi *Letters* 41, 85. Serif (1989: 181–182).
32 The role of bay'a as a marker of hierarchical networking is not restricted to Sufi networks in expansion to the West. In an example from South Asia, the Israr Ahmed movement, Tanzeem-e Islami, an Islamist circle at a certain point began to emphasize the important of taking bay'a to an amir. Of course this is one version of political organizing based on the model of the golden age of Islam where the khalifa received bay'a. While absent from the model of modern nation states, it is revived in some contemporary Islamic movements.
33 The Naqshbandi influence in the life and writings of Nursi is evident going back to Shaikh Ahmad Sirhindi through the Khalidi-Naqshbandis. See, for example, Algar (1979). In the case of Fethullah Gulen, one may intuit a Mevlevi current as well, although no direct initiation or influences are claimed.
34 Loras is the son of a Turkish Mevlevi shaikh from Konya who came to the United States in the 1980s and leads a "New Age" version of Mevlevism.

35 Kabir Helminski is an American Mevlevi who heads an organization known as the Threshold Society.
36 Reinhertz (2001).
37 Webb (1995).
38 For example, typologies have been suggested by Hermansen (1997); Webb (1995: 251–252); Chittick (1995).
39 For example between the sons of Inayat Khan and between the son (Ali Nader) and daughter (Nahid) of Shah Maghsoud Angha in the case of the Shah Maghsoudi Uveyysi.
40 Hermansen (2004).
41 Stark and Bainbridge (1980).
42 This movement is discussed in Hermansen (2005).
43 Kinney (1994). Schuon is given a biographical notice in Rawlinson, *Book of Enlightened Masters* (Chicago: Open Court, 1997), 517–524.
44 Brief bio-bibliographies of Guenon, Schuon and his circle may be found in Borella (1992). Frithjof Schuon's more well known writings on Islam are *Understanding Islam* (1963) and *Islam and the Perennial Philosophy* (1976).
45 Danner briefly discussed the connection of Rene Guenon (Shaikh Abd al-Wahid Yahya) with the former Shaikh al-Azhar, Abd al-Halim Mahmud, himself a Shadhili. Mahmud mentions the diffusion of Shadhili teachings in the West in *Qadayyat at-Tasawwuf: ul-Muḥ usa al Shadhiliyya* (1988: 281–362). Danner (1991: 47).
46 Stoddart (1986).
47 Mark Sedgwick, "Western Sufism and Traditionalism". Online, available at: www. aucegypt.edu/faculty/sedgwick/trad/write/WSuf.html (accessed 24 September 2005).
48 See Lings (1971). Nasr mentions that Schuon met al-'Alawi in 1932 (1986: 53).
49 Schuon apparently has a special affinity for native American traditions and has written a work, illustrated with some of his own paintings, *The Feathered Sun* (1990). See also Wilson (1993).
50 Nasr (1986).
51 Chittick (1995).
52 An early publication of Abdal Qadir was entitled *Islam: A Manifesto*, in emulation of Karl Marx's work on Communism.
53 The Darqawis are in the same lineage as the 'Alawiyya-Shadhiliyya. See Schleifer (1997).
54 A brief reminiscence of this period may be found in Sardar (2005).
55 al-Jamal (1977).
56 Kose (1996: 181).
57 Maurer (2002) treats the Murabitun and e-dinar in the context of alternative currencies.
58 Abdalqadir al-Murabit, Preface to Umar Vadillo, "The Return of the Gold Dinar". www.geocities.com/Athens/Delphi/6588/gpreface.html. Viewed March 5, 2009.
59 Garvin (2005).
60 Reaction in Spain to these developments has been mixed. See Smith (2003). The mosque opening was hailed widely the first official return of Islam since 1492.
61 For example, Abu Ammar, "Principles of Dawa". Online, available at: http://iic. netuse.co.uk/dawah.htm.
62 Geaves (2002).
63 *Letter to an Arab Muslim*, (Palma de Mallorca: Kutubia Mayurqa, 2000), 62.
64 Abdülkadir el-Murabit, *Diyalektigin Sonu Gelmekte Olan Insan Için* (n.d.) and *Muhammedi Yol* (n.d.).
65 www.ulumulhikmekoeln.de/Dallas.htm is a Turkish article on Dallas and his thought.
66 The only site seems to have been superceded in 2003 by the Mosque of Granada site as a vehicle for Murabitun identity and outreach in Spain. Online, available at: www. mezquitadegranada.com (accessed 24 September 2005).

67 www.islamhariini.org (Jakarta) (accessed 24 September 2005).
68 'al-Rahman Shaghuri (1998). His obituary by Keller is available at: www.israinterna-tional.com/library/topics/2004/nov.php (accessed 24 September 2005).
69 Najjah al-Naubani (1997).
70 www.islamfortoday.com/keller.htm.
71 Boumediene Hamzi, "Notes on the History of Orthodox Sufism in the United States", unpublished paper.
72 *Reliance of the Traveler* (Evanston: Sunna Books, 1993) and al-Nawawi, *Maqasid* (Evanston: Sunna Books, 1994).
73 A phenomenological description of some aspects of this movement and Keller's teachings may be found in Sahin (2003).
74 Geaves (2001). Shaikh Nazim and his teachings have been attacked directly by a senior member of the Murabitun, Umar Vadillo (2003).
75 This is not a new element in Murabitun ideology but reprises an article by Abdal Qadir in which he characterized the Sufism of (Ahmad) Koftaru, (Hisham) Kabbani and (Martin) Lings as "neo-batinism that puts the experience of mar'ifa on par with the shari'a". Abdal Qadir as-Sufi, "El Nuevo Ismailismo". Online, available at: www.cislamica.org/ultimahora.asp?Id=21 (accessed 17 September 2005).
76 Some global Sufi movements embrace aspects of traditional culture, and nostalgia for this aspect of tradition in the personal sphere at the same time as they embrace moder-nity in the operational one.
77 Hermansen (2003).
78 Quintan Wiktorowicz, *Islamic Activism: A Social Theory Approach* (Bloomington: Indiana University Press), 16. The debate favouring either the economic (rational choice, material circumstances) vs. community of discourse (ideological) models of explanation goes on in World History circles regarding historical examples of net-works. Loimeier (2000: 64).
79 Among global Sufi movements the tightest networks are among the followers of convert shaikhs and their (largely) Western followers due to the element of world-denying orientation and protest.

References

Agai, Bekim "The Educational Network of Fethullah Gulen: The Flexible Implementa-tion of Modern Islamic Thought: A Comparison of Three Countries", *Istanbuler Alma-nach* 5 (2001): 7–10.
Agai, Bekim, *Zwischen Netzwerk und Diskurs. Das Bildungnetzwerk um Fethullah Gülen* (Hamburg: EB-Verlag, 2004).
Algar, Hamid, "Said Nursi and the *Risale-i Nur*", in *Islamic Perspectives Studies in Honour of Sayyid Abu'l-A'la Mawdudi*, Khurshid Ahmad and Zafar Ishaq Ansari (eds) (Leicester: The Islamic Foundation, 1979), 313–333.
al-Jamal, Sidi 'Ali, *The Meaning of Man* (Norwich: Diwan Press, 1977).
al-Rahman Shaghuri, 'Abd, *Diwan al-hada'iq al-nadiyya fi-al-nasamat al-ruhiyya* (Damascus: Dar fajr al-'uruba, 1998).
Appadurai, Arjun, *Modernity at Large: Cultural Dimensions of Globalization* (Minneapo-lis: University of Minnesota Press, 1996).
Arberry, A.J., *Sufism: An Account of the Mystics of Islam* (New York: Harper & Row, 1950).
Balci, Bayram, "Les Ecoles Neo-Nurcu de Fethullah Gulen En Asie Centrale: Implanta-tion, Fonctionnement Et Nature Du Message Vehicule Par Le Biais De La Coopera-tion Educative", *Revue des Mondes Musulmans et de la Mediterranee* 101–102 (2003): 305–330.

Borella, Jean, "Rene Guenon and the Traditionalist School", in *Modern Esoteric Spirituality*, Antoine Faivre and Jacob Needleman (eds) (New York: Crossroad, 1992), 330–358.

Buehler, Arthur. *Sufi Heirs of the Prophet: the Indian Naqshbandiyya and the Rise of the Mediating Sufi Shaykh* (Columbia: University of South Carolina Press, 1998).

Chittick, William, "Sufism", in *Encyclopedia of the Modern Islamic World IV*, John L. Esposito (ed.) (New York: Oxford, 1995), 107–108.

Danner, Victor, "The Shadiliyyah and North African Sufism", in *Islamic Spirituality II: Manifestations*, Seyyid Hosein Nasr (ed.) (New York: Crossroad, 1991).

el-Murabit, Abdülkadir, *Diyalektigin Sonu Gelmekte Olan Insan Için* (Yayina Hazirlayan, n.d.)

el-Murabit, Abdülkadir, *Muhammedi Yol* (Yayina Hazirlayan, n.d.).

Eickelman, Dale. "The Art of Memory: Islamic Education and its Social Reproduction", in *Comparing Muslim Societies: Knowledge and the State in a World Civilization*, Juan I. Cole (ed.) (Ann Arbor: University of Michigan, 1992), 97–132.

Fusfeld, Warren, "Naqshbandi Sufim and Reformist Islam", in *Ibn Khaldun and Islamic Ideology*, Bruce Lawrence (ed.) (Leiden: Brill, 1984).

Garvin, Natascha, "Conversion and Conflict: Muslims in Mexico", in *ISIM Newsletter*, 15 (Spring 2005): 18–19.

Geaves, Ron, *Sufis of Britain* (Cardiff: Cardiff Academic Press, 2002).

Geaves, Ron, "The Haqqani Naqshbandis: a Study of Apocalyptic Millennialism within Islam", in *Faith in the Millennium* (Sheffield: Sheffield Academic Press, 2001), 215–231.

Geertz, Clifford (1976) "From the Native's Point of View: On the Nature of Anthropological Understanding", in *Meaning in Anthropology*, Keith H. Basso and Henry A. Selby (eds) (Albuquerque: University of New Mexico Press).

Gellner, Ernst and Waterbury, John, *Patrons and Clients Mediterranean Societies* (London: Duckworth, 1977).

Hermansen, Marcia, "Mystical Paths and Authoritative Knowledge: A Semiotic Approach to Sufi Cosmological Diagrams", *Journal of Religious Studies and Theology*, 12, 1 (1992): 52–77.

Hermansen, Marcia, "In the Garden of American Sufi Movements: Hybrids and Perennials", in *New Trends and Developments in the World of Islam*, Peter Clark (ed.) (London: Luzac, 1997), 155–178.

Hermansen, Marcia, "How to Put the Genie back in the Bottle: 'Identity Islam' and Muslim Youth Cultures in North America", in *Progressive Muslims*, Omid Safi (ed.) (Oxford: One World, 2003).

Hermansen, Marcia "What's American about American Sufi Movements?" in *Sufism in Europe and North America*, David Westerlund (ed.) (London: Routledge, 2004) 36–62.

Hermansen, Marcia "The Other Shadhilis of the West", in *The Shadhiliyya – Une voie Soufi dans le monde*, Eric Geoffroy (ed.) (Paris: Maisonneuve et Larose, 2005) 481–499.

Kinney, Jay, "Sufism Comes to America", *Gnosis Magazine* 30 (Winter 1994): 21

Kose, Ali, *Conversion to Islam: A Study of Native British Converts* (London and New York: Kegan Paul International, 1996).

Lings, Martin, *A Sufi Saint of the Twentieth Century: Shaikh Ahmad al-Alawi* (London: Allen and Unwin, 1971).

Loimeier, Roman, *Die Islamische Welt aus Netzwerk: Moglichkeiten und Grenzen des Netzwerkansatzes im islamischen Kontext* (Wurzburg: Ergon, 2000).

Mahmud, Abd al-Halim, *Qadayyat at-Tasawwuf: al-Madrasa al-Shadhiliyya* (Cairo: Dar al-Ma'arif, 1988), 281–362.

Maurer, Bill. "Chrysography: Substance and Effect", *The Asia Pacific Journal of Anthropology*, 3, 1 (2002): 49–74.

Motahhedeh, Roy, *Mantle of the Prophet: Religion and Politics in Iran* (New York: Pantheon Books, 1985).

Najjah al-Naubani, Muhammad, *Al-'Arif b-ill'h Muhammad Sa'id Kurdi* (Amman: Dar al-Mana'hij, 1997).

Nasr, Seyyed Hossein, *The Essential Writings of Fritjof Schuon* (Amity: Amity House, 1986).

Rawlinson, *Book of Enlightened Masters* (Chicago: Open Court, 1997), 517–524.

Reichmuth, Stefan, "Netzwerk und Wltsystem: Konzepte zur neuzeitlichen 'Islamische Welt' und ihrer Transformation", in *Die Islamische Welt aus Netzwerk*, Roman Loimeier (ed.) (Wurzburg: Ergon, 2000), 64ff.

Reinhertz, S., *Women Called to the Path of Rumi: The Way of the Whirling Dervish* (Prescott, Ariz: Holm Press, 2001).

Rosen, Lawrence, *Bargaining for Reality: The Construction of Social Relations in a Moroccan Community* (Chicago: University of Chicago Press, 1984).

Sahin, Inayet, "The Experience of Turning to a Spiritual Path and Healing the Emptiness", unpublished Master's thesis, University of Maryland, 2003.

Sanyal, Usha, *Devotional Islam and Politics in British India: Ahmad Riza Khan Barelwi and his Movement, 1870–1920* (Delhi and New York: Oxford University Press, 1996).

Sardar, Ziaddin, *Desperately Seeking Paradise: Journeys of a Sceptical Muslim* (London: Granta Books, 2005).

Schmidt, Garbi, "Sufi Charisma on the Internet", in *Sufism in Europe and North America*, David Westerlund (ed.) (London: Routledge, 2004), 109–126.

Schleifer, Abdullah, "Sufism in Egypt and the Arab Middle East", in *Islamic Spirituality II: Manifestations*, Seyyid Hossein Nasr (ed.) (New York: Crossroads, 1997), 194–205.

Schuon, Frithjof, *Islam are Understanding Islam* (London: Allen and Unwin, 1963).

Schuon, Frithjof, *Islam and the Perennial Philosophy* (London: World of Islam Publishing, 1976).

Schuon, Frothjof, *The Feathered Sun: Plains Indians in Art and Philosophy* (Bloomington: World Wisdom Books, 1990).

Serif, Mardin. *Religion and Social Change in Modern Turkey: the Case of Bediüzzaman Said Nursi* (Albany: State University of New York Press, 1989).

Smith, Craig S., "Where the Moors Held Sway, Allah Is Praised Again", *New York Times International*, 21 October 2003.

Stark, Rodney and Bainbridge, W.S., "Networks of Faith: Interpersonal Bonds and Recruitment to Cults and Sects", *American Journal of Sociology*, 85 (1980): 1376–1395.

Stoddart, William, *Sufism: the Mystical Doctrines and Methods of Islam* (New York: Paragon House, 1986).

Vadillo, Umar, *Esoteric Deviation in Islam* (Cape Town: Madinah Press, 2003).

Webb, Gisella, "Sufism in America", in *America's Alternative Religions*, Tim Miller (ed.) (Albany: State University of New York Press, 1995), 249–259.

Wiktorowicz, Q. *Islamic Activism: A Social Theory Approach* (Bloomington: Indiana University Press), 16.

Wilson, Peter Lamborn, "The Shaikhs have Two States: Loose-Strung Meditations on the Problems of Sexuality and Authority in Modern Sufism", in *Sacred Drift* (San Francisco: City Lights Books, 1993), 108–112.

Yavuz, Hakan, "Matrix of Modern Turkish Islamic Movements: The Naqshbandi Sufi Order", in *The Naqshbandis in Western and Central Asia*, Elisabeth Ozdalga (ed.) (London: Curzon Press, 1999).

Yavuz, Hakan, "Nur Study Circles (Dershanes) and the Formation of New Religious Consciousness in Turkey", in *Islam at the Crossroads: On the Life and Thought of Bediüzzaman Said Nursi* (New York: State University of New York Press, 2003).

Yavuz, Hakan and Esposito, John (eds), *Turkish Islam and the Secular State: The Gülen Movement* (Syracuse: Syracuse University Press, 2003).

4 Globalizing the soundworld

Islam and Sufi music in the West

Michael Frishkopf

An Egyptian Shaikh's reception in Edmonton

I first met Shaikh Mohamed el-Helbawy (b. 1946) in 1995, while researching the Hamidiyya Shadhiliyya tariqa (Sufi order) in Cairo.[1] At that time he served as that tariqa's lead munshid (chanter of hymns), as well as principal muqri' (Qur'an teacher and reciter) at their large mosque in the upscale Mohandiseen neighborhood. Shaikh Mohamed is an established Qur'an reciter well-versed in the Egyptian tradition of mujawwad (melodically elaborate tilawa, Qur'anic recitation), regularly performing at mayatim (funeral gatherings) and specializing also in several genres of inshad dini (religious hymnody), especially tawashih (semi-composed dialogues between solo munshid, and choral bitana) and ibtihalat (improvised supplications and praises), as well as the adhan (the Muslim call to prayer); he regularly performs ibtihalat and adhan on Egyptian national radio. He also performs staged versions of these genres with his Firqat al-Inshad al-Dini (Religious Hymnody Group), comprising vocalists, duff (frame drum), and nay or kawala (reed flute). Most Egytians consider such an ensemble, and its musical sound, to be a representation of Islamic turath (heritage). This perception is reinforced by Shaikh el-Helbawy's traditional dress, training, and milieux. Raised in the medieval Cairo neighborhood of Bab al-Shi`riyya – a district brimming with sights and sounds of mosques, madrasas, saint shrines and Sufi orders – he absorbed the styles and repertoires of traditional Islamic recitation and hymnody from the greatest performers of the twentieth century – Shaikh Mustafa Isma`il, Shaikh `Abd al-Basit `Abd al-Samad, Shaikh Taha al-Fashni, Shaikh Sayyid al-Naqshabandi – and from the senior munshidin in the Hamidiyya Shadhiliyya tariqa. More formally, he studied tilawa at the venerable al-Azhar University (established under the Fatimids *c*.975), and Arabic music theory with co-tariqa member, composer and musicologist Dr Soliman Gamil (see Figure 4.1).

Shaikh Mohamed embodies the traditional intersection, formerly broad, between art and spirituality in Egyptian society. Though locally known primarily for his abilities as a religious performer, he is also indisputably significant as a musical artist, as measured not only by intuitive knowledge and skill in Arab music, but also through extensive concertizing – in Cairo's cultural centers, and

Figure 4.1 Shaikh Mohamed el-Helbawy: teaching in Edmonton (March 2005; left), and reciting pre-dawn ibtihalat at the mosque of Sidi'Ali Zayn al-'Abidin in Cairo, for broadcast on Egyptian radio (April 2007; right) (photographs by the author).

on the World Music circuit in Europe (including the Institut du Monde Arabe in Paris) – and through publication of several compact-disc recordings in Europe (e.g. Chazili, 1982; El Helbawy, 2003; "Mozart in Egypt," 2002). Though his recordings present varying proportions of "music" and "Islam" (from World Music fusion to ethnographic representation of Sufi ritual) all are directed primarily toward a non-Muslim market and filed under "World Music" in record shops.[2]

In December of 2003, while on a year's research leave in Cairo, I began mulling a plan to bring Shaikh Mohamed el-Helbawy to the University of Alberta, in Edmonton, Alberta, Canada, where I presently teach in the Department of Music. The University of Alberta provides generous funding for visiting lecturers, and looks especially favorably upon those who would benefit the broader Edmonton community. In the post-9/11 world I felt certain that bringing a Muslim spiritual artist, projecting a humane image of Islam, would receive university support. However I also knew that I would be expected to demonstrate interest from the Muslim community of Edmonton, both on campus and beyond.

Greater Edmonton is a diverse urban community, within the Canadian province of Alberta. According to the 2001 census, Edmonton's population was

666,104; Alberta's 2,974,807 (StatsCan, 2001c).[3] Overall, both Edmonton and Alberta contain a high proportion of Muslims, exceeded in Canada only by Ontario, and the percentage has increased sharply over the previous ten years (see Figure 4.2); the 2001 census indicates 18,790 Muslims in Edmonton (2.9 percent) and 49,045 in Alberta (1.7 percent). These percentages are almost entirely due to the larger urban areas of Edmonton and Calgary (2.8 percent Muslim), and the study and work opportunities they provide; the rest of Alberta (mainly rural) is only 0.3 percent Muslim (StatsCan, 2001a, 2001b, 2001c).

In December 2005, the University of Alberta comprised approximately 32,000 full-time students, of which the graduate student population (4,356) was about 40 percent non-Canadian, including a conspicuous population of immigrant students from Muslim-majority countries, many from the Arab Middle East. By contrast, the undergraduate population is only about 8 percent non-Canadian. Figuring conservatively, the number of undergraduate Muslim students should be about 600 (2.2 percent of the undergraduate student body), 29 percent of these first-generation immigrants and 71 percent non-immigrant Canadians. The number of graduate Muslim students should be about 234 (5.4 percent of the graduate student body), 81 percent of these first-generation immigrants and 19 percent non-immigrant Canadians.[4]

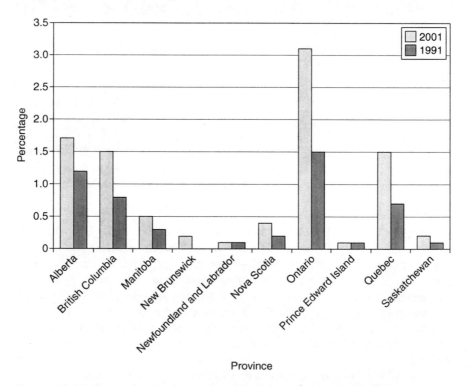

Figure 4.2 Muslims in Canada, by province (2001) (source: StatsCan, 2001b).

Muslims began to emigrate to Canada during the late nineteenth century, although in 1931 there were still reportedly only 645 Muslim residents in Canada, mostly Arabs; Canada's first mosque (al-Rashid) was founded in Edmonton in 1938, by 20 Lebanese Muslim families (Abu Laban, 1983: 138–139). Drawing heavily on the Middle East and South Asia, Muslim populations across Canada expanded rapidly after 1990, particularly in Alberta. Today, Edmonton's pioneering Muslim umbrella organization, the Edmonton Council of Muslim Communities (ECMC), represents nine Muslim organizations, and Edmonton houses over ten places of Muslim worship, including six Sunni mosques, and others serving Shia, Ismaili and Ahmadi communities.

In public, Muslim leaders tend toward tolerance and liberality; these attitudes are best demonstrated by the remarkable ECMC. But within the mosques themselves, out of the public eye, a different atmosphere often prevails. Over the course of some eight years living in Edmonton, I have heard even practicing Muslim friends and acquaintances complaining about "Salafi" attitudes prevailing in local Edmonton Sunni mosques. Sermons often (although not always) exhibit a conservative and sometimes even intolerant line: railing against liberal society; warning against making non-Muslim friends; generally opposing "us" (Muslims) to "them" (others). From the perspective of such sermons, the Sunni community appears relatively closed; Shiites are hardly recognized as Muslims, and Ismailis not at all. Fear of bida (innovation, i.e. heresy) is rampant. Sufism is not acknowledged in official mosque discourse, and informally statements rejecting Sufism (e.g. "Sufism has nothing to do with Islam") are commonly heard. Even when not hostile to outsiders, the wisdom of caution lies heavily upon the community's public practice.

Clear boundaries between "Sufi" and "orthodox" Islam, so carefully inscribed both by orientalist and Islamic reformist discourses, hardly exist in Egyptian Muslim practice. This ambiguity is best demonstrated in the soundworld,[5] that affectively charged sonic–social intersubjectivity, where sharp boundaries between "Sufi" and "non-Sufi" sound and practice cannot be located. Rather, the whole of Islam is suffused with sonic practices, including tilawa (Qur'anic recitation), du'a' (supplication), adhan, ibtihalat and inshad, mediated or live, as associated with daily prayer, life-cycle events and religious holidays, as well as with liturgies of the Sufi orders, indicating the interpenetration of Sufi and "mainstream" Islam. Aside from exceptional instances featuring unequivocally mystical texts, and outside of explicitly Sufi contexts, it is impossible to say whether Shaikh el-Helbawy's repertoire is "Sufi" or "orthodox," because the same recurrent themes (supplication, praise, exhortation, devotion) permeate all Islamic religious poetry and are featured in all Islamic performance contexts. These genres of Islamic vocal performance are highly melodic, powerfully expressive and deeply affecting. The unarticulated, unremarkable prevalence of these sonic forms mediates social relations by linking individual and group experience in an integrated, affectively rich soundworld.

Yet, Islam in Edmonton – as in most North American cities – is comparatively silent. In public, outside the mosque, this silence reflects Muslims' minority status. In large cities of the Muslim world, calls to prayer, Qur'anic recitation, religious hymns and sermons are broadcast in the streets, and via radio and television media. With few exceptions, such broadcast is controversial where Muslims comprise a social minority.[6]

But in Edmonton even the interior of the mosque is relatively silent. When I arrived in Edmonton in 1999, I wondered why there was no tilawa prior to Friday prayer, a custom which is nearly universal in Egypt. One Egyptian friend told me that some Edmonton Muslims believed such a practice to be bida (heretical), an attitude which spread rapidly as representing the "safe side" on which to be. Whereas Ismailis recite a sacred poetic corpus (ginan (see Gillani, 2004)), no religious poetry is recited in connection with any Sunni ritual practices I have attended in Edmonton, unlike common practice in Egypt (where ibtihalat precede dawn prayer, and Sufi orders are everywhere). On Fridays Muslims gather in the university mosque, sitting or reading Qur'an individually. The call to prayer – object of melodic elaboration in Cairo – is here perfunctory, rarely even elongated, much less beautiful. The sermon is performed in ordinary speech; Qur'anic passages are not melodically elaborated as is often the case in Egypt. Following prayer, all disperse; there is no public khitam al-salat (closing) by the imam, a passage often performed melodically in Cairo. During Ramadan the mosques often hire an Egyptian preacher (who may or may not possess a good voice), but never a dedicated Qur'an reciter. Sufism typically carries its own sonic forms, but Sufism plays an exceedingly marginal role among Edmonton's Muslims. There are no Sufi groups operating openly, and in my experience Sufism has never been the subject of weekly sermons or mosque lectures and study groups. (This fact is in stark contrast to other large Canadian cities; for instance, a number of Sufi orders are active in Montreal, often with highly musical hadras.)

Such an Islam is not to the liking of several immigrant Muslim acquaintances whose concept of Islam remains defined by practices they grew up with. Nor is it acceptable to the more liberal-minded among them. Some of these have therefore abandoned the mosques. Others attend Friday prayers as a matter of habit, without expecting much spiritual sustenance. Among the second (and subsequent) generation Muslim community, however, the "silence of the mosque" is more accepted, since many have not experienced anything else.

In arranging to obtain letters of support for Shaikh el-Helbawy's visit, I enlisted the help of a Muslim Egyptian-Canadian friend, who expressed the liberal attitude of cultural rapprochement which I had expected to prevail in multicultural Canada, particular among second or third generation Muslims. In an email, she wrote:

> Salam Michael
> You have my support in bringing Shaykh Mohamad El-Hilbawi. I think it is a great idea and his presence will add another dimension to the religion that is not known to most. People aren't aware that there could be singing and music in Islam. Please, start working on it and I will get you all the letters you need starting with myself.

She suggested I solicit other letters from the president of the Canadian Islamic Center (Edmonton's oldest and largest mosque), the president of the Edmonton Council of Muslim Communities (ECMC), the president of the Canadian Arab Friendship Association, president of the Canadian Egyptian Society of Edmonton, and president of the Canadian Arab Professional and Business Club.

I proceeded to write to these individuals, explaining Shaikh el-Helbawy's esteemed position in Egyptian Muslim society, describing his recitational talents and emphasizing the multiple value of his visit: spiritual, educational, aesthetic. Perhaps regarding the issue as primarily a matter of turath – cultural heritage – the three non-denominational associations responded positively without delay, despite their multiconfessional memberships. However, the president of Edmonton's oldest (and Canada's first) mosque, al-Rashid, reportedly refused at first, without explanation. Subsequently, my letter to the president of the ECMC stirred a general discussion. The organization's president is well known as a relatively liberal Muslim, eager for dialogue with the wider Canadian society; under his leadership, the organization produced a letter. As a consequence, the mosque also agreed to support the visit.

Having secured the needed funds, and hoping that the university and Edmonton Muslim communities could receive maximal benefit from Shaikh el-Helbawy's visit, now set for March 2005, I sought to identify community groups to be included in his complex schedule of lectures, lecture-demonstrations, workshops and performances. Though the Egyptian community association invited Shaikh el-Helbawy to dinner, the Arab associations did not respond to my scheduling offer.

The Muslim Community of Edmonton mosque – representing primarily the Muslim student body, including a large proportion of immigrants – expressed interest, inviting Shaikh el-Helbawy to recite Qur'an prior to Friday prayer, a most uncommon event. Many worshippers were moved to tears by his performance, and mosque officials (mainly first-generation immigrants) were eager for him to return the following Friday, when he was scheduled to recite at Edmonton's older mosque, al-Rashid, run by non-immigrant Muslims. Here the welcome was decidedly cooler. Shaikh el-Helbawy expressed a clear preference for the first mosque, and – accompanying him – I understood why. The Egyptian Students' Association, comprising almost exclusively male Muslim immigrant graduate students (nearly all of them engineers), invited Shaikh el-Helbawy to lead their weekly maqra' (Qur'an recitation session). There followed a fascinating conversation in which several students (evincing Salafi discourse) objected to the shaikh's associating with music; he adopted approximately al-Ghazali's neutral stance: what is forbidden in it is forbidden; what is permitted in it is permitted. But an atmosphere of genuine respect for his skill and common Egyptian patrimony prevailed, and he felt welcomed.

His reception by the University of Alberta Muslim Students' Association (MSA[7]) was at first ambivalent, finally negative. Leadership of the University of Alberta MSA has tended to alternate between undergraduate students (most of whom are not immigrants) and graduate students (who generally are). At the time I contacted them, the former situation prevailed. I had emailed the MSA president in the autumn of 2004 about the proposed visit, but received no reply.

Finally, in early January 2005, I attended Friday MSA prayers on campus, following which I succeeded in speaking to a thoughtful undergraduate student, who suggested that I write the group's leader (not present) in order that the request be taken up at the following meeting.

Our short email exchange ran as follows:

Assalamu 'alaykum,
al-Hamdu lillah, I have secured funding from the University's Distinguished Visitor program to bring a renowned muqri', mubtahil, and munshid (specialist in inshad or anashid) from Cairo to the U of A campus this coming spring, for ten days (March 7th to 17th), insha'Allah. His name is Shaykh Mohamed el-Hilbawy. His visit is now pending visa approval from the Canadian Embassy in Cairo.

If possible, I would like to work with the MSA to plan some special events during his stay, for instance durus[8] in tajwid and adhan, either in the evening or during the day, especially directed towards MSA members.

Shaykh Mohamed will also be working daily with a group of students and members of the community to develop a full program of anashid diniyya, to be presented in Convocation Hall on March 17th. I invite members of the MSA with strong and good voices to join this group; we will begin preparation on Mondays evenings starting in January, insha'Allah, since his stay is too short to provide sufficient training.

On the two Fridays that he will be spending in Edmonton, I would also like to escort him to Friday prayers either on campus or at MCE mosque, where he could also conduct some study sessions if there is interest.

I welcome other ideas you may have. If possible let's talk by phone or in person; please send me a contact number. Mine are below.

wassalamu 'alaykum.
Michael

I neither requested – nor required – any financial support or official endorsement. My message was merely to offer an opportunity. A pregnant pause of about ten days followed. Then on January 25 I finally received the following reply:

WaAlaikum Assalaam Brother Michael,
Im sorry for the delay in getting back to you. As the MSA we are responsible in insuring that those whom the MSA endorses, and those who are using the MSA for specific purposes meet guidelines that do not transgress the boundaries of the Quraan and Sunnah. After investigation, we feel that Shaikh Mohammed el-Hilbawy practices certain things that are considered innovations in the religion, and other matters which are highly doubtful and

debatable and these matters should be avoided. Therefore, the MSA executive body has agreed that we cannot support this proposed program with the Sheikh. Please do not take any offence to this position we are adopting; we simply choose to remain on the side of caution.

Jazaakallaahu Khairan Wassalaamu Alaikum,
Muslim Students Association – President

Seeking elaboration of those "certain things," I promptly answered as follows:

Assalamu alaykum brother Abdulmelik,
Of course I fully respect whatever position the MSA may choose, and thank you for considering the issue. I further sympathize with your felt need to err on the side of caution, and certainly take no offence. In fact as a Muslim you have raised certain doubts in my own mind about this program. I am therefore wondering if you can explain how your investigation led you to conclude that Shaykh Mohamed's practices may be bida, or at least doubtful from the perspective of shari'a. After all, he recites Qur'an and inshad on national Egyptian radio, with the blessings of al-Azhar university. Furthermore practices of tilawat al-Qur'an al-karim and anashid diniyya are well-established even in the most conservative Islamic countries, such as Saudi Arabia. I realize that music itself has often considered haram[9] among Islamic scholars, although even widely respected authorities such as Shaykh al-Qaradawi have endorsed the right of Muslims to hear and perform music so long as it is respectable from an ethical standpoint.
I await your response with sincere interest.

jazaakallahu khayran wassalamu 'alaykum.
Michael

In retrospect, it is perhaps unsurprising that my questions went unanswered, because, as I came to understand, the MSA's affective subtext is not belligerent, didactic nor even well-informed – rather it is anxious, expressing the fear of uncertainty which seeks safety in conservatism. Often contrasted with "hope" (raja'), the emotion of fear (khawf) occupies an central position in Islamic – and especially Sufi – piety. One fears God, while placing one's hopes in Him. But the fear expressed by the MSA leadership does not appear to be of this sort at all, as signalled by their unwillingness to enter into any sort of discussion regarding the precise source of his supposed bida, and their neglect of his mainstream position in Egyptian society. The MSA's fear, then, appears to be a social rather than a spiritual fear, a fear of what others might say – what might equally be described as "peer pressure" – a stance which accords with their desire to "remain on the side of caution."

I hasten to add that social fear as a motivation for action (or inaction) is certainly not exclusive to the MSA (or indeed to Islam): in a climate of sanctimony, many fear what others may say or think of their behavior; they therefore conform (outwardly at least) to the way others behave. The result is a feedback cycle of fear, propagating within Muslim social networks, as each Muslim impels network "neighbors" (friends, co-workers, family members) to appear more conservative than his or her peers (or than he or she really wants to be).[10] Such a cycle is checked to some extent in traditional Muslim societies by the inertial force of continuous oral tradition which suffuses the same social network. This force is absent, however, in immigrant societies where Muslims constitute a small minority.

Accordingly, in this era and an immigrant social context – to draw upon an established Islamic triality – it is "islam" (outward ritual performance) that prevails over "iman" (inner faith) and "ihsan" (the continual awareness of God), or (to draw upon a duality in the ladder of Sufi maqamat – spiritual stations) – it is "fear" that prevails over "hope." This attitude of social fear accentuates the external (zahir) – precisely the contrary of Sufi emphasis upon the internal (batin). Fear creates a vicious cycle whose logical endpoint is a retreat to literalism, the relative safety of certainty in the canonical texts, according to maximally conservative interpreters, denying the Islamic cultural heritage which is solidly rooted in oral tradition. Thus Sufism's own terms reveal the anti-Sufi perspective of the Islamist Salafi position.

On the other hand, a local Christian college went furthest in providing a warm welcome to Shaikh el-Helbawy, featuring him as guest speaker, and even providing lunch. I organized an "inshad ensemble," which quickly grew to over 20 members, despite a demanding rehearsal schedule (almost daily for over a week), culminating in a final concert. This ensemble included a significant Muslim component, though nearly all were Egyptian immigrants feeling a strong cultural link to the inshad tradition.

On the whole, the visit itself was, by many measures, a great success, benefiting both the university and broader Edmonton communities. However many events were under-attended, particularly by Muslims, and the final concert performance drew a rather meager Muslim crowd. And interest among undergraduate Muslims was nearly non-existent.

Clearly in the case of Shaikh el-Helbawy, the trigger of disputation was a word carrying a long history of controversy in Islam, but which has lately become a kind of acid test for Muslim conservatism: "music," a word which may have been invoked not only by the Shaikh, but also by my own departmental affiliation. Yet members of the MSA certainly listen to music (including Arab music); it is only within the sphere marked "Islam" that different rules apply, especially in response to increasing conservatism of Islamic practice worldwide. So their objection cannot simply be to music per se from an Islamic perspective. Rather, they object to music *in* (or considered *as*) Islam. Music appears not as forbidden by Islam but rather as dangerous *to* Islam. More generally, the silence of Islam in Edmonton cannot be attributed simply to the general Islamic ambivalence about music. For one thing, Shaikh el-Helbawy's sonic practices are, by and large, accepted as mainstream in Egypt, even by the more conservative

Muslims. For another, his performances and teaching of tilawa, filling the silent spaces of Edmonton's mosques, were welcomed by many, mainly first-generation immigrants.

As for "Sufi music" – it is popular among alternative music connoisseurs and spiritual seekers, but not among most Muslims, for whom the combination of words may even appear oxymoronic. A world-famous American Middle-Eastern historian of Egyptian descent once told me that there is "no such thing as Islamic music." Likewise in Edmonton; the category appears at best to mark two non-overlapping categories; at worst pejorative. A recent Edmonton concert featuring "spiritual" Sufi-inflected performances by the late Nubian artist Hamza el Din and the raucous Gnawa of Hassan Hakmoun drew an enthusiastic world-music crowd. But the Egyptian Muslims I know – liberal-minded Muslims with a strong interest in music – didn't appreciate it at all; for them it didn't represent music of the Arab world, and it certainly didn't represent Islam. And while they appreciated Shaikh el-Helbawy, they'd certainly never heard of him before – perhaps because his persona in the West (like his CDs) is to a great extent manu-factured through interaction with, and concern for, a Western non-Muslim audience. While he is a deeply religious man, he also demonstrates considerable skill in communicating to such audiences, in his discourse, in his performances and in his dress – which during his visit oscillated between traditional shaikhly robes (jubba and quftan) and a rather dapper tailored suit topped off with a Central Asian cap.

What is going on here? Why was Shaikh el-Helbawy rejected by some, and welcomed by others, within the Muslim community? Why is "Sufi music" pri-marily marketed for – and consumed by – non-Muslims in the West? And why is Islamic practice in Edmonton so silent?

My argument is that Shaikh el-Helbawy's own journey from Cairo to Edmon-ton retraces two fundamental trajectories by which the "soundworld" of Islam in Muslim societies has been – and continues to be – globalized: through global migration, and through global media. In order to make such an argument, I now must make a brief side-excursion into theory.

Soundworld: soundscape: lifeworld: ethnoscape

By analogy to the lifeworld of Schutz and Luckmann (1973: 3ff.) and Habermas (1984: 113ff.), I define the *soundworld* to be the affectively charged sonic–social intersubjectivity, that lived social world of empathetic understanding, intuitive communication and shared values, as developed, expressed and reproduced in the social experience of pre-linguistic sound.[11] By definition the soundworld links sonic and social aspects, mediated through individual aural experience, an experience that is primarily implicit and affective, and which cannot therefore be rendered in discourse without distortion. Indeed the soundworld references a non-specific semantic domain, which is also somatic, and thus very far from the rational domain of language. The sonic aspect of the soundworld features per-formed sound, particularly music, the most complexly organized form of humanly-organized sound, to use ethnomusicologist John Blacking's classic formulation (1973), and is carried primarily by oral tradition. The social aspect of the soundworld centers on face-to-face interactions, through a social network comprising them, which also provides the basis for inertial continuity of the oral tradition.

Now a few theoretical corollaries can be drawn at once. Several stem from biological facts: the soundworld cannot (usually) be selectively silenced; it is pervasive – even more so in an age of amplified media technology. And though it can be the focus of attention, its presence (and effects) frequently remain out of active awareness.[12] The soundworld does not center upon symbolically referential units, in the precise sense exploited by language; though its non-linguistic sounds may acquire symbolic meaning, they do not consistently shift attention from signifier to a signified (as language does), but rather allow consciousness to remain fixed upon the "signifier" without requiring any active effort at resistance (as listening to the sound of ordinary spoken language does).

This fixity enables the soundworld to develop a powerful emotional force; particularly as music, non-discursive sounds become affectively potent "presentational symbols," offering the "form of feeling," as Susan Langer observed (1960: 97, 101, 235). The emotion of sound becomes associated too with the context of its listening, and the soundworld thereby provides emotional coloring to all perceptions within its scope. Though defined in subjective terms, the soundworld is also hardly ever a solitary experience (at least prior to the headphone); this property derives in part from the physical fact of sonic diffraction. Unlike light (which proceeds in approximately straight lines), sound navigates around even large obstacles, thus becoming maximally inclusive, and often excluding competing linguistic communications. Unlike vision, hearing thus facilitates an intersubjective social experience through the mere fact of physical proximity. In face-to-face experience, we rarely see the same sights, but we nearly always hear the same sounds. This fact of corporate listening experience, charged also with the emotion of listening, bestows an affective valence upon social relations, providing the "collective effervescence" cited by Durkheim as reinforcing group solidarity (1976: 434). The soundworld is socially powerful, even – through its formalisms, apparent innocuousness and blockage of alternative point-to-point communications – coercive, especially in apparently innocuous corporate music-making; as Maurice Bloch once observed, "you can't argue with a song" (1974).[13]

In affectively supporting the social network, the soundworld becomes a principal pathway for cultural localization. Cultural formations, always mobile, frequently global (even in the past), are fixed in particular socio-affective coordinates by their association with sound experience. Even though the humanly-organized soundworld is theoretically subject to discursively-transmitted norms, in practice it tends to resist them, because it constitutes a separable, quasi-autonomous communicative system. Though speech is expressed through sound, at a theoretical level speech and sound are autonomous systems, incommensurate modalities which always fail to comment on each other precisely.[14]

No better example exists than the various manifestations of the Islamic soundworld in various cultures and places throughout history, and in particular in relation to Islamic globalization. I suggest that from a theoretical point of view this globalization be regarded in two phases (rather unequal in duration). In the first phase (from the early Islamic empires through the eighteenth century), when the Islamic world was globally central, flows of people and sound were carried together – only people could carry the sounds of Islam – mostly from center to margin. During this period what I'll shortly term the soundscape and the ethnoscape were inextricably linked in a soundworld. In the more recent phase, starting with globalizing discourses of nineteenth-century pan-Islamic reform movements but especially with the advent of latter twentieth-century postmodern globalization, and under pressure from Islamic reformism, soundscape and ethnoscape have disengaged, and the soundworld has become undone.

During the first phase, Islamic globalization took place, ironically enough, via localization. It was precisely the adaptability of Islam which enabled its expansion, the ability to absorb local cultures without losing its élan, and this property in turn required a flexible, non-literal interpretation of Islamic practice and doctrine. Sound – and hence the soundworld – was a critical feature enabling such localization. Islamic tradition has always comprised a complex synthesis of oral and written. Only the latter can (potentially) be fixed and universalized; oral transmission is inherently dynamic, ramifying and localizing. The authoritative written sources – primarily Qur'an and Hadith – do not, and indeed cannot, specify sonic dimensions of Islamic practice completely – this limitation pertains of course not merely to Islam but to any tradition, as a consequence of the independence of sonic and linguistic systems. There thus necessarily exist "free variables" in the multidimensional space of sound which cannot be precisely regulated through any discursive mechanism, but only through non-discursive oral transmission.[15] Oral transmission in turn occurs via face-to-face interactions through a social network, closely integrated with the soundworld in each locale.

As Islam encountered foreign cultures and adapted to their local conditions (sonically, and otherwise), sacred sonic dimensions of Islam tended to ramify, while a parallel sacred discursive textual tradition (especially Qur'an and Hadith) remained relatively fixed. Local musical practices were everywhere absorbed, as is evident from a cursory listen to the Islamic soundscape today: Turkish and Iranian tilawa sounds entirely different from Egyptian. Cultural locale is expressed in contrasting timbres, ornaments and modal systems, while the sacred words themselves are identical.

But it was within the context of Sufi groups, themselves absorbing local social structures and ritual practices, that the most distinctive Islamic soundworlds developed, from the elite Ottoman Mevlevi, to the more popular rhythms of the Rifa`iyya in Cairo.

In this phase of Islamic globalization, the core messages of Islam were broadly disseminated, in a million outward guises. This process itself constituted a kind of Sufi message: a single inner meaning (batin) clothed everywhere in variant outward forms (zahir). Functionally, this multiplicity of forms served, rather than undermined, Islamic globalization, not only by facilitating adaptation but also by enabling Islam to develop affective, social vibrancy in each location, a consequence – to a great extent – of the soundworld, and its affective integration of social and sonic systems.

To appreciate the force of such integration it suffices here to consider the Islamic soundworld of Egypt as it developed over the past century (see Frishkopf, 2002). In the early twentieth century a broad domain of overlap obtained between musical and religious performance, as indicated for instance by the title "shaikh." The shaikh demonstrated religious knowledge through public oral performance, as imam (prayer leader), khatib (preacher), 'alim (scholar), munshid (inshad specialist), mu'adhdhin (caller-to-prayer), or qari` (Qur'an reciter). The art of the latter three practices, though never termed musiqa (music) or ghina' (song), was nevertheless judged by musical criteria, which these religious practices also helped to shape. Vocal training took place primarily via tilawa and inshad, and late nineteenth/early twentieth-century secular singers who received such training often retained the title "shaikh" (e.g. Shaikh Sayyid Darwish 1892–1923, Shaikh Zakariya Ahmad 1896–1961). Meanwhile, specialists in tilawa and inshad frequently crossed into the domain of elevated amorous song. Such performers, such as Shaikh Ali Mahmud (b. 1881) or Shaikh Yusuf al-Manyalawi (b. 1847), also active at the turn of the twentieth century, often specialized in the Sufi repertoire whose mystical love poetry, taken out of context, might in any case be misconstrued as speaking of ordinary love. Such performers were called upon to sing for life-cycle rituals (weddings, circumcisions), as well as religious holidays. Egyptian Muslim life was thus suffused with aesthetically powerful sound; an extended Islamic soundworld that not only integrated individual and society, but also blurred the distinction between secular and sacred spheres. Indeed, religious training served as a touchstone for a performer's authenticity (Danielson, 1991). This entire tradition of sacred sound was localized, drawing upon specifically Egyptian musical types (e.g. local concepts of melodic mode, or maqam), and orally transmitted, especially via the kuttab (traditional Islamic school) and the Sufi halaqat dhikr (dhikr circles), twin crucibles for the formation of specialists in both secular and sacred sonic performance. The same processes produced localized Islamic soundworlds throughout the Islamic sphere, from North Africa to Indonesia.

But since the mid-twentieth century a bifurcation has developed in the soundworld of Muslim societies, a consequence of twin (though not unrelated) forces of capitalism (specifically the commodification of mediated music) on the one hand, and Islamic reformism on the other. The common ground inhabited by the artist-shaikh (and still represented by Shaikh el-Helbawy), has largely eroded, a result of market forces (always pandering to the most physical, hence most dependable, of human drives) applied to newly commodified music, and Muslim reformist critiques (calling for Islamic purity and unification of the Umma via the deculturization – delocalization – of Islam). The soundsphere has thus developed paradoxically – yet characteristically – postmodern ironies: on the same Egyptian television one hears light love songs on one channel, and Muslim preachers denouncing them on the next. Popular music "videoclips" featuring scantily clad singers blare from one local café's wall-mounted television, aurally juxtaposed with tilawa emanating from the café next door.

Despite this bifurcation, a characteristically Islamic soundworld persists throughout Muslim societies – most affectively potent through tilawa, adhan and du`a' – suffusing ordinary life in a wash of aesthetically and spiritually charged sound, mediating individual and group, binding both together through a felt sense of belonging. Indeed, even if – due to the commodification of popular music – the sonic span of the new Islamic soundworld has contracted, its intensity is all the greater: the number of mosques and the power of their broadcasts has increased, not only via omnipresent loudspeakers, but new specialized religious channels throughout broadcast media (especially satellite radio and television) as well. Quotidian sonic experience is marked by the regular performance of adhan, iqama and tilawa, often in elaborately melodic styles. On Fridays the sounds of tilawa and prayers in progress filter through every Egyptian neighborhood. One regularly passes funeral tents, erected in side-streets, marking a death ceremony – maytam (funeral), arba`in (fortieth-day memorial), or dhikra sanawiyya (yearly memorial); such occasions are accented with tilawa, and sometimes with inshad. Likewise, the saints populating cemeteries of villages and cities alike are set aglow in an annual mawlid festival, ringing with the sound of recitation and inshad; here the localization of sound, centering on a shaikh's tomb, is particularly striking. While some of these contexts and sounds – maytam, mawlid, excessively melodic tilawa, excessively musical inshad – are condemned by the Muslim reformers as bida, the inertial force of continuous oral tradition allows them to persist.

The traditional soundworld is a harmonious integration of sound with social network, mutually reinforcing one another: the former providing socialized affect (collective effervescence), the latter the social capacity of reproduction. In its pure form, the soundworld is completely localized (without necessarily being local in extent), adaptively supporting a kind of social homeostasis. The soundworld is a critical factor in the dialectical formation of the Islamic *habitus*, to use that keyword popularized by Pierre Bourdieu (1977: 72ff.) to represent the individual's collection of non-discursive yet strongly inculcated dispositions, values and strategies – structuring social structures, even as it is structured by them. In Muslim societies, even its discursive intellectual detractors often harbor sentimental emotional attachments to the soundworld, which has shaped their spiritual *habitus* from earliest childhood.

The Islamic soundworld is attenuated in the second phase of Islamic globalization, as Islam and Muslims participate in the broader currents of postmodern globalization, a phenomenon many critics and scholars have treated, in respect of the vast scope, speed and quasi-independence of its flows, as qualitatively new.

Anthropologist Arjun Appadurai has aptly applied the metaphor of "landscape" to processes of post-modern globalization, deploying the "-scape" suffix to convey the fluidity, irregularity and subjective nature of contemporary global flows. "Landscapes" of finance, ideology, technology, ethnicity and media (his so-called finanscape, ideoscape, technoscape, ethnoscape and mediascape) are the building blocks of what he terms (following Benedict Anderson (2006)) "imagined worlds," the multiple worlds constituted by the historically situated imaginations of persons and groups around the globe. What is significant about contemporary globalization is the growing disjunctures between these multiple "scapes," and the ways in which global flows occur in and through them; at unprecedented speed, scale and volume, following increasingly non-isomorphic paths within the labyrinthine global system (Appadurai, 1996: 33–37). Implicit in his analysis is "a theory of rupture that takes media and migration as its two major, and interconnected, diacritics and explores their joint effect on the *work of the imagination* as a constitutive feature of modern subjectivity" (Appadurai, 1996) Global media and migration – the mediascape and ethnoscape – are the focal points of my chapter as well, because they account for the fracturing of the soundworld into independently-flowing sonic and social components, tracing different global trajectories and accumulating contrastive meanings.

Here I'd like to introduce a theoretical refinement to Appadurai's paradigm, a subgenus of the mediascape that I call the *soundscape*. At the same time, I want to indicate a paradigm linkage, by proposing that *soundscape is to soundworld as ethnoscape is to lifeworld*. Whereas the "scapes" suggest the disengagement (politically- and market-driven) of objective relations and meanings to which they were once deeply, even "inextricably" connected, the "worlds" suggest holism. If the ethnoscape is the fragmentation of the lifeworld into an unmoored, even chaotic array of tourists, guestworkers, immigrants, exiles and refugees, for which stable social networks and communications have frequently broken down, equally the soundscape results when the the sonic aspect of the soundworld disengages from its social, semantic and somatic groundings, and is thereby freed to flow globally.

Both ethnoscape and soundscape irregularly join (sometimes driven by, sometimes driving) global flows of capital, technology and ideology. In the transition from "world" to "scape" is the disruption and distortion of what was once a *relatively* functional, stable integration of individual within social group, through the mediation of communicative media which no longer effect real integrative communication, but rather serve rational–quantitative forces accumulating capital and power.

In both cases, globalization of the "scape" proceeds through the agency of broader technical–rational systems. The ethnoscape is shaped by systems of technology, law and force (e.g. immigration policy) regulating the flow of people around the globe, while the soundscape depends upon the international entertainment industry, especially its systems of legal regulation (e.g. intellectual property law) and distribution (media technology).

Mobilizing these three theoretical concepts – soundworld, ethnoscape, soundscape – we may better understand the relations between Sufi music and Muslims in Edmonton, Canada, and perhaps elsewhere as well. Postmodern globalization has induced a fracturing of the Islamic soundworld, a rupture between formerly interpenetrating social and sonic aspects, by which these aspects, formerly integrated, have disengaged and begun to circulate independently – through an ethnoscape and a soundscape, respectively – unmoored from their original contexts and meanings. Though rapid global circulation virtually ensures that such flows will re-cross one another, such re-crossings are typically non-interactive. Ethnoscape and mediascape have been shaped by the global system to very different purposes, so that reintegration cannot occur. On the contrary, the crossing point often goes unrecognized, or may even be the site of social strain, as the Shaikh el-Helbawy example illustrates.

The Islamic soundworld and the Muslim ethnoscape

Again, my argument is that Shaikh el-Helbawy's own journey from Cairo to Edmonton retraces two fundamental trajectories by which the "soundworld" of Islam in Muslim societies has been – and continues to be – globalized: through global migration (the ethnoscape) and through global media (the soundscape). His simultaneous embodiment of both – as a temporary guest within the Muslim diaspora, and as a producer of Islamic world music – accounts for the multiple, at times contradictory, attitudes toward him. In this section I consider the ethnoscape in greater detail.

To begin, it is necessary to view Islam in North America against the backdrop of early modern Islamic reform. As a response first to Western military power, and subsequently what appeared as an overwhelming technical–civilizational superiority, late nineteenth and early twentieth-century Muslim reformers, so-called salafis, sought to reunify the Islamic world on the "sound" basis of reason, usually returning to the early Muslim community (al-salaf al-salih), as understood through canonical texts, as a model for a new pan-Islamism. The sociopolitical weakness of Muslims, it was argued, stemmed from their failure to unify around their principles. Unable to recognize the ways in which local adaptations via oral traditions, operating in the spaces left by the "free variables" of discursive Islamic regulations, had actually paved the way for expansion during Islam's long period of strength, for the reformists difference could only lead to weakness. The new unity the Muslim Umma required must be a textual, practical unity, a unity of outward discourse and practice, as opposed to an inward spiritual–aesthetic unity. Reformers thus tended to reject cultural localizations, expressed above all in the sonic dimension of Islamic practice.

This move naturally came at the expense of the Islamic soundworld, in both its mystical and aesthetic aspects, which, operating in the discursive spaces was not only diverse (thus presenting the appearance of disunity), but lacking explicit discursive justification within the sacred texts. To the reformist way of thinking, oral traditions not directly supported by recourse to Qur'an and Sunna (or Hadith) constituted heresy, bida. Not only Sufism, but all taqlid (imitation), the basis for locally adaptive oral traditions, generated unwelcome accretion, which should be eliminated in order to restore Islam's pristine purity and unity. A logical corollary – accelerated perhaps by growing literacy – was a gradual shift of authority: from an oral tradition (embedded in a social network of authorship), to a written tradition (embedded in an intertext).[16]

The soundworld began to contract as a response, particular in the heartlands of such reformism, e.g. in Egypt where performances by the munshidin became increasingly regarded as a "folk" phenomenon, characterizing the backwardness of the peasantry and the farther anti-modern reaches of Upper Egypt. Whereas the early reformers – e.g. Shaikh Muhammad ʿAbdu in Egypt – could be liberal-minded, "opening the door of ijtihad" (independent interpretation of Qur'an and Sunna) in order to re-establish Islam on a rational basis, reformism's institutionalization, e.g. in the Muslim Brothers in the late 1920s coincided with a predictably anti-intellectual turn. Given the pressing need for unity, the door of ijtihad was once again firmly shut, in favor of a new taqlid (imitation) of reformism itself. With the concurrent rapid social transformations which have continued to the present, it is not surprising that religion and professional life have, especially in recent years, often been clearly demarcated into non-interacting spheres. Technical knowledge is compatible with religion in a way that humanistic (or even scientific) inquiry is not, particularly in its historical and social critical forms. It is not surprising then that the Brothers have thrived particularly among those – lawyers, doctors and engineers – whose critical intellectual training operate within well-defined, closed, ahistorical systems (law, the body, technology). And it is perhaps not entirely coincidental that it was upon precisely this technical class that push and pull forces of migration to the West were most strongly felt.

To further unravel this story requires some understanding of the Muslim ethnoscape, and the emergence of enormous Muslim minorities in non-Muslim countries, primarily in the West. As Roy writes:

> The phenomenon of Muslims living as a minority is not new, but historically it has been a consequence of conquests or reconquests … trade and conversions … or loss of political power … what is new is the choice made by individual Muslims to migrate to a country knowing that they will live there as a minority.
>
> (Roy, 2004: 18)

Here an important distinction must be observed between postwar immigration to Europe, and to North America. Postwar Europe required immigration to offset labor shortages and depopulation. With European sources unavailable, many countries turned to immigration from ex-colonies from all social strata, presumed linguistically and culturally compatible, hence assimilable. Many of these sources were Muslim; France drew extensively on North Africa; Britain absorbed South Asians (Hollifield, 1986: 116; McNeill, 1998). North American immigration policy – unencumbered by a colonial past – has recently been more influenced by rational economic analysis, setting minimal technical–economic criteria designed to boost economic output, and less concerned with assimilation than productivity. In practice, skill-based immigration policies have tended to favor professionals, especially engineers who (unlike lawyers or doctors) generally do not require recertification. Intellectuals, artists and the poor have been largely excluded, except in the case of familial reunification.

Contemporary Canadian immigration dates to 1967, when a rationalized "point system" was established, taking into account education, training and demand, as well as family ties. This regulatory system continues to form the framework of Canadian immigration policy to the present (Green and Green, 1995: 1007–1008). Laws governing Canadian immigration today thus effect a kind of "high pass filter" favoring admission of those possessing significant quantities of in-demand technical or financial capital, primarily engineers. Since technical requirements are applied without regard to ethnicity, Muslim immigrants to Canada find themselves juxtaposed with other Muslims representing a wide array of cultural and linguistic groups. These conditions on Canadian immigration exist in dialectical relation to Canada's self-proclaimed "multicultural mosaic" model (itself in dialectical relation to what Canadians tend to portray as the USA's assimilationist "melting pot"), celebrating cultural difference.

Ironically, the cultural politics of Canadian multiculturalism pressures minority groups to unify internally as a means of translating "minority capital" into political capital. In the case of Islam, the new North American Muslim community is unprecedented in its cultural diversity. The intra-community juxtaposition of cultural contrasts – for instance the soundworld of the Egyptian as against the Pakistani or Indonesian – highlights the need to erase cultural differences among Muslims, in order to emphasize the purely religious basis for unity. This process, I would argue, is structurally compatible with the strategies of the Muslim reformers, who have for the past century likewise sought to erase internal difference: to homogenize as a means of achieving outward unity of the Umma (not only eliminating Sufi orders, but even seeking to homogenize the multiple schools of law, or madhahib). While Islamism, strongly driven by prosperous Muslim communities in the West, has moved in the direction of universalization and homogenization worldwide since the nineteenth-century reformers (a point underscored by Roy (2004: 59)), the process is only intensified in North America where it is precisely those socio-occupational classes (mostly engineers) most partial to Islamic reformism, and least knowledgeable about local oral traditions (whether Sufi or otherwise) who have been selected to immigrate in North America, particularly Canada, either as students or permanent migrants.[17]

The impact of such migration on the Islamic soundworld in Canada has been drastic. Muslim sound specialists – those carriers of the oral traditions who recreate the Islamic soundworld in each succeeding generation – have largely been excluded from Canadian immigration process; while mosques may request a full-time imam, they are unlikely to obtain (or, increasingly, even desire) a qari' or mu'adhdhin. Engineer immigrants, accustomed to closed, internally consistent systems governed by logical principles, are typically reformist in outlook, favoring the presumed deculturization as a means of purifying and strengthening Islam, and regarding only an extremely narrowed (largely silent) soundworld as legitimate in the first place. And multicultural politics, ironically enough, seems to contribute real social pressure towards Islamic unity; to criticize (even constructively) the local mosque is a kind of disloyalty. The same factors imply that Sufism itself, spiritual source and practical scene of so much of the Muslim soundworld, does not easily take root in Canada; Sufi activities in larger, more diverse cities (especially Toronto and Montreal) are constantly threatened by more powerful reformist ideology eyeing their activities as un-Islamic, and seeking to unify the Umma on a more "rational" basis.

The strength of oral tradition over a rich social network in traditionally Muslim societies, combined with the affective logic of the soundworld itself, ensures its inertial survival despite the depredations of reformism, and is here compatible with internal unity, since localization is by definition locally unified; there is no social juxtaposition of difference. However, in an immigrant society, this inertia is reduced or eliminated, even as the need to eliminate internal difference is felt more acutely, and equated with the negation of Islamic localizations as a means of seeking a common Islamic denominator. Thus while reformist ideology is longstanding, this erasure of difference due to juxtaposition is unprecedented on such a scale, when not only rapid communication but also immigrant societies tend to facilitate the active perception of difference among the Muslim community. In the context of Muslims' perception of social and political weakeness, the deculturization of Islam becomes increasingly rapid, particularly within its marginal position in Western Canada.[18] In the absence of the soundworld, itself providing the most visceral, non-discursive, refutation of its critics, the fear-driven tendency towards conformity, avoidance of anything that might possibly be labelled as bida, and hence converging upon maximally conservative Islamic interpretations, is relatively free to propagate unchecked within Muslim social networks

Newer, resource-driven cities such as Edmonton (whose economy is fueled by oil sand deposits located in the northern regions of the province) are especially susceptible to the domination of reformist ideologies and the propagation of conservative conformism. Whereas larger, older, more diversified cosmopolitan centers such as Montreal and Toronto contain much greater absolute numbers of Muslims, and thus an irreconcilable plurality of ideological voices and diversity of sound specialists, Edmonton is far smaller, lacking the critical mass to develop alternative points of view. It is not surprising that the establishment of a Muslim umbrella organization (the Edmonton Council of Muslim Communities) first succeeded here. Furthermore Canadian immigration policy, combined with the technology-based Edmonton economy, tends to attract engineer immigrants who readily adopt the reformist posture (see Figure 4.3). Meanwhile, second and higher generation Muslims, cut off from the Islamic soundworld, but increasingly interested in their Islamic roots (in keeping with the general revival) have been learning about Islam through dissemination of reformist discourse, outside the soundworld and its affective-oral traditions.

I suggest that first-generation Alberta immigrants do not actively support the traditional Islamic soundworld for two reasons. In part they are unable to do so,

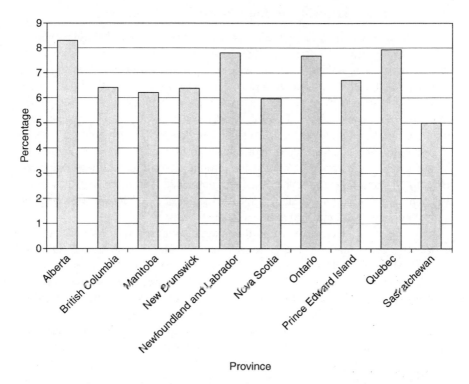

Province

Figure 4.3 Percentage of the labor force working in natural and applied sciences (source: StatsCan 2001d).

because immigration policy, and more specifically labor conditions in Alberta, do not favor its carriers. In part they may discursively oppose it, due to reformist tendencies which tend to become intensified following immigration. Nevertheless, this group's *habitus* has been strongly conditioned by the Islamic soundworld in their countries of birth, and the sound of Islam elicits a strong emotional response. It is for this reason, I believe, that I found tremendous affective receptivity to Shaikh el-Helbawy among first-generation Muslim students and professionals in Edmonton, even when they opposed his musical-artistic persona. On the other hand, non-immigrant Muslims are not merely cut off from the Islamic oral tradition. They have become practicing Muslims in an environment devoid of the Islamic soundworld, an environment suffused on the contrary by discursive signs of Islamic reformism. Therefore they tend to reject a carrier of the traditional soundworld wholeheartedly, as at worst bida and at best doubtful – and when in doubt it is best to "remain on the side of caution." Hence the Muslim Students' Association (whose leadership at this time was primarily composed of non-immigrant undergraduates) and the venerable al-Rashid mosque (run by Edmonton's long-standing Canadian Muslim community) were far less receptive to Shaikh el-Helbawy's religious arts than the immigrant-dominated Muslim Community of Edmonton.

The Islamic soundworld and the World Music soundscape

If the Islamic soundworld (a sonic–social whole) is drastically attenuated in Canada, the Islamic soundscape is not. Certainly Qur'anic recitation has magnificently retained its vibrancy at the level of global distribution (lately via the Internet), first with Egyptian reciters serving as primary models, though more recently (in an anti-musical turn) a newly popular Saudi model has gained primacy (Frishkopf, 2007). Islamic children's recordings are a particularly important feature of the Western Muslim soundscape, due to their key role in transmission of religious values in a non-Muslim society; the British Muslim Yusuf Islam (formerly Cat Stevens) has produced some of the best examples. But this "Muslim directed" material traces global paths primarily within Muslim social networks; though available in local mosques and on Muslim websites, one cannot purchase such material in one's local record store.

More generally accessible within the Islamic soundscape is "Islamic music," especially "Sufi music," filed in record stores under the broader heading of "World Music," produced within an increasingly concentrated, integrated and oligopolistic transnational music industry.[19] Such music is not manufactured for Muslims per se, but rather for World Music consumers, the vast majority of whom are non-Muslim Europeans and North Americans of eclectic musical tastes. "World Music" is thus not music of the world as such, but music drawing upon the vast range of non-Western sounds – suitably selected, transformed and fused so as to appeal to a Western audience.

Clearly that audience represents only a tiny slice of the overall marketing pie. But it is a terribly significant slice because World Music answers to the inclination among select, thinking music consumers to use their purchasing power in order to resist the global music media system and its totalizing control. World Music is the industry response: an attempt (if not by the owners of the music world-system then by others under their virtual control) to commodify precisely those qualities which most unequivocally signify the denial of a globalized, totalizing world-system of music, by pointing to that which appears to lie beyond the range and control of that system. Among those qualities are pre-modern Tradition ("roots," "authenticity"), Otherness ("exoticism"), Spirituality ("metaphysics," "New Age"), and Creative Fusion ("East meets West") – whatever appears to defy the dominance of the world system, breaking free through sound and meaning, or, to be more succinct: whatever appears to *relocalize globality*. The farther afield the music, the more loudly it trumpets such a message. World Music thus stands as a kind of "public service announcement;" in producing World Music, the global music industry proclaims its respect for cultural diversity, while simultaneously closing the leaks in its oligarchic control. Successful marketing of World Music effects a recapture unrecognized by the captive.

In embracing "Sufi music," the music industry tends to return to the pre-bifurcated soundworld of Islamic societies, to the aesthetic–spiritual appeal of that ambiguous performative zone delicately balanced between art and Islam. In this way, the global music system has recourse to the pre-modern integration of music as art, and sound as spirituality, to construct a soundscape of much greater appeal to non-Muslims (for whom the aesthetic is typically an entrée to exploration of unfamiliar cultural or sacred terrain), and much lesser appeal to contemporary Muslims living in the West (most of whom were raised in the post-bifurcation media world in which "music" and "sacred performance" do not overlap). This crossing (from "traditional Islam" to "contemporary non-Islam") is a significant structural feature of this particular global process (analogous to the appeal of Sufism to non-Muslims in the West).

Understood in this way, it is clear that "Sufi Music" instantiates the ideal "World Music," a rich admixture of Tradition, Otherness and Spirituality. Synthesizing art and the sacred, the Divine yearning of sama` (Sufi spiritual audition) is the perfect embodiment – or "ensoundment" – of World Music qualities. As a consequence its uptake into the global soundscape, if not significant in comparison to the whole, has certainly been remarkably rapid. Besides a wave (mostly earlier) of "ethnographic" recordings issued by specialized scholarly labels with limited distribution, including Arion, Ocora (French radio), Inedit (the French Ministry of Culture's Maison des Cultures du Monde), Long Distance, Auvidis UNESCO, Harmonia mundi[20] and culture centers (e.g. the prolific Parisian Institut du Monde Arabe[21]) came a second wave of music-centric spiritual–aesthetic ones, produced by major music industry labels (e.g. Atlantic, Island, Nonesuch, Rykodisc and Real World), geared more toward listening (the ecstasy of sonic experience) than cultural learning, and hence bereft of detailed contextualizations provided by scholarly liner notes.[22] Ironically it is the latter (focused on non-discursive immersion and insight through the listening experience itself) that is somehow closer to the spirit of the Islamic soundworld (and the Sufi sama`), even if a reactivation of its religious meanings is well-nigh impossible under such radically transformed listening conditions.[23] Indeed it is not only the listening context that is transformed, but the sound as well – minimally due to exigencies of the commodified recording (for instance, the need to select 60 minutes (or, worse, five) out of an all-night sama`), and maximally when sounds emitted by multiple soundworlds are fused together ("east and west," or "east and east") in a newly creative act of audio hybridity (two examples are "A prayer for the soul of Layla," 1997; "Hadhra," 2000).[24]

The rapid uptake of multiple Islamic soundworlds, disengaged from the social network, selectively filtered and transformed into an Islamic or Sufi soundscape, then distributed throughout the globe, has occurred nearly independently of Muslim migrations within the ethnoscape. The various recordings of Shaikh Mohamed el-Helbawy, centered on an early twentieth-century Sufi aesthetic enjoying little popularity among Muslims today (particularly those living in the West), provides a typical instance of that which World Music marketers favor, and most contemporary Western Muslims eschew: the sounds of Sufi ritual, spiritual Arab music and east–west fusion (including a remarkable alignment of Mozart's Requiem K. 626 and Sufi dhikr).[25] Such acclaimed World Music artists as the Egyptian Hamza Ala al-Din, who point (sonically and discursively) to Sufi inspirations, are almost completely unknown within Muslim (or even Egyptian) communities. Whereas a significant fraction of the Muslim mainstream (especially pronounced among the second generation) in Canada appears to yearn for the deculturization of Islam in order to unify the Umma, *to globalize locality*, World Music/Sufi music consumers seek precisely the opposite: to culturally reparticularize mass-culture, *to localize globality*. For the most part, these two "imagined worlds" coexist without interacting, circulating in disjunctive global fields (a social ethnoscape, a media soundscape), while their messages may occasionally clash. Occasionally the two worlds, projected into a common frame, are forced into interaction, as when a single individual, entering temporarily into the Muslim immigrant community, yet carrying the strains of Islamic World Music, seeks acceptance, and Islamic music stirs nostalgia (among first-generation immigrants) or refusal (among the second).

Conclusion

Thus locally adaptive soundworlds in Muslim societies have globalized, their sonic and social components disengaging, as Muslims diffuse through the ethnoscape, and as – almost completely independently – Islamic music (mainly "Sufi music") diffuses through the soundscape, both converging in the West: two contrastive trajectories – driven by completely different forces – with a common destination.

In the Muslim ethnoscape of North America, strongly influenced by reformism, seeking unity and the overcoming of cultural difference through deculturization, filtered by immigration policies effectively eliminating carriers of local oral tradition, the Islamic soundworld is largely silenced. Older, larger Muslim communities in Toronto or Montreal, more densely populated, and perhaps better established before the present wave of Salafism hit so strongly, have developed branches of Sufi orders and on occasion nutured (or imported) sonic specialists, (particularly within those orders) – though these represent a minute fraction of the Muslim community (Qureshi, 2003). But in the Canadian West, where the Muslim community represents a smaller proportion of a more geographically dispersed urban population, where the vast majority is "white" (even in urban areas) and immigration is more recent, where pull factors select for technical expertise, such specialists hardly exist, and the number of Sufi-minded individuals falls far short of the critical mass required to form sustainable orders. While the first generation population may maintain some sentimental attachment to the soundworld, they cannot (and perhaps do not wish to) reproduce it. Those who are raised within "Canadian Islam" do not even know it, their Islamic *habitus* having been inculcated without it, even against it. In the absence of the powerful, inertial affective force of the soundworld, which makes received Islamic tradition "sound right" despite the critiques of reformers, fear of social difference (the "bida") propagates unimpeded through the Muslim community, resulting in social conformity converging on the "side of caution," the most conservative possible stance as judged by prevailing discourse. Hence the relative silence of Islam in Edmonton.

Meanwhile the localized Islamic sounds of Muslim-majority countries, especially those sounds taken to represent a pre-modern harmonious "cosmos" (idealized for a disenchanted, spiritually thirsty West) in which the full spectrum of expressive representations was supposedly infused by spirituality – that "pre-bifurcation" era alluded to earlier – have flowed into an Islamic soundscape. Such sounds, detached from their social sources (though this fact tends to be masked) are absorbed into the "World Music" component of the global Islamic soundscape, marketed to non-Muslims of the West, by emphasizing a generalized spirituality, exoticism and traditionalism. None of these values is particularly attractive to devout Muslims, particularly in Alberta.

The irony of immigration lies in the following. While many Muslims of Edmonton seem to want a deculturized Islam, freed of the ramification of oral tradition, it is precisely the "culture" concept which is every immigrant group's ticket to wider recognition, since it is only in their *cultural* distinction (not belief, much less truth) that contrasting groups can share the "stage" of public space under multiculturalism. This strategy dovetails with that of Islamic reformism generally. Many Canadian Muslims – at least those with influence – seek a literalist universality, in a deculturized Umma, purified of "cultural" differences. As a consequence, non-discursive spiritual forms, those whose resistance to textual formulation implies they can never be entirely unified, including the soundsphere, tend to be erased. Second-generation Muslims in particular would globalize all locality by deprivileging oral tradition, a purification of Islam in search of a more powerful social and political position in the world.

Conversely, the consumer of World Music, and of Sufi music in particular, occupies precisely the opposite position. He or she is typically a Western non-Muslim, someone enjoying all the benefits of political and social supremacy and finding it lacking. In seeking out the exotic, the authentic, the transcendently spiritual, he or she is seeking to localize globality – to seek refuge (however fleeting) from the world's universal material forces (primarily economic and political rather than religious), through immersion in the *representation* of a localized soundworld, a seamless synthesis of sound and social practice, conspicuously operating in a particular place and time (however imaginary), and – thus grounded – poised to catalyze some form of metaphysical transcendence.

At a more abstract level of interpretation – not likely to occur either to Muslim immigrant or World Music consumer – perhaps the apparently contrastive meanings animating Islamic ethnoscape, and Islamic soundscape are not so contrary as it would seem. Both are utopian imaginings of a spiritualized world, but differently shaped by differential access to power. The appeal of a globalized Islam is now inextricably intertwined with a spiritualized search for political empowerment, for Divinely-sanctioned socio-economic justice in a patently unjust world in which a small minority enjoys complete physical security and comfort, the West at the expense of the rest. By contrast, the appeal of Sufi music in the West stems largely from the bourgeois search for meaning in a capitalist society in which basic material needs have largely been met, and in which a certain spiritual–aesthetic longing, pointing nostalgically or creatively outside of this system, remains unfulfilled. But, again, this equivalence is only an abstraction. For Muslims in Edmonton, as for consumers of World Music, the soundscape and the ethnoscape are disjunctive, worlds apart.

So long as the soundscape is mediated, while the ethnoscape is populated, the two scapes need not interact at all, despite geographical overlap. Not far from my local mosque, it is possible to purchase Sufi World Music on CD. But with the appearance of Shaikh Mohamed el-Helbawy in Edmonton, simultaneously an agent of Islamic soundscape and Islamic ethnoscape in Edmonton, some interaction was bound to occur, throwing subtle differences among Edmonton's Muslims into sharp relief, depending on which of his identities was given priority. Socially, the Shaikh could be engaged primarily as a fellow Muslim (or Egyptian), in which case his performance might be accepted. Or he could be engaged primarily as a purveyor of Islamic World Music, in which case it might be rejected. This ambiguity, due to his journey's retracing the trajectory of both ethnoscape and soundscape, is what makes the nuanced reactions to his presence so interesting to observe. Shaikh el-Helbawy became a kind of litmus test of the silence of Islam in Edmonton.

In particular, his presence revealed significant discrepancies between first and subsequent generations of Muslims in Edmonton. For first-generation immigrants, silence is born of necessity as much as of ideology. First-generation Muslims frequently harbor a deep-seated, though usually unacknowledged, nostalgia for the lost soundworld, which is embedded in their spiritual *habitus*. Their (common enough) discursive adoption of the reformist ideology, by which Islam must be deculturized and (thereby) unified in order to succeed, is belied by the deeper, pre-discursive dispositions of this *habitus*. At an emotional level at least, Islam comprises a set of relatively open texts, unvoweled (as it were), "vocalized" through locally elaborated cultural traditions, orally transmitted, filling discursive gaps with non-referential, affective sound. But the Islamic soundworld is not merely an oral tradition accepted (tacitly) along with the canonic texts; it is intrinsic to these Muslims' core affective identity. Yet, being non-discursive, its absence can scarcely be articulated (or may be actively repressed by competing ideologies) and thus goes unacknowledged – until the missing soundworld is suddenly invoked by the sounds of its presence, for instance when a figure such as Shaikh Mohamed el-Helbawy appears momentarily on the ethnoscape. Only then, with a sudden recognition of what one has lost through emigration, do the tears begin to flow. The intellectual fear of difference ("but music in Islam is bida") is emotionally appeased, by the affective certainty of what one "feels" to be right.

But for the second and subsequent generations – represented by MSA and al-Rashid leadership – this is an ideological silence, a silence of the *habitus* itself. This generation has been raised in the silent Islam of Canada, isolated from the oral traditions received by parents or grandparents. No localized Islamic soundworld occupies its deepest memories; many have not even been raised in religious households, but rather experienced the need to return to Islam as young adults. The spiritual *habitus* is disconnected from the sound of Islamic tradition, and – logically enough – finds no discursive reason to seek a reconnection, since the loss is purely affective. Returning to Islam, this generation perforce seizes upon its texts – not only the sacred sources of Qur'an and Hadith, but Islamic books generally, including the new wave of Salafi publications. Unlike previous generations of Muslims, this one's Islamic identity is recreated almost exclusively via such texts, developing the basis for a new oral tradition detached from the old. Lacking access to the soundworld, discourse is consequently elevated to much higher position than in traditional Muslim societies; texts become, in my theoretical terms (see below), "closed." Oral culture is not invoked to fill gaps, not only because such culture is lacking – but due to the prevailing ideological stance against cultural variation within Islam, as a means of unifying the worldwide Umma. These second-generation Muslims, rediscovering their Muslim roots, but lacking access to the multidimensional Muslim tradition, are driven by fear and conformity to a position of extreme conservatisim, a fact consistent with Roy's claim that Western Islam has generated its own neo-fundamentalist forms (Roy, 2004).

I wish to offer a final theoretical distinction, between "open" and "closed" texts. I take it as self-evident that no text is ever complete, in the sense of offering an unequivocal representation. Texts always contain gaps, whether or not they are recognized as such, spaces to be filled by their "readers." Hence "openness" and "closure" are never properties of the text as such, but rather of textual perception or attitude: these are in effect social rather than textual properties. Lacunae of "open texts" are interpreted creatively, elaborated with additional (often non-discursive) meanings, allowed to develop via oral transmission. In Islamic culture, the paradigm is provided by the ambiguity of an unvocalized (unvoweled) Arabic text, a visual–sonic metaphor for the relation between text and social vocalization more generally. The vowels, termed harakat (movements) in Arabic, have evolved to a great extent as an oral tradition, varying from one place to another.

Thus the authoritative Qur'anic recension – the 'Uthmanic mushaf – lacks all diacritics (dots, vowels and other marks). Though carefully prepared, and preserved since the seventh century, this mushaf lacks semantic meaning until completed by an oral tradition of readings (qira'at) which determine the missing diacritics. Even this much is not sufficient to enable its recitation, which requires additional information from the oral tradition, for instance phonetics (as preserved in the ahkam al-tajwid, rules of recitation), and melodic modes (maqamat). Necessarily, such vocalization may vary from place to place. But this oral tradition is never open to individual determination, because it is preeminently social, part of an intersubjectively negotiated soundworld, a sonic–social whole.

In Islam, the Qur'an is but the most salient instance of this phenomenon. More broadly, one finds in Islamic culture a careful balance between discursive texts and local culture. Textual openness enables local culture to fill textual gaps, hence – in the context of globalization – the production of difference, perhaps even leading to conflict. But this openness also offers an adaptive relation to the global system, an embedding in the soundworld, and hence in the *habitus*, a psycho-social rooting reaching into the very heart of each individual, and thereby connecting them all. Conflicts over practice are resolved by the recognition of the priority of the batin (inner meaning) over the zahir (external meaning), the immutability of essence despite external multiplicity. Since no text is ever complete, it follows that the "closed" text can only be that whose gaps go unrecognized, or whose gaps are denied. Such gaps can be filled only with silence.

Notes

1 The Hamidiyya Shadhiliyya has been extensively documented by Gilsenan (Gilsenan 1973), and at least two CD recordings featuring Shaikh el-Helbawy are available.

2 On the first of these, Shaikh el-Helbawy performs anonymously with the munshidin (chanters) of the Hamidiyya Shadhiliyya order; the disc was recorded in Paris while the group toured there (a visit arranged by Dr Soliman Gamil). On the second Shaikh el-Helbawy is featured prominently with a professional group of musicians and chorus (who are not munshidin by training). The third contains a remarkable fusion of ibtihalat with Mozart's Requiem.

3 In April 2007, Alberta's population was estimated at 3,455,062 ("About Alberta").

4 University of Alberta statistics are inferred from the University of Alberta Databook for 2005–2006 ("University of Alberta Databook for 2005–2006," 2006). The university does not collect statistics on religious affiliations, but these can be roughly approximated by using population-wide Muslim percentages for Canadians, and by counting according to country of origin (a statistic which is tabulated) for immigrants.

5 This term will be more rigorously defined below.

6 See for instance the culture wars that erupted in Hamtramck, Michigan, over plans to broadcast the call to prayer in a local mosque there ("Mosque's calls to prayer signal Hamtramck change," 2005).

7 The Muslim Students' Association of the US and Canada was formed at the University of Illinois (Urbana-Champaign) on January 1, 1963; the organization mobilizes and coordinates student Muslim organizations at college campuses throughout North America ("MSA National").

8 Lessons.

9 Forbidden by Islamic law.

10 I would furthmore argue that this "social fear" is a principle force driving so-called "fundamentalism" in the contemporary wave of Islamism worldwide – at least as powerfully as revolutionary politics or heartfelt faith. Donning the veil among women, like removing gold wedding bands among men, is an expression of conformity at least as often as it is an expression of piety.

11 By "pre-linguistic" I do not mean to exclude linguistic sound, but rather to consider such sound primarily as sound, not as discourse, i.e. consider such sound in its phonetic, timbral, tonal and rhythmic aspects.

12 This fact may only be tautological, in the sense that it is only the discursive portion of experience of which one is usually said to be actively aware.

13 The social nature of the soundworld is confirmed also by research demonstrating that the blind (participating more or less fully in the soundworld) find social integration much more readily than the deaf. And the coercive power of amplified sound was adequately demonstrated during the Panama "intervention" (1989–1990), when the US Marines deployed high decibel rock music as a weapon against General Manuel Noriega, holed up in the papal Nunciatura; this track has since been replayed by the FBI in their 1993 standoff with Branch Davidians at Waco, Texas, and with the use of AC/DC by Marines in 2004 during the Iraq War ("U.S. deploys loud music, insults in Fallujah," 2004).

14 The limitations of language to comment upon music was eloquently noted by the eminent musicologist-philosopher Charles Seeger as an instance of the "linguo-centric predicament" (Seeger, 1961), and can also be formulated in systems theoretic terms: language and music communications may be regarded as a pair of structurally-coupled operationally closed autopoietic systems (Luhmann, 2000: 107–108).

15 Such is the case for instance in Qur'anic recitation: discursive *ahkam al-tajwid* (rules of recitation) regulate only that which can be talked about, leaving free multiple variables such as tonality, melody, tempo, rhythmn, and timbre (see Frishkopf, 2009).

16 I have coined the term *interauthor* to denote this social network of authorship (Frishkopf, 2003), in contrast to the textual network, or *intertext*.

17 Here an important difference between Canada and the US comes into play: whereas in both countries universities actively solicit international students to fill their technical graduate programs, only in Canada are students allowed to apply for immigration while on a student visa. However such visas are unlikely to be granted in non-technical fields, due to limited employment opportunities. Typically, then, immigrant graduate students studying science and engineering in Canada become Canadian citizens prior to completing the doctorate, and many of these stay on.

18 A counter-outcome is the development of "ethnically based" mosques, e.g. in Edmonton where one mosque draws primarily South Asians (with a khutba in Urdu). But this fact only underscores the inability to tolerate difference within any particular Muslim community.

19 The transnational music industry is currently dominated by the "big four:" Sony BMG, EMI, Universal and Warner.

20 (Hear, for instance: al-Tuhami, 1998; "Soufi songs from Tunisia: Ensemble de Cheikh Abdelaziz ben Mahmoud," 2000; "Sufi songs of Damascus," 1993; "Transe Soufie d'Alep," 2003; "Turkish Sufi music: folk lute of Anatolia,"; "Turquie: musique soufie: Ilahi et nefes," 1991).

21 (Hear: "Algeria: Ahallil de Gourara: sacred songs from the Sahara," 1994; El Helbawy, 1999; "Maroc: Rituel de transe: Les Aissawa de Fes," 1995; "Syrie: Chants d'Alep," 1994; "Tunisie: Chants soufis de Tunis," 1999; "Yemen: Chants sacres de Sanaa," 2001).

22 (Hear: Brothers, 1990; "Gnawa music of Marrakesh: night spirit masters," 1990; Lo, 1995; "Music of the Whirling Dervishes," 1987; N'Dour, 2004; "The passion of Pakistan: Iqbal Jogi & party," 1997).

23 The fact that ethnomusicological–ethnographic production (much of it with governmental support) typically takes place in France, while music-oriented discs are usually issued by American and British labels, is itself a noteworthy reminder of the need to nuance generalizations about "the West." France, lacking the global financial and political clout of the Anglo-American alliance, often seeks to strengthen its world position through cultural exchanges. Another noteworthy trend is for African and South Asian sounding Sufi music to be decontextualized by larger music producers for its aesthetic/entertainment value (e.g. Nusrat Fateh Ali Khan, Youssou N'Dour), while Arab Sufi music tends to be presented more ethnographically; this tendency follows the lines of world music popularity generally: first African and African-linked (Latin, Caribbean), then South Asian.

24 A more comprehensive taxonomic frame might be developed as follows. Muslim-directed Islamic music comprises traditional genres, plus new studio-oriented ones (e.g. Sami Yusuf), flowing within limited networks worldwide; the overall intention is always spiritual and pedagogical. Western-directed Islamic music comprises at least three mixable intentions (pedagogical/scholarly, aesthetic, spiritual), freely combining in at least four representational forms (ethnographic recording on-site, specially arranged performance on-site, staged concert recording, studio recording) of varying distance from the "original," with the additional factors of fusion and creative

interpretation (mixing traditions, or inventing new ones) tending to weaken the connection to any particular pre-mediated tradition.
25 (Hear: al-Chaziliyya, 1992; El Helbawy, 1999, 2003; "Mozart in Egypt," 2002).

References

"A prayer for the soul of Layla" (1997). USA: Alula.

"About Alberta." Online, available at: www.gov.ab.ca/home/about_alberta.cfm (last accessed October 31, 2007).

Abu Laban, Baha (1983). "The Canadian Muslim community: the need for a new survival strategy." In E.H. Waugh, B. Abu-Laban and R. Qureshi (eds.), *The Muslim community in North America* (pp. 75–92). Edmonton: University of Alberta Press.

al-Chaziliyya, al-Hamidiyya (1992). "Al-tariqa al-hamidiyya al-chaziliyya." On *Musique soufi =: Sufi music: Musique soufi (Compact discs)*. France: Arion.

al-Tuhami, Shaykh Yasin (1998). "The magic of the Sufi inshad." France: Long Distance.

"Algeria: Ahallil de Gourara: sacred songs from the Sahara" (1994). France: Institut du Monde Arabe.

Anderson, Benedict (2006). *Imagined communities: reflections on the origin and spread of nationalism* (rev. edn). London and New York: Verso.

Appadurai, Arjun (1996). *Modernity at large: cultural dimensions of globalization*. Minneapolis: University of Minnesota Press.

Blacking, John (1973). *How musical is man?* Seattle: University of Washington Press.

Bloch, Maurice (1974). "Symbols, song, dance and features of articulation: is religion an extreme form of traditional authority?" *Archives Européenes Sociologiques*, 15, 55–81.

Bourdieu, Pierre (1977). *Outline of a theory of practice*. Cambridge and New York: Cambridge University Press.

Brothers, The Sabri (1990). "Ya Habib." Britain: Real World.

Chazili, L'Order (1982). "Egypte: L'Order Chazili." On *Musique Soufi*. France: Arion.

Danielson, Virginia (1991). "'Min al-Mashayikh': a view of Egyptian musical tradition." *Asian Music*, 22(1), 113–127.

Durkheim, Emile (1976). *The elementary forms of the religious life*. New York: The Free Press.

El Helbawy, Mohamed (1999). "Sufi chants from Cairo, Egypt." France: Institut Du Monde Arabe.

El Helbawy, Mohamed (2003). "Hossam Ramzy presents Egyptian Sufi: Arc music."

Frishkopf, Michael (2002). "Islamic hymnody in Egypt." In V. Danielson, S. Marcus and D. Reynolds (eds.), *The Garland encyclopedia of world music* (Vol. 6). New York: Garland.

Frishkopf, Michael (2003). "Authorship in Sufi poetry." *Alif: Journal of Comparative Poetics: Intersections: Literature and the Sacred*, 23.

Frishkopf, Michael (2009). "Mediated Qur'anic recitation and the contestation of Islam in contemporary Egypt." In L. Nooshin (ed.), *Music and the play of power in the Middle East, North Africa and Central Asia*. Burlington: Ashgate.

Gillani, Karim (2004). "The Ismaili Ginan tradition from the Indian subcontinent." *Bulletin of the Middle East Studies Association*, 38(2), 175–186.

"Gnawa music of Marrakesh: night spirit masters" (1990). USA: Axiom-Island Records.

Green, Alan G. and Green, David A. (1995). "Canadian immigration policy: the effectiveness of the point system and other instruments." *Canadian Journal of Economics*, 28(4b), 1006–1041.

Habermas, Jurgen (1984). *The theory of communicative action, Vol. 2.* Boston: Beacon Press.

"Hadhra" (2000). France: Quoi Qu'Il en Soit.

Hollifield, James F. (1986). "Immigration policy in France and Germany: outputs versus outcomes." *The Annals of the American Academy of Political and Social Science,* 485, 113–128.

Langer, Susanne Katherina Knauth (1960). *Philosophy in a new key: a study in the symbolism of reason, rite, and art* (3rd edn). Cambridge: Harvard University Press.

Lo, Cheikh (1995). "Ne la thiass." USA: Nonesuch.

Luhmann, Niklas (2000). *The reality of the mass media.* Cambridge: Polity Press.

McNeill, Tony (1998). "Immigration in postwar France." Online, available at: www.sunderland.ac.uk/~os0tmc/contemp1/immig2.htm (last accessed August 1, 2006).

"Maroc: Rituel de transe: Les Aissawa de Fes" (1995). France: Institut du Monde Arabe.

"Mosque's calls to prayer signal Hamtramck change" (February 23, 2005). *The Detroit News.*

"Mozart in Egypt" (2002). Virgin Classics.

"MSA National." Online, available at: www.msanational.org (last accessed October 29, 2007).

"Music of the Whirling Dervishes" (1987). USA: Atlantic.

N'Dour, Youssou (2004). "Egypt." USA: Nonesuch.

Qureshi, Regula (2003). "Lineage, shrine, qawwali, and study circle: spiritual kinship in transnational Sufism." *Religious Studies and Theology,* 22(1).

Roy, Olivier (2004). *Globalized Islam: the search for a new Ummah.* New York: Columbia University Press.

Schutz, Alfred and Luckmann, Thomas. (1973). *The structures of the life-world, vol. 1.* Evanston: Northwestern University Press.

Seeger, Charles (1961). "Semantic, logical and political considerations bearing upon research in ethnomusicology." *Ethnomusicology,* 5.

"Soufi songs from Tunisia: Ensemble de Cheikh Abdelaziz ben Mahmoud" (2000). France: Arion.

StatsCan (2001a). "Community highlights for Calgary." Online, available at: www12. statcan.ca/english/Profil01/CP01/Details/Page.cfm?Lang=F&Geo1=CMA&Code1=82 5__&Geo2=PR&Code2=48&Data=Count&SearchText=Edmonton&SearchType=Begi ns&SearchPR=48&B1=All (last accessed March 3, 2009).

StatsCan (2001b). "Religions in Canada: provincial and territorial highlights." Online, available at: www12.statcan.ca/english/census01/Products/Analytic/companion/rel/ provs.cfm (last accessed October 29, 2007).

StatsCan (2001c). "Community highlights for Edmonton." Online, available at: www12. statcan.ca/english/Profil01/CP01/Details/Page.cfm?Lang=E&Geo1=CSD&Code1=481 1061&Geo2=PR&Code2=48&Data=Count&SearchText=Edmonton&SearchType=Be gins&SearchPR=48&B1=All&Custom= (last accessed October 29, 2007).

StatsCan (2001d). *Labour Statistics: Statistics Canada, CANSIM tables 282–0069 and 282–0073.*

"Sufi songs of Damascus" (1993). France: Long Distance.

"Syrie: Chants d'Alep" (1994). France: Institut du Monde Arabe.

"The passion of Pakistan: Iqbal Jogi & party" (1997). USA: Rykodisc.

"Transe Soufie d'Alep" (2003). France: Le Chant du Monde: Harmonia mundi.

"Tunisie: Chants soufis de Tunis" (1999). France: Institut du Monde Arabe.

"Turkish Sufi music: folk lute of Anatolia." USA: Lyrichord.

"Turquie: musique soufie: Ilahi et nefes" (1991). France: Inedit: Maison des Cultures du Monde.

"University of Alberta Databook for 2005–2006" (2006). Online, available at: www.ualberta.ca/IDO/databook/05–06/.

"U.S. deploys loud music, insults in Fallujah" (April 16, 2004). *Globe and Mail*.

"Yemen: Chants sacres de Sanaa" (2001). France: Institut du Monde Arabe.

5 Pluralism and authenticity

Sufi paths in post-9/11 New York

Markus Dressler

Based on research in the New York City area, this chapter explores the ways in which Sufi-Muslim identity is negotiated in a North American metropolitan context post-9/11.[1] It aims to clarify the impact of a secular pluralist framework on the negotiation of religious boundaries between Muslims, with a focus on Sufi Muslims. Particularly, it asks how Sufis engage with the challenges and opportunities within a non-Muslim majority context that is both secular and pluralist. Engaging questions of religious boundary construction, the chapter reflects on the impact of the post-9/11 era on Muslims and Sufis within US identity politics. It then discusses three ideal-typical Muslim Sufi reactions to American society and culture ranging between seclusion from and appropriation of American lifestyles and values, and finally elaborates on those characteristic features of Western Sufism that seem to be furthered by the secular and pluralist situation.

Identity politics: pluralism, Islam and 9/11

It can be argued that one of the major aims of US patriotism is to transcend ethnic and religious differences. The ethnic inclusivism of US patriotism, as expressed in the melting-pot metaphor, is based on an implicit model of layered identities and loyalties, espousing a civic patriotism that aims at integrating ethnic identities into the American national mainstream and demanding loyalty to the nation's symbols and values. Throughout the last century, with the inclusion of Catholics and Jews into the American mainstream, the religious landscape of the US has become more diverse. This is reflected in successive identity transformations as a Protestant, Christian and finally Judeo-Christian nation.[2] Most recently, mainstream political rhetoric shows attempts to include Muslims into the American religious narrative by pointing to the common roots of Jews, Christians and Muslims as Abrahamian religions – a rhetoric which I suggest calling *Abrahamianism*.[3]

The ethnic and religious inclusivism of American nationalism is, however, fragile. The layered identity model fails in times when national values and interests are being seen in conflict with those of particular religious or not-yet-Americanized ethnic communities. This is what happened after 9/11, when

Muslims in the US found their loyalty to the country questioned on religious grounds. The suspicions directed against Muslims were often interwoven with racial profiling, especially for people of – supposed or real – Arab or Middle Eastern background. Following the public pressure to position themselves vis-à-vis vague notions of Islamic terrorism and American values, Muslims were forced to identify their cultural and political locations and allegiances. The wide array of different responses reflects the political and religious heterogeneity of American Muslims.[4]

The pressure on American Muslims is heightened in the case of Sufi Muslims, since they are in a marginalized position within the Islamic discourse. The experience of this double or triple marginalization was expressed by several participants of a focus group interview with members of New York Sufi communities in 2003.[5] As with other Muslims, these Sufis, too, claimed that the Muslims of America – divided like other Americans along ethnic, racial, religious and class lines – have moved closer together in the aftermath of 9/11. American Muslims in general have reported increased participation in ritual and social activities of local mosques, as well as an increase in inter-religious dialogue, civic participation and even an increase in conversions to Islam. However, in addition to these widely acknowledged developments, the above-mentioned Sufi group interview also revealed less well-known dimensions of the Muslim post-9/11 experience, namely increasing tensions between Muslims along political and religious lines. Even if they have come into sharper light more recently, these tensions already existed prior to 9/11. An example is the uproar among American Muslims caused by a Sufi leader's public remarks in 1999. On January 7 of that year, Hisham Kabbani, the American head of the Haqqani branch of the Naqshbandi order, remarked at an US State Department Open Forum on the Evolution of Extremism that "there are more than 2,000 mosques in the U.S … and 80 percent of them are being run by extremist ideologies."[6] Unsurprisingly, his remarks were vehemently criticized by Muslims throughout the country who felt that they were unjustly attacked and victims of Kabbani's political ambitions. In fact, his remarks have to be seen as part of a strategy to establish himself as a main representative of a "moderate" Islam. In a sense, Kabbani benefited from 9/11, since his allegations now came in handy to justify the heightened scrutiny directed against Muslims.[7] He received unprecedented media attention, which he used to spread his staunch criticism of Wahhabi Islam.[8] Kabbani reiterates his order's polemic against Wahhabism and the influence that this revivalist and thoroughly anti-Sufi brand of Islam has been able to wield worldwide due to potent Saudi Arabian sponsorship – a criticism that resonates well with the American public's increased suspicion of the US–Saudi economic and military alliance in the wake of 9/11. In his religious fervour, Kabbani is part of a movement of self-proclaimed traditionalist Muslims who reject Wahhabi and Salafi exclusivist claims on Islamic orthodoxy and defend the Islamic legitimacy of Sufism.[9]

There is no question that, following more than a century of anti-Sufi propaganda from modernist Muslims as well as Muslim revivalists, Sufism is today in a defensive position.[10] Modernist Muslims often disregard Sufism as superstitious and irrational and see in the powerful Sufi networks a threat to their ideals of modern and secular nation-states. Muslim revivalists, on the other hand, in their aim for a return to a pure and uncorrupted Islamic utopia, aspire to purge Islam from what they see as non-Islamic – and thus illegal – innovations (bida). After a century of being under such attacks from both modernists and revivalists, Sufism has become contested within Islam to an unprecedented extent, and Sufis have to prove their legitimacy vis-à-vis the Islamic mainstream. In many Muslim-majority countries, especially in the Middle East, it has lost much of its legitimacy and significance both as a religious path and as a form of social organization. Only in Egypt are Sufi orders officially recognized by the state.[11]

In the non-Muslim majority countries of Europe and North America, Sufism is even more contested insofar as universalist and reformist interpretations of Islam are here comparatively strong. There are several reasons for this. For one, it is not in each case possible to maintain the cultural traditions of the homeland unless there is a critical mass of Muslims with the same cultural background that allows for maintaining a specific Muslim culture, as, for example, in the case of Turkish migrants in Germany. In addition, for second- and third-generation Muslim migrants, the cultural practices of their parents and grandparents lose evidence; therefore, they often tend toward homogenized and universalist interpretations of Islam. The thusly achieved de-ethnicization or de-culturalization of Islam allows in a second step for notions such as "American," "British," "German" and "European" Islam to emerge.[12]

Before 9/11, New York Sufis put emphasis on issues such as education and health, economic empowerment and outreach to local Muslim and non-Muslim institutions.[13] 9/11 and its aftermath shifted the priorities. Sufis were now, like other Muslims, confronted with increasing suspicion and sometimes xenophobic attacks by parts of the non-Muslim public. The anti-Islamic rhetoric can certainly increase the sense of belonging to a universal Muslim community (umma). However, in the age of the "War on Terror," the pressure from the non-Muslim public also increased competition and antagonisms between Muslim groups, as the example of Hisham Kabbani's remarks illustrates. These tensions are strongly felt by Sufi Muslims, who find themselves in a double-minority position facing two critical and powerful others: the Muslim mainstream as well as the non-Muslim public. In a way, the ambivalence of a Sufi Muslim identity became even more pronounced:

9/11 forced us to say who we are ... We were forced to be brothers and sisters because, you know, we all said "We're Muslim." But instead of saying who we are, at that time we had to defend who we weren't. So it's kind of a negative identity ... I think now Sufis can come out and talk more about what Islam really is, because it's the heart of Islam.[14]

The contestation between Muslim and Sufi identities within Islam brings up the question of the boundaries of the Islamic tradition.[15] One challenge that has accompanied me throughout my research is how to distinguish between Muslim Sufis and non-Muslim Sufis. I suggest focusing on how boundaries are constructed and negotiated in Muslim discourse and practice. I perceive both mainstream Muslims and Sufi Muslims as participants in a dynamic debate on the meanings and boundaries of Islam.[16] In other words, I regard as part of the Islamic tradition all those Sufis who participate – be it through their practice or through intellectual debate – in the negotiation of Muslim belief, identity and practice. This definition includes those Sufis accused of heresy, or bida. Apologetic accusations are in a discursive sense extremely important for the construction of an Islamic subject since they highlight the boundaries of the tradition. In the language of Islamic law, it is the semantic shift from heresy to unbelief, from bida to kufr, that makes the difference. Thus, I consider *non-Muslim* only those Sufis who do not bother relating themselves to the Islamic tradition and are also ignored by mainstream Muslim discourse.[17]

Sufi-Muslim appropriations of the secular and pluralist situation

The pluralist situation of Western Europe and North America opens new possibilities for Sufis,[18] as a Turkish member of the Jerrahi order expressed in the following way:

> The fact that I was in Turkey until I was 24 was a curse and blessing at the same time. The fact that, I mean, pretty much I was surrounded by the flavour of *tasawwuf* [i.e. Sufism] … It was in the culture. It was in the food I ate, it was in the music I listened to – I was not aware … I felt more free to join and practice Sufism in the United States than I was in Turkey … I mean, although I was living in it [in Turkey], I did not have the courage, I did not have the identity to associate myself with Sufism at the time … I came here, I felt more relaxed and free to seek the truth … that would put me in peace.[19]

He was seconded by another Turkish immigrant, himself from the Naqshbandi order, who explained: "New York is a place where you can find yourself … I mean this is the place that we live our religion freely, freely. I mean you can not live your religion in Turkey … this safe, you know."[20]

The relationship between a Sufi-Muslim and an American identity can be experienced in a variety of ways: as a clash of identities, as a compartmentalization of identities or as an amalgamation of identities. Accordingly, I suggest distinguishing between three ideal-typical Sufi-Muslim responses to the unregulated, pluralist American situation:

1   criticism of and seclusion from the American society and culture;
2   appropriation of and active involvement within American society by maintaining a distinctive identity defined through religious and cultural particularisms; and

3 amalgamation of Sufi-Muslim identity with American identity, or Americanization of Sufism as part of an "American Islam."

1 Criticism of American lifestyle and seclusion: the Naqshbandi-Haqqani circle of Shaikh Abdul Kerim

The Naqshbandi-Haqqanis in New York are split into two branches. The larger one meets at a place in midtown Manhattan led by the Turkish-Cypriot Shaikh Abdul Kerim, who also owns a Sufi convent in Sidney Center in upstate New York and claims to be a khalīfa (authorized to take on students and continue the lineage) of Shaikh Nazim al-Haqqani from Cyprus.[21] In average between 30 and 50 people seem to be attending the weekly Manhattan gatherings. The second group does not recognize the leadership of Abdul Kerim – although I have met New York Sufis who attend, if irregularly, both circles – and is directly affiliated to Shaikh Hisham Kabbani, the order's official American representative. This considerably smaller group gathers for weekly dhikr ("remembrance" – the central Sufi ritual in which God is remembered through invocation of his names) at Masjid al-Aqsa in Harlem under the leadership of Imam Suleiman Diomande. The loose structure of the Haqqani network appears to be partially the result of a lack of centralized leadership, which allows for a large degree of autonomy of local circles led by authorized muqaddams (members of the brotherhood authorized to teach the order's tradition).[22]

Shaikh Abdul Kerim has a reputation for his patriarchal and authoritarian leadership style. While I met New York Sufis who complained about his strong ego, and doubted his authenticity as shaikh, others see in him an authentic and charismatic leader with deep and sincere knowledge of tasawwuf. His understanding of Sufism is firmly centred in sharia as a necessary precondition for tariqa (the Sufi path).[23] I witnessed a meeting of the circle at which roughly 35 people attended, roughly two-thirds of which were men. Attendees appeared to have been mostly from Turkey, the Middle East and South Asia. There were also some African-Americans and some Caucasians. The women were sitting separately, though in the same room, and all but one were covered. Abdul Kerim elaborated extensively on the evils of dunya – the profane world – warning especially the attending immigrant Muslims not to get involved beyond the necessary with the dangerous American way of life.[24] Among the most dangerous evils of dunya he identified Wahhabism and Zionism – emphasizing several times that the two were interrelated – as well as feminism and communism. He warns of shaytan, who appears to be omnipresent in the American culture. A further characteristic feature of the group is its strong sense of millennialism: the end of days is believed to be very close. Here as well as his in his warnings of dunya, Abdul Kerim closely follows the teachings of Shaikh Nazim.[25] The millenarian expectations of the group serve as pretext for not getting involved with societal and political affairs – the time left would be limited – and everybody would be better off concentrating on his/her personal perfection as a Muslim. The expressed political restraint distinguishes this group strongly from the activist approach of the main branch of Naqshbandi-Haqqaniyya in the US, led by Hisham Kabbani.

The meeting I attended was overall not very harmonious. A first issue of contention was the apparent inequality in the treatment of the male and female members during the meal, which was consumed after dhikr. First, the shaikh was served an opulent meal, then the male attendees were served a simple plate with bread and chicken. While the women were serving the food, it was not clear whether they would also be able to participate in the meal, and the women expressed their unhappiness through a male middleman.[26] Shaikh Abdul Kerim now got very angry and started lecturing about the evils of feminism, the emergence of which he connected with the French Revolution. The male disciple, who had transmitted the women's complaint, especially drew the shaikh's anger.[27] In a following conversation with me, the shaikh distanced himself from the Naqshbandi-Haqqanis of Hisham Kabbani, emphasizing the need for discipline, especially in the American environment with all its material and sensual temptations.

2 Appropriation of the American context while maintaining a particularist identity: the Murid community

Very different from Shaikh Abdul Kerim's Naqshbandi circle, the Murid community aims at an integration of its particularist identity into American society. The Murid strongly value family and community and do not seem to interact much with other Muslim or Sufi communities. The center of Muridism is in Touba, Senegal, and a vast majority of the Murid in New York (roughly 1,000 people) are Wolof from Senegal.[28] Nevertheless, the Murid stress that the message of their patron saint Ahmadou Bamba is universal and that Muridism would not be restricted to black people or Wolof Senegalese. There are some African-American converts; and I was also told of Caucasian converts, the number of which appears, however, to be rather negligible.

The rhetoric of the community comprises both universalist and pan-African ideals. On the one side, according to their self-representation, American Murid seem to be able to successfully harmonize their own values and interests with what they perceive as American values and interests. American and Murid culture would share values such as hard work, democracy, solidarity, freedom, tolerance and piety.[29] The dominant theme of a Murid conference at the United Nations I attended in July 2003 was that Muridism should be regarded as an example for America, i.e. as a means for a successful purification of the American society from its social, spiritual and economic illnesses. This could be achieved by concentration on certain key values, especially a puritan work ethic, education, spirituality and community.

The former itinerant salesmen's community[30] has by now settled in New York as well as in other urban centers of North America, and they clearly begin to see themselves as part of American society where they establish their own permanent Murid spaces. In many streets of Harlem and other neighborhoods of New

York, the names of Murid-run shops and businesses point to the sacred center of the Murid universe: from "Touba Hair-Braiding" to "Touba Business Network," from "Touba African Clothing" to "Touba Books and Tapes," to give just some random examples. Touba is the holy city of the Muridiyya in Senegal, where the tomb of Ahmadou Bamba is located. Another example of how New York's Murid incorporate New York City space into their religious landscape can be observed on Harlem's official Ahmadou Bamba Day, celebrated since 1990 every year on July 28. On this day the Murid organize a colourful parade on Seventh Avenue, marching through Harlem, chanting qasaid from Ahmadou Bamba, and doing loud dhikr. The chanting and the carrying of large pictures of Ahmadou Bamba and his sons – who consecutively replaced him as the leaders of the Murid community – renders Seventh Avenue into a Murid space. At the same time, by carrying the American flag as well as the Senegalese flag – making sure that they are caught next to each other by the lenses of the attending journalists – the Murid express both their loyalty to America and their connection to their home country.

The universalism as claimed in the official Murid rhetoric contrasts, however, with strong Murid voices of Black-African particularism, which appear to be furthered by the group's aim to reach out to and proselytize among the African-American community. At Ahmadou Bamba Day in 2004, Muhammad Balozi Harvey, an African-American convert to Islam and current Chairman of the Murid Islamic Community in America, gave a speech in front of the Adam-Clayton-Powell Building in which he put strong emphasis on the brotherhood between black people and, in particular, on the duty of the Murid toward African-Americans: "The Sheykh said what we have to do. Convert them [African-Americans] to Islam."[31] African-Americans should be taught the teachings of Ahmadou Bamba, and in fact, "Shaikh Ahmadou Bamba has to be shared with every human being that has common sense ... [S]ome of his most worshipped followers will be those who don't speak Wolof." Again addressing African-Americans, he urged that "until we don't get into the hearts and the minds of our brothers and sisters here, we won't have done the work that was set out for us to do."[32]

3 Amalgamation of Sufi-Muslim and American identities

"There is a need to develop ... an *American-Islamic identity*, an Islam that is orthodox in its religion, in its theology, in its practice, but culturally American and Western" (Feisal Abdul Rauf).[33]

Feisal Abdul Rauf, Imam of Masjid al-Farah in downtown Manhattan, is the New York Muslim who advocates the notion of an American Islam most passionately. He leads a local Sufi circle in the tradition of a Moroccan branch of the Shadhili-Qadiri order.[34] Imam Feisal, known to a larger public through his engagement in inter-faith dialogue and his activism for an American-Muslim identity, emphasizes the common roots and values of the Abrahamic religions.[35] He is the founder and CEO of ASMA Society, which he leads together with his wife, Daisy Khan, ASMA's executive director.[36] ASMA is dedicated to inter-religious dialogue, Muslim youth leadership development, and reconciliation of Islamic and American values and identities expressed in the programmatic notion of an "American Islam."[37] ASMA advocates religious tolerance and is dedicated to the development of a new American Muslim leadership espousing its ideas and values. Until 2005, ASMA stood for American Sufi Muslim Association. The recent name change to American Society for Muslim Advancement reflects the increasing public role of Imam Feisal and Daisy Khan and the broader goals of the organization, namely reaching out to non-Sufi audiences.

Universalist Mysticism, too, offers ways to bridge the gap between seemingly colliding religious identities. Going beyond Abrahamianism, Sufi Mysticists argue that on a spiritual level the outward differences between the religions disappear since they are but different paths ultimately leading to the same goal in the Divine/God. In this spirit, the Nur Ashki Jerrahi Sufi order, based in lower Manhattan, promises on its website to "joyfully welcome seekers and students of all religious and non-religious paths."[38] The head of the Nur Ashki Jerrahis, Shaikha Fariha (born Philippa de Menil), is one prominent example of a Sufi who employs the language of Mysticism to explain the location and role of Sufism in America. She shares the New Age consciousness insofar as she expects the era of spiritual awakening to be inaugurated in the West, as expressed in the following verses of Shaikh Nur al-Jerrahi (alias Lex Hixon, d. 1995), the preceding leader of the circle:

> Sun that rises from the East awakens now within the West...
> Eagle soaring in the West, True Kaaba whirling in the West...[39]

Thus, in strong opposition to the separatist Naqshbandi circle of Shaikh Abdul Kerim, who sees in the US society a threat to Muslim identity, Sufi teachers like Imam Feisal and Shaikha Fariha appreciate the secular and pluralist society as an opportunity for the Muslim community to concentrate on spiritual growth and civic integration. Both the Abrahamian and the universalist approaches embrace hyphenated "Americanized" identities – in stark contrast to the featured Naqshbandi-Haqqani circle, which perceives Americanization as a threat. The Murids' position is more ambivalent. While they aspire to reconcile American and Murid values, they also maintain their particularist and communitarian identity politics as a means for creating authentic Murid space in America. The Murid express their loyalty to the US, but their social, cultural and economic interests differ considerably from that of Imam Feisal and Shaikha Fariha. Unlike the Naqshbandi Abdul Kerim, however, they do not appear to feel threatened in the American environment and promote active engagement in it. Their community is based on ethnic kinship – a kinship, however, in which African-Americans are invited to share based on an implicit notion of common African origins. For them, the creation of their own Murid microcosm within American society does not appear to be a symbol of seclusion, but rather a solid communitarian basis for their own contributions to the American society. The Jerrahi circle of Spring Valley, led by Shaikh Tosun Bayrak al-Jerrahi, is similar in this regard, displaying both cultural and ethnic cohesion – Turkish in this case – and strong civic engagement within US society.[40]

Pluralism and Sufi-networking

The American context challenges pre-migration cultural and religious identities. While the secular and pluralist situation provides opportunities for immigrant Muslims unknown in many Muslim countries, it also creates the problem of how to establish and maintain Islamic authenticity in a non-Muslim and, in the aftermath of 9/11, often hostile environment. For those traditional Sufi orders, which have their roots and mother organizations in more or less strongly authoritarian and centralist Muslim majority countries, the move to a secular and pluralist system brings to the forefront questions of cultural, religious, social and political location – especially in a society in which more or less explicit notions of race and religion have a strong impact on the social positioning of individuals and groups. Some Sufis see an adaptation of race and class politics in the Muslim community and point to tendencies to gather along ethnic lines and to exclude individuals based on internalized racialist categories.[41]

This is, however, only one side of the story. The non-regulated religious field, which can be described with the metaphor of the market, also offers new opportunities. In the following I will elaborate on five features characteristic of Western Sufism – features that I see as furthered by the pluralist situation. These mutually connected and asserting features are:

1   the unquestioned legitimacy of Sufism;
2   the possibility of advertisement and outreach activities;
3   the commodification of Sufism;
4   Sufi travelling and intra-Sufi competition; and
5   the regularity of multiple affiliations and intra-Sufi networking.

1 Legitimacy

Due to the secular-pluralist situation, there is no competition between the different Sufi communities in terms of legitimacy vis-à-vis the state. Sufi communities do not have to defend their legitimacy against an authoritarian state that fears their potential to create and/or organize opposition; neither do they have to prove themselves against a state-endorsed definition of Islam that criminalizes Sufi practice.[42] Due to their marginal status, Sufism in the US is politically less significant – even if some Sufi leaders might aspire to a more political role.

2 Advertisement and outreach

In Western Europe and North America, Sufi circles face no particular restrictions with regard to religious organizing and gathering or public activities and speech.

Some Sufi groups put information regarding their meeting times and location on their websites and are thus relatively easy to contact and access. The extent to which advertisement is used depends on the openness/inclusivism of a particular circle and the acceptance of modern ways of dawa[43] as appropriate to Sufi etiquette.[44] The unrivalled champion of Sufi dawa on the Internet is the Haqqaniya branch of the Naqshbandiyya order, which entertains several complex and cross-linked websites.[45] In one of its numerous webpages, titled "Naqshbandia America," not only do we find a concise narrative of the order's history in the Americas but we are also informed that its local leader, Shaikh Hisham Kabbani, has brought more than 40,000 Caucasian Americans and more than 20,000 non-Caucasian Americans to Islam; in addition, we learn that he initiated more than 20,000 immigrant Muslims into the Naqshbandi order.[46] The head of the order, Shaikh Nazim al-Haqqani, visited his followers in the US several times. His last visit in August 2000 is covered in great detail on the webpage of the American Haqqanis. We are, for example, informed that on August 27 Shaikh Nazim led prayers at Masjid al-Aqsa on Eighth Avenue in Harlem, and,

> witnessed by 2500 participants ... 250 young men and women recited the shahada [confession of faith] together, entering Islam in one moment. Following the mass shahada ceremony, the entire congregation of the mosque joined their hands in taking initiation into the Naqshbandi Sufi Order.[47]

In a report covering a dhikr evening led by the visiting shaikh at the Haqqani centre in midtown Manhattan, we are told that "the center was filled to its 1,000 person capacity."[48] However, these numbers seem widely exaggerated. Already the pictures of the respective events on the webpages make us question their accuracy. I would, in fact, doubt that it is even possible to get as many people into the two respective locations. If we were to rely on the website information covering the visit of Shaikh Nazim, we would get the impression that the Haqqani group in the US and also in New York constitutes a Muslim mass movement. The impression given by these webpages complies neither with my own observations nor with the information I could gather from other sources. I was told by one ex-member of Abdul Kerim's circle that these numbers on the webpages had even been a source of amusement among the group members.[49] Aminah Mohammad-Arif reports that when she visited the group in 1995, she was told there were about 10,000 adherents of Shaikh Nazim in the US, roughly 1,000 of whom lived in New York; however, she counted barely 50 people at the meeting she attended.[50]

3 Commodification of Sufism

The lines between Sufi outreach and commodification of Sufism are often difficult to draw. In the European West and North America, Sufi poetry, music and practices are advertised and sold under the labels of esoteric globalization such as "Eastern Spirituality," "Wisdom of the East," "World Music" and "Islamic

Mysticism."[51] The most common examples of the success of Sufi products are the bestselling poetry of Jalaluddin Rumi, the artistic performances of the Whirling Dervishes of the Turkish Mevlevi tradition who tour North American and West European concert halls, popular Sufi music like the qawwali singers from Pakistan (most prominently Nusrat Ali Fateh Khan, d. 1997), and popular books on Sufi Mysticism, as for example the books by Idries Shah.[52] Of course, this kind of capitalist re-branding of Sufism happens largely independent of contemporary Sufi movements, especially when it comes to the commodification of Sufi poetry and music. But some Sufi circles try to get their own – if mostly small – share of the Sufi market. Doing so, they can capitalize on their authority as authentic transmitters of Sufi knowledge, and thusly use the esoteric market as a means for both dawa and business.[53] Many Sufi websites sell books online, some also sell videos and music CDs as well as other Sufi/Muslim utensils like Muslim clothing, perfume and incense.[54] A more recent phenomenon is Sufi tourism, where Sufi groups organize pilgrimages to sacred places in the Islamic homelands.[55]

It appears that the willingness to participate in the commodification of Sufism correlates positively with the openness to Western society in general. A brief look at the websites of some of the earlier-discussed groups suffices to validate this point. While the website of the West-critical Naqshbandi Shaikh Abdul Kerim does not offer Sufi products for sale, the main line of the order in North America externalized their commercial activities and created an extra website for it: the Islamic Shopping Network.[56] The official website of the Murid community in Harlem, which is rather exclusive and selective in its proselytizing efforts, does not feature commercial products.[57] ASMA Society, on the other side, offers books as well as talks (on CD) by Imam Feisal for sale, as well as a serious of documentaries on Islam and Muslims in America.[58] The products correspond with the educational outreach approach of the organization. The Nur Ashki Jerrahi order does not feature commercial products on its main website, but has established its own small publisher house, Pir Press, which features mainly books and audio materials from within its own tradition.[59] Its sister organization in Spring Valley does offer a huge list of recommended books on Islam and Sufism, but does not sell them directly.[60] A link leads the potential buyer to amazon.com; the page clarifies that the provisions generated from book sales will be used for relief projects.

Sufism has with no doubt become an established trademark within the New Age/esoteric market. "Spirituality" sells well in West European and North American societies,[61] and it is not surprising that both traditionalist Sufi-Muslims as well as Sufi Mysticists use the available commercial opportunities. The positive side effect of the commercialization of Sufism and its compartmentalization in consumable Sufi products is that it helps to foster an interest in Islam that focuses more on aesthetics than on terrorism – as long as Sufism is still seen as part of the Islamic tradition.

4 Travelling and competition

Ethnically homogeneous groups where kinship and cultural bounds are very strong such as the Senegalese Murid appear to be very consistent and self-contained. However, travelling between Sufi groups in search for an ideal fit – labelled "baraka-surfing" by Marcia Hermansen[62] – is rather common, especially among converts. Some practitioners visit different circles at the same time. I even met Sufis who visit both Sunni and Shiite circles. At least in New York, there appear to be many cross-tariqa connections and allegiances on a personal level – and interestingly not only between members of circles with a similar understanding of Islam and Sufi practice. For example, one local Sufi practitioner had, after he converted to Islam and became interested in Sufism, temporarily visited the circles of the universalist Nur Ashki Jerrahi order before participating in a more traditionally organized Qadiri circle. Then he became a disciple of a traditionalist Naqshbandi circle.[63] At a certain point, he got disillusioned with his shaikh and continued his search, looking for a new, authentic and powerful shaikh with whom he felt comfortable to take a vow of allegiance. While on this search, he also visited the New York branch of the Shiite Nimatullahi Order, apparently not too strongly influenced by the strong anti-Shiite stance of the Naqshbandi order he previously belonged to. The ongoing search of F. is not that atypical. During my fieldwork, I met several Sufis who told similar stories. A huge number of these continuous searchers appear to be converts.

The relative openness of the individual orders should, however, not convey the image of unanimous harmony. Sometimes hostilities between certain groups are relatively openly expressed. Brad Gooch reports an incident when a Sufi gathering of the Nur Ashki Jerrahi community was seriously disturbed where a "young man from West Africa ... [with] a black turban ... threateningly approached the shaikha [Fariha], shouting, 'This is *bidah*.'"[64] The same incident has also been related to me by a former member of the Naqshbandi circle to which the offender belonged. His narration illustrates how contested Islam sometimes is, even among Sufi-Muslims and especially with regard to orthopraxy:

> One brother ... went to the Jerrahi mosque, the one in Lower Manhattan; he heard from ... saying that in that mosque they do everything different than Islam – female shaikh, praying with the men, and dancing with men and all that stuff, you know. He went there with the turban – he is all turban, he was just Naqshibandi – he went there with the jalabiya, like a long robe. He went there and went among them, sort of screaming, yelling about: "This is not Islam, Islam is not supposed to be like this, Islam is different."[65]

More often, however, animosities are of a more subtle nature, as expressed in the following disillusioned comment by S., a Sufi practitioner who is not initiated with a particular order and who at another instance expressed to me his serious doubts about what he perceives as an exaggerated influence of the shaikhs:

I have gone to many different groups. I hear from one group, they say: "Oh, you know, that group, it does all those things, that's not good ... We do this." You go to the next group, it's: "Our group..." You go to another group, it's: "Our group..." ... There's no embracing.[66]

It appears to me that the tensions between Sufi circles are accelerated by the pressures Sufi practitioners experience as a marginalized tradition within Islam, where their Islamic orthodoxy and thus legitimacy is often questioned. In some instances, the pressure to legitimate themselves appears to increase intra-Sufi competition and animosities. Accordingly those Sufis, who, like the Naqshbandis and the Turkish Halveti-Jerrahi Order, put obedience to Islamic law first and appear to be more likely to criticize the more universally oriented Sufis.

5 Multiple affiliations and networking

You seem to be ambassador of different *tariqa*s, I want you to continue with that.

The above quote from Shaikh Nur al-Jerrahi was narrated to me by his disciple Abdul Qudus, who took Shaikh Nur's word to heart. In his own words, Abdul Qudus tries to make "a concerted effort to maintain relations with frequent different orders." He aims to "keep in contact with them because we are all about the same work."[67] In fact, while initiation in different Sufi traditions is not the rule, it appears to be very common. An impressive example is Laurence Galian, who claims on his current website to be shaikh of the Nimatullahi and Khwajagani Sufi orders and provides a list of Jerrahi shaikhs (both of the Spring Valley and Manhattan lineages) with whom he has studied and taken hand (i.e. the act of establishing a teacher–student relationship).[68] In an earlier version of his personal website, he also claimed membership in the Rifā'ī-Ma'rūfī order.[69] Here he listed a total of nine shaikhs with whom he claims to have studied or taken hand, mostly from the Jerrahi tradition. He also claims to have received initiation by Khidr (the legendary Islamic trickster figure with much appeal in popular Islam and Sufism – there is a tradition of Sufis who claim to have met him and/or having been initiated by him or having been granted shaikhhood through him; I met, for example, a Turkish lady in New York City, herself leader of a Sufi circle, who told me about her meetings with Khidr). If Galian's webpage is compared with the older version of the same page, we find that he appears to have shifted his main allegiance to the Turkish Jerrahi tradition slightly – in 2003 he had introduced himself as a student of the Halveti-Jerrahi order, claiming to have studied at their center in Spring Valley and not even mentioning Manhattan's Ashki Jerrahis.[70] In the most recent version of his website, he explains that in September 2003 he,

> reestablished his connection with Hazreti Pir Muhammad Nureddin Jerrahi (the founder of the Jerrahi Order – born in Istanbul 1678 CE) by renewing his hand with Shaykha Fariha al-Jerrahi, the lineage bearer in the Americas (with the help of Shaykha Amina and the khalifas and circle leaders of the Order).[71]

From these observations emerges the picture of a complex informal network based on personal contacts among New York Sufis. With some important qualifications, this can be extended to the national level. Formalized contacts exist especially between the more Americanized Sufi groups. An example is the annual "Sufi Conference" organized regularly since 2001. Regulars on this conference, the idea for which was born in the Sufi Book Store of lower Manhattan (which was run by the Nur Ashki Jerrahis),[72] are representatives of organizations inspired by Pir Inayat Khan (such as the Sufi Order International, the Sufi Islamia Ruhaniat Society and the Dances of Universal Peace movement), the Nur Askhi Jerrahi Sufi Order, the Bawa Muhaiyaddeen Fellowship, the Golden Chain Naqshibandi Order and the Threshold Society (a Mevlevi organization).[73] The participants of the Sufi Conference for the most part represent organizations that are dominated by American converts to Islam and have a very wide, universalist understanding of Sufism as Islamic Mysticism – in some cases deliberately challenging the boundaries of the Islamic mainstream discourse. Of similar kind in terms of its Islamic orientation and thus attracting a similar group of participants is the annual Sufism Symposium, organized regularly since 1994, by the International Association of Sufism (California), an organization sponsored by the Uwaiysi tariqat, which is dedicated to promote the heritage of the Iranian Shiite mystic Shah Maghsoud (d. 1980).[74] For 2006, even the relatively conservative Naqshbandi-Haqqanis announced the participation of Hisham Kabbani at the Sufism Symposium.[75]

A different, clearly more mainstream Muslim-Sufi audience is addressed at the annual "Maulidu-n-Nabi" conferences organized by the Islamic Studies & Research Association International (ISRA). Here we find representatives of the Shadhili tradition (Noorouddeen Durkee), the Tijaniyya, as well as the Haqqani-Naqshbandiyya. ISRA, which operates transnationally, defines its goal as "presenting Islam as a comprehensive deen [religion] based upon islam [surrender], iman [belief], and ihsan [spirituality] (tasawwuf)"[76] and is thus clearly dedicated to defend Sufism as a legitimate and indispensable part of the Islamic tradition. The Haqqani-Naqshbandis also organized two "International Islamic Unity Conferences" in 1996 and 1998, to which they invited a rather broad array of Sufi and Sufi-friendly Muslim representatives, scholars of Islam and politicians. The first conference took place in Los Angeles and the second in Washington DC, and they exemplify the ambition of the group to establish itself as a major Islamic player in the US.[77]

Sometimes there are also high-level contacts between Sufi representatives with very different understandings of Sufism. The Naqshbandi shaikh Abdul Kerim, for example, also used to visit the dhikr meetings of Tosun Bayrak's Jerrahi circle.[78] The conservative Abdul Kerim is connected in a friendly manner with Shaikh Abdul Qudus, African-American convert to Islam and representative of a Senegalese Qadiri branch, who has himself been initiated into Sufism through the Mysticist Shaikh Nur al-Jerrahi.[79] Shaikh Nazim met with Pir Vilayat Khan at New Lebanon (NY) when he first visited the US in 1991.[80] A prolonged and more intimate relationship has been established between the traditionalist Jerrahi Shaikh Tosun Bayrak and the more universalist Sufi teacher Bawa Muhaiyyaddeen (d. 1986) from Sri Lanka.[81] As I was told by a New York member of the Bawa Muhaiyyaddeen fellowship,[82] Shaikh Tosun used to visit Bawa Muhaiyyaddeen regularly and "they [the Jerrahis, MD] accept Bawa as their shaikh."[83] In fact, a picture of Bawa Muhaiyyaddeen is prominently displayed in the Spring Valley Jerrahi lodge.[84] There are, nevertheless, limitations to intra-Sufi dialogue. It appears that the more traditionalist orders on the one side and the more universalist Sufis on the other for the most part stay within their own circles.

Sufi-networking can not be discussed without considering the implications of the increasingly global use of the Internet and the new forms of communication it enables. By its very nature transnational, although sometimes restricted by language, the worldwide Sufi web offers a wide range of opportunities for advertisement, apologetic discourse, as well as exchange of information and ideas.[85] We can find seemingly countless cross-traditional as well as traditional Sufi discussion lists,[86] blogs,[87] newsgroups and Sufi resource sites posting local or transregional information on Sufi events.[88] What will be interesting to follow in the long run is the impact of the medial revolution on Sufism. Will it change the traditional ways of shaikh–disciple relationships? How successful can web-dawa be? To which extent can a Sufi shaikh's charisma be mediated through an email or electronic video clips? Will it at some point become possible to get initiated online? While the idea might seem off at first hand, a visit to the website of the Philadelphia-based Bawa Muhaiyyaddeen Fellowship provides the Sufi-surfer with access to an online membership form.[89] The question is what an online membership can actually mean for an individual as well as for a thusly connected "virtual" community.

Conclusion

It should have become apparent from this chapter that Sufism is extremely contested within the Islamic discourse and also between competing Sufi groups. While this contestation can be observed on a global scale, its local forms vary and reflect engagement with the specific cultural, socio-political and legal frameworks of particular environments. As for the Sufi Muslim scene in New York, to the admittedly limited extent that it could be presented in this chapter, it is very heterogeneous with regard to its understanding of doctrinal and ritual matters as well as with regard to how different Sufi groups position themselves toward American society and culture. The pluralist and secular definition of the public space in the US accentuates questions of authenticity and belonging. At the same time, however, it offers opportunities largely unknown in many Muslim majority countries in which religion is often state-regulated and where discourses on religious and cultural orthodoxy tend to be defined much more narrowly. By using the opportunities the secular and pluralist US society has to offer – such as public outreach and open networking – Sufi Muslims both continue and expand traditional modes of Sufi activities. It will be interesting to see in the long run to which degree emerging Sufi Muslim identities in the West will be able to integrate potentially conflicting cultural heritages and how successful they will be in establishing Western Sufi identities without loosing their bonds to the Islamic tradition.

Notes

1　This chapter is mainly based on fieldwork been between 2002 and 2004 as part of Columbia University's Muslims in New York Project (MUSNY) funded by the Ford Foundation. I am thankful to everybody involved in the organization of the project and even more so to the New York Sufis, who allowed me to visit their meetings and shared their stories, experiences and ideas with me.
2　Cf. the standard of Herberg (1983).
3　For just one typical example of this rhetoric I refer to a recent essay by Brian Cox (2006), an Episcopal Priest and Senior Vice President of the International Center for Religion and Diplomacy in Washington, DC, in which he urges for a shared effort of the "children of Abraham" to overcome current religio-political challenges.
4　Cf. Hermansen (2004).
5　Sufi Focus Group Interview, MUSNY Project, Columbia University, June 2, 2003, transcript.
6　Curtiss (2006); see also Witham (1999).
7　Cf. Dressler (2006).
8　Hermansen (2004: 85f.).
9　Cf. Geaves (2005); see also Chapter 6, this volume.
10　Sirriyeh (1999).
11　Ess (1999: 43).
12　Cf. Chapters 2, 4, 6 and 10, this volume.
13　MUSNY Sufi Focus Group Interview, Columbia University, September 12, 2000, transcript.
14　Sufi Focus Group Interview, 2003.
15　"Islamic tradition" I understand discursively following Asad (1986).
16　Drawing on examples from my fieldwork, I suggested elsewhere to distinguish between different approaches to Sufism based on the respective groups' understanding of sharia and the degree of their inclusivism/exclusivism. Dressler (forthcoming).
17　For a concise historic essay on the inner-Islamic debate about Sufism's legitimacy see Sedgwick (2000), especially Chapter 5; for a more detailed account see Sirriyeh (1999).
18　I think this holds generally true, even if there are certain legal and bureaucratic issues that may sometimes limit the freedom of Sufi-Muslim expression as pointed out by Ernst (1997: 210f.).
19　Sufi Focus Group Interview, 2000.
20　Sufi Focus Group Interview, 2000.
21　See the webpage of this branch, the Osmanli Dergahi, www.naksibendi.org (last accessed March 10, 2006).
22　Internal splits and tensions between competing local circles are quite typical for the Haqqaniyya; see Nielsen *et al.* (2006).
23　Examples of his teachings in the form of lecture transcripts can be found at Osmanli Dergahi, www.naksibendi.org/sak_sohbets.html (last accessed March 11, 2006).
24　Fieldnotes, June 20, 2003.
25　On the tariqa's millennialism see Geaves (2001). Shaikh Nazim's khalifa in the US dedicated a whole book to the theme of millennialism; see Kabbani (2003).
26　Afterwards I was told by other participants that the meal issue had been contested for a while and created much unrest among the circle's women, who complained that

there was either no or not enough food for them and that they ought not to be treated differently than the male members on that subject.

27 A second phase of tension occurred when a female attendee – herself a regular dhikr attendee, but not initiated in the order – challenged the harsh language the shaikh used in his dismissal of Saudi Arabia (in this context seen as the epitome of Wahhabism and anti-Sufi propaganda), in which he drew a rather negative picture of the Saudi royal family. Against the growing anger of the shaikh, the female attendee remained rather staunch in her defense of the Saudi family, some of its members she happened to have met in person.

28 The community in New York City is large enough to be able to offer certain services a small community never could afford: the New York Murid have their own mosque and community center in Harlem, the "House of Islam" (see Murid Islamic Community in America, www.micawebsite.org/house.htm2001, last accessed July 22, 2006); they offer among other things Koran classes on Sundays (70 children enrolled in 2003), and daira ("circle") meetings twice a week, where they chant the qasaid (hymns) of Ahmadou Bamba, the founder of the order.

29 Dieng (2006).

30 Cf. Ebin (1996).

31 La Marche 2004, DVD, Nouha Video Production: New York, 2004.

32 Ibid.

33 Dede (2002).

34 For a description of the Sufi biography of Imam Feisal, including a description of his dhikr meetings, which have the reputation of being more sober than the rather ecstatic gatherings of, e.g., the Nur Ashki Jerrahis, see Gooch (2002: 351–360).

35 Rauf (2002, 2004); ASMA Society, "Amrahamic Ethics," www.asmasociety.org/religion/abrahamic.html (last accessed March 12, 2006).

36 Cf. ASMA Society, www.asmasociety.org.

37 PBS, "Frontline. Muslims[:] Interview [with] Imam Feisal Abdul Rauf" (March, 2002). Online, available at: www.pbs.org/wgbh/pages/frontline/shows/muslims/interviews/feisal.html (last accessed March 12, 2006); *Zion's Herald*, "ZH interviews[:] Feisal Abdul Rauf" (November/December 2002). Online, available at: www.zionsherald.org/Nov2002_interview.html (last accessed March 12, 2006).

38 Nur Ashki Jerrahi Sufi Order, www.nurashkijerrahi.org/main.htm (last accessed July 11, 2006).

39 "Tariqat, the West, and the Path of Ease. A talk by Shaykha Fariha al-Jerrahi, 1999," www.nurashkijerrahi.org/teachings/sfariha_002.htm (last accessed March 6, 2006).

40 Cf. their website Halveti-Cerrahi Order of Dervishes, http://jerrahi.org (last accessed July 22, 2006); for a comparison between the Nur Ashki Jerrahis and the Spring Valley Jerrahis see Dressler (forthcoming).

41 As one New York Sufi put it:

> The American culture is a racist culture, is a class culture … We would not allow you to call the *azan* [call to prayer] in the *masjid* [mosque] if you're not of that ethnic *masjid*, in some cases. These are realities that we have to deal with.
>
> (Sufi Focus Group Interview, 2000)

42 Recently, the media reported harsh measures by Iranian authorities against Sufis in Qom in what has been interpreted as a move to encounter the growing popularity of Sufism in Iran; Amnesty International, Public Statement, "Iran: urgent investigation required into security forces violence against Sufi Muslims in Qom" (February 17, 2006), www.amnestyusa.org/news/document.do?id=ENGMDE130162006. As for Saudi Arabia, there were recently signs of a more tolerant approach to Sufism; Faiza Saleh Ambah, "In Saudi Arabia, a resurgence of Sufism," *Washington Post* (May 2, 2006), www.washingtonpost.com/wp-dyn/content/article/2006/05/01/AR2006050101380. html. In Turkey, Sufi orders are legally banned since 1925, but orders are usually

tolerated as long as they don't enter the public arena and declare their practices as cultural rather than religious.

43 Dawa (lit. invitation), is the Islamic concept of outreach and proselytism in the name of Islam.

44 Criticism is voiced, for example, by a New York Tijani Sufi, who explained that "in the Western country they used ... the newspaper. The Sufi don't use. Our *dawa* is not like this. We can not send it by newspaper. It is heart-to-heart" (Sufi Focus Group Interview, 2000).

45 These are the Naqshbandi Sufi Way, www.naqshbandi.org; The Islamic Supreme Council of America, http://islamicsupremecouncil.org; The as-Sunnah Foundation of America, http://sunnah.org/; and the Islamic Shopping Network, www.isn1.net/.

46 Http://islamicsupremecouncil.org/Spirituality/Naqshbandi/naqshabandi_america.htm (last accessed March 12, 2002).

47 www.naqshbandi.org/events/us2000/20000827/alaqsa/default.htm   (last   accessed March 6, 2006).

48 www.naqshbandi.org/events/us2000/20000827/alaqsa/default.htm   (last   accessed March 6, 2006).

49 Interview with F., July 22, 2003.

50 Mohammad-Arif (2000: 240).

51 For the commodification of Sufism see also Chapter 4 in this volume.

52 Cf. Ernst (1997: xviii).

53 The Islamic Shopping Network reported proudly the success of Shaikh Hisham Kabbani as a guest speaker at the International New Age Trade Show; www.isn1.net/ketodiki.html (last accessed September 11, 2005).

54 For a discussion of the Internet merchandising of the Haqqaniyya see Schmidt (2004: 114f.).

55 Hermansen (2006: 39).

56 The website offers a huge span of products, from Sufi books – many of which they produce themselves – to home décor; www.isn1.net (last accessed July 11, 2006).

57 www.micawebsite.org (last accessed July 22, 2006).

58 www.asmasociety.org/shop/index.html (last accessed July 11, 2006).

59 Pir Press: Sufi Books and Music, www.pirpress.com (last accessed July 11, 2006).

60 www.jerrahi.org/jerrahi_books.htm (last accessed July 11, 2006).

61 See Carrette and King (2005).

62 Hermansen (1997); see also Hermansen (2006: 38–40).

63 Interview with F., July 22, 2003.

64 Gooch (2002: 350f.).

65 Interview with F., July 22, 2003. F. also reported that his shaikh repeatedly made negative statements about the Nur Ashki Jerrahi order, rejecting especially its female leadership.

66 Sufi Focus Group Interview, 2003.

67 Interview with Abdul Qudus, June 24, 2003.

68 Laurence Galian's homepage, http://home.earthlink.net/~drmljg/id12.html   (last accessed June 15, 2006).

69 www.quiddity-inc.com/id1.html (last accessed February 4, 2005).

70 Accessed July 7, 2003.

71 Laurence Galian's homepage.

72 Sufi Conference, 'About the Sufi Conference', www.suficonference.org/About Conference.html (last accessed September 17, 2005).

73 See www.suficonference.org (last accessed September 17, 2005).

74 See www.ias.org (last accessed March 13, 2006). For another example of such cross-tariqat connections click at the pictures at www.sufimexico.org/htm/historia/f_historia.htm (last accessed September 17, 2005); the pictures show the heads of the Nur Ashki Jerrahi order with prominent representatives of other religions and other

Sufi orders such as the Turkish Rufai order (Shaikh Sherif Baba), the Senegalese Murid order (Shaikh Yei), and the Sufi Order of the West (Pir Zia Inayat Khan).

75 Email message, naqshbandi_network@yahoogroups.com, March 18, 2006.
76 www.israinternational.com (last accessed September 11, 2005).
77 www.sunnah.org/nl/v0101/unity.html (last accessed June 20, 2006); www.naqshbandi.net/haqqani/events/conf98.htm (last accessed June 20, 2006).
78 Fieldnotes, conversation with S., June 20, 2003.
79 Interview with Abdul Qudus, June 24, 2003.
80 Kabbani (1995: 394, 396).
81 Bawa Muhaiyyaddeen's mausoleum in East Fallowfield, 40 miles outside Philadelphia, is the first Sufi shrine on US territory, and has a reputation as an important sacred location not only for Bawa Muhaiyyaddeen Sufis.
82 For more information on the Bawa Muhaiyyaddeen fellowship see Webb (1994, 2006).
83 Interview with Ali, August 15, 2003.
84 Personal observation, July 5, 2003.
85 A useful link collection is the List of the Sufi-related Resources on the Internet, http://world.std.com/~habib/sufi.html (last accessed March 6, 2006).
86 See for example Sufis without Borders: Sufism w/o Ism, http://groups.yahoo.com/group/sufis_without_borders (last accessed June 15, 2007).
87 For example Sufi News and Sufism World Report, http://sufinews.blogspot.com (last accessed June 15, 2007).
88 An example of the latter is the page http://groups.yahoo.com/group/sufi-events (last accessed September 17, 2005).
89 www.bmf.org/fellowship/membership.html (last accessed March 2, 2006).

References

Asad, T., *The Idea of an Anthropology of Islam*, Washington: Center for Contemporary Arab Studies Georgetown University, 1986.
Carrette, J. and King, R., *Selling Spirituality. The Silent Takeover of Religion*, London: Routledge, 2005.
Cox, B., "The third way of 'Abrahamic Reconciliation'," *The Review of Faith & International Affairs* 4, 2006.
Curtiss, R.H., "Dispute between U.S. Muslim groups goes public," *Washington Report on Middle East Affairs*, April/May 1999, pp. 71, 101. Online, available at: www.washington-report.org/backissues/0499/9904071.html (last accessed February 20, 2006).
Dede, M., "Islam: the spiritual matrix, page II," *The Lightmillenium* 2002 (Summer). Online, available at: http://lightmillennium.org/summer_02/mdede_spiritual_matrix_p2.html (last accessed March 12, 2006).
Dieng, A., "Islam as a model of society: the example of Muridiya," talk delivered at the Murid Conference at the UN, New York City, July 28, 2003. Online, available at: www.micawebsite.org/mouridism.htm#MURID%20COMMUNITY (last accessed July 15, 2006).
Dressler, M., "Election polemics," *The Revealer*, November 2, 2006. Online, available at: www.therevealer.org/archives/timely_002693.php.
Dressler, M., "Between Islamic exclusivism and mysticist universalism: negotiating Sufi Muslim identity in New York City," in L. Cristillo (ed.), *Muslims in New York City*, New York: New York University Press, forthcoming.
Ebin, V., "Making room versus creating space. The construction of spatial categories by

itinerant Mouride traders," in B.D. Metcalf (ed.), *Making Muslim Space in North America and Europe*, Berkeley: University of California Press, 1996, 92–109.

Ernst, C.W., *The Shambhala Guide to Sufism*, Boston: Shambala, 1997.

Ess, J.v., "Sufism and its opponents. Reflections on topoi, tribulations, and transformations," in F. de Jong and B. Radtke (eds.), *Islamic Mysticism Contested. Thirteen Centuries of Controversies and Polemics*, Leiden: Brill, 1999, 22–44.

Geaves, R., "The Haqqani Naqshbandis: a study of apocalyptic Millenialism within Islam," in S. Porter, M. Hayes and D. Tombs (eds.), *Faith in the Millenium*, Sheffield: Sheffield Academic Press, 2001.

Geaves, R., "Tradition, innovation, and authentication: Replicating the 'Ahl as-Sunna wa Jamaat' in Britain," *Comparative Islamic Studies* 1, 2005, 1–20.

Gooch, B., *Godtalk. Travels in Spiritual America*, New York: Alfred Knopf, 2002.

Herberg, W., *Protestant, Catholic, Jew: An Essay in American Religious Sociology*, Chicago: University of Chicago Press, 1983.

Hermansen, M., "In the garden of American Sufi movements: hybrids and perennials," in P. Clarke (ed.), *New Trends and Developments in the World of Islam*, London: Luzac Oriental, 1997, 155–178.

Hermansen, M., "The evolution of American Muslim responses to 9/11," in R. Geaves, T. Gabriel, Y.Y. Haddad and J.I. Smith (eds.), *Islam and the West post 9/11*, Aldershot: Ashgate, 2004, 77–96.

Hermansen, M., "Literary production of Western Sufi movements," in J. Malik and J. Hinnells (eds.), *Sufism in the West*, London: Routledge, 2006, 28–48.

Kabbani, M.H., *The Naqshbandi Sufi Way: History and Guidebook of the Saints of the Golden Chain*, Chicago: KAZI, 1995.

Kabbani, M.H., *The Approach of Armageddon: an Islamic Perspective*, Washington, DC: Islamic Supreme Council of North America, 2003.

Mohammad-Arif, A., *Salam America: l'Islam Indien en diaspora*, Paris: CNRS, 2000.

Nielsen, J., Draper, M. and Yemelianova, G., "Transnational Sufism: the Haqqaniyya," in J. Malik and J. Hinnells (eds.), *Sufism in the West*, London: Routledge, 2006, 103–114.

Rauf, F.A., *What's Right with Islam. A New Vision for Muslims and the West*, San Francisco: Harper, 2004.

Rauf, F.A., "A call to bridge the Abrahamic faiths: Judaism, Christianity, Islam. Sermon at al-Farah Mosque," September 6, 2002. Online, available at: www.cuii. org/911sermon.htm (last accessed March 12, 2006).

Schmidt, G., "Sufi charisma on the internet," in D. Westerlund (ed.), *Sufism in Europe and North America*, London: Routledge, 2004, 109–126.

Sedgwick, M., *Sufism: The Essentials*, Cairo: American University of Cairo Press, 2000.

Sirriyeh, M., *Sufis and Anti-Sufis. The Defense, Rethinking and Rejection of Sufism in the Modern World*, Richmond: Curzon Press, 1999.

Webb, G., "Tradition and innovation in contemporary American Islamic spirituality: the Bawa Muhaiyaddeen Fellowship," in Y.Y. Haddad and J.I. Smith (eds.), *Muslim Communities in North America*, New York: SUNY Press, 1994, 75–108.

Webb, G., "Third-wave Sufism in America and the Bwa Muhaiyaddeen Fellowship," in J. Malik and J. Hinnells (eds.), *Sufism in the West*, London: Routledge, 2006, 86–102.

Witham, L., "Muslim cleric stands by statement on extremists; He accuses group of threatening him," *Washington Times*, March 2, 1999, p. A8.

6 A case of cultural binary fission or transglobal Sufism?

The transmigration of Sufism to Britain

Ron Geaves

A number of scholars have been utilising the phrase 'transglobal' or 'transnational' to describe the formation of diaspora communities. For example, Pnina Werbner refers to the Pakistani communities in Britain as 'transnational communities of co-responsibility'.[1] Sufism has arrived in Britain as part of the process of migration which has seen the creation of South Asian diasporas, now supplemented by communities from Turkey, Malaysia, North and sub-Saharan Africa, all places where Sufism in the Muslim context flourishes. Consequently it would be accurate to assert that the dominant form of Islamic expression in Britain is a traditional version of the religion highly influenced by Sufism.

Most of the major tariqas exist in Britain, including several forms of Naqshbandiya, Qadiriya, Chishtiya, Alawiya, Tijaniya to name but a handful of those present. However, unlike the USA, Sufism has made little impact on the original non-migrant non-Muslim population, and with the exception of the Haqqani Naqshbandis, led by the charismatic Shaikh Nazim, very few outside of the Muslim migrant communities have been attracted. Even Shaikh Nazim has not had the success he achieved in Germany or North America.

I would argue that the main contributory reason for this lack of success up to the end of the twentieth century is that Sufism in Britain remained tightly bound up with ethnic identity, a means of maintaining traditions and customs closely linked with localities in the place of origin that can be limited in boundary size to areas only as large as a village shrine. Thus Sufism has functioned not so much as a transmission of mysticism within Islam, able to cross over to a universal mysticism sought by Western seekers, but as a boundary mechanism primarily concerned with the transmission of cultural and religious traditions. Sometimes these traditions are duplicated so effectively in the diaspora situation, providing a mirror image of village customs and practices, that I have preferred to use the term 'cultural binary fission' to describe the process of reproduction. The term 'binary fission' is borrowed from biology and refers to the most basic reproductive method known to nature, where amoeba simply divide their cells and split in two to create a duplicate of themselves. I am not arguing that the attempt is fully successful as there will always be transformations that take place in a new environment, and some of these will be explored, but that the *tariqas* have primarily functioned as attempts to duplicate the cultural forms of the locality of origin.

I would argue that a true 'transglobal' phenomenon occurs, at least in the religious realm, when a tradition succeeds in breaking its geographical confines, spreading its teachings far and wide, but successfully adjusted to a variety of cultural and social formations. Sufism is capable of doing this and demonstrates prominent examples in its history. Sufi migrants are not unknown before the twentieth century and indeed transnational movements have been started by them. The most famous example would be Rumi who arrived in Turkey as a migrant, fleeing from political disturbances in his place of birth. Others have migrated in order to carry the teachings of their shaikh or to proselytise the teachings of Islam, and the transglobal nature of the Naqshbandiya is testimony to the success of this movement. Indeed considerable geographical spread can be partly attributed to the Sufi ideal of travel to seek a teacher who can initiate one into the effective means of communion with Allah.

Pnina Werbner also points out in an earlier piece of work that the development of a Sufi tariqa follows a pattern in which there is a constant historical process of 'waxing' and 'waning' amongst the local cults within the broad encompassing tariqa. She suggests that new cults appear, 'energised through the emergence of a charismatic saint', which revitalises the tariqa.[2] She argues that the shrines of departed saints cannot function in this way:

> Although shrines of illustrious saints, once established, remain points of personal pilgrimage and seasonal ritual celebrations, such shrines no longer extend as organisations far beyond a relatively localised area, and cannot continue to control, as the cult founder did, a series of sub-centres, and sub-sub-centres over a vast region.[3]

If Pnina Werbner is correct in her assertion of a repeated cyclical pattern of development amongst Sufi cults in the subcontinent and elsewhere in the Muslim world, then it takes the presence of a living charismatic pir or shaikh to create a genuine religious Sufi transglobal movement within Islam, maintaining control over centres and sub-centres across the world. Thus by this process, genuine transglobal movements come into existence within Sufism, but usually waning into a series of localised traditions orbiting around the location of the shrine of the founder after his death. However, the processes of migratory spread of religions are different, not least because the motivations for displacement are not the same. Amongst such economic or political migrants, the primary purpose for transmigration of religion initially, at least, is to maintain cultural identity, to protect ethnicity by serving as a boundary marker. The thrust of the religious dimension involved when a charismatic saint is alive is able to subsume culture, whilst creating diverse forms of the religion each bearing the hallmarks of the subsumed cultural ambiance. However, new formations are beginning to take root in Britain since the advent of the twenty-first century that undermine both of types of development described above. The chapter will chart the various attempts in Britain to rally around the idea of the Ahl-e Sunnat wa Jama'at, first successfully utilised by Ahmad Riza Khan Barelwi (1856–1921) in Northern

India as a strategy of resistance against reformist critiques from Deobandis, Ahl-e Hadith and others who were opposed to popular Sufi practices and beliefs.[4] However, Ahmad Riza Khan Barelwi did not undermine the traditional tariqa structure but merely provided a common umbrella identity which promoted Sufism and its sympathisers as the mainstream of Muslim tradition. These strategies have continued unbroken in amongst British Sufis of South Asian origin and to an extent have pulled in Sufis from places of origin elsewhere in the Muslim world. However, as we will see, new developments on the Internet provide sites for the globalisation of the identity issues and new possibilities for a transglobal identity that transcend cultural binary fission with a new emphasis on scripturalisation and an emergence from tariqa as the primary location of belonging for Sufis.

Religion and ethnicity

In *Sufis of Britain*, I conducted a number of ethnographic studies of various tariqas, particularly focusing on the relationship of religion and ethnicity.[5] The following information is a summary of some of its conclusions. The study of Sufi tariqas that were introduced into Britain through the process of migration provides a useful tool with which to investigate the complex relationship between religion and ethnicity. Many of the tariqas have developed as localised groups with strong loyalties to a particular family tradition imbued with sanctity through their lineal association with a deceased saint. The focus on worship at the tomb of the saint reinforces this geographical location of sacredness and maintains the nucleus of local support. Sometimes the participation at the tomb can radiate out to include a wider network of international pilgrimage as in the case of more famous shrines. However, this can serve to reinforce the sense of loyalty and pride felt by the people who reside in the vicinity of the tomb. It is also likely that their Islam will include time-honoured customs associated with the adab of the tariqa and the hagiography of the founding saint.

If, as in the case of Britain, members of such communities move their location into specific districts of British cities through the processes of chain migration, then it is likely that they will gather around the lifestyle and leadership provided by the shrine cult. These will function as significant maintainers of boundary mechanisms associated with ethnic identity. In this sense, the unique customs, the presence of influential leaders related to the family of the saint, and new sacred spaces in Britain linked to the original shrine help to maintain a connection to the history and geography of a sanctified place of origin. The soil of the villages of origin is made sacred by the presence of the shrine and journeys are made not only to visit relatives but also to recharge the spiritual batteries by undergoing a pilgrimage. The landscape of the shrine very often becomes the location of significant dreams, visions and prophecies that are taken back to the new place of residence and used to recreate variant religious forms of the original shrine cult.

These forms of religious expression can all reinforce ethnic identity and maintain boundaries not only against a perceived hostile non-Muslim indigenous community but also to the wider Muslim presence in Britain, including even those from the same nation that houses the shrine. However, the change of location to a non-Muslim environment has resulted in an important adaptation taking place in many of the tariqas transferred to Britain. Whereas, in the place of origin, the focus of attention is the shrine itself, in the new location this is not possible. The priority in a non-Muslim environment has shifted to protecting and maintaining Islam itself, especially in regard to the new British-born generations. Thus many of the leaders associated with family membership of the shrine cults have used their traditional authority to promote Islam. This renewal of the original proselytising intention of the founding saint has rejuvenated the tariqa and widened its participation to include followers from outside the original location of the shrine. Thus religion can become a means to recreate a new sense of loyalty that extends the original ethnic base of membership. In turn the shrine in the original place of location is visited by the new membership, who have no ancestral history associated with the region. In this way the shrine is also rejuvenated as its reputation spreads to a wider geographical base and it begins to attract international pilgrims.

The traditional pattern of 'waxing and waning' identified by Pnina Werbner that takes place in the tariqas when new institutional forms develop after the death of charismatic leaders is transformed by migration. The typical pattern of 'waning' after the death of the original saint can be negated by the urgent motivation to promote Islam in the new environment. The thrust of this new dynamic can revitalise the old shrine cult and lead to a revival or 'waxing' that does not necessarily involve the appearance of a new charismatic saint. On the other hand, the new location of a Muslim community in a non-Muslim nation can inspire the charismatic saint to relocate in order to propagate Islam. Since the beginning of Islam, Sufis have travelled to non-Muslim territory in order to proselytise. It is in this way that many new communities of Muslims have developed, and on the death of the saint, new locations of sacred space have appeared. However, the motivation is blurred where large-scale migration has taken place. In effect, the promotion of Islam takes place only within the migrant community, and usually only on a localised scale. Consequently, it is often the case that Islam is in actual fact utilised as a resource for maintaining the reproduction of ethnic patterns of behaviour.

This pattern is developing as charismatic Sufi masters either visit or settle in Britain. Those who have settled in Britain have formed around themselves strong followings that have been able to transcend to some extent localised regional loyalties, although generally their core following retains a strong local ingredient. This impacts on their ability to gain followers from outside the ethnic group, as incomers may be resistant to socialising into the core values, also they will be not be able to integrate fully, perceived as 'high-value' outsiders. Even where some success has been achieved in gaining adherents from outside the localised area of origin, there has been little success in moving outside the confines of national allegiance. This is often the result of an unfamiliarity of culture or the difficulties of negotiating unknown languages. The Muslim world may exist in a microcosm in the new terrain of Britain but it is still represented by a range of cultures and languages that may have little in common except their religious affiliation.

British-born Muslims are often impatient with this diversity of culture and language crossing over into the realm of religion. Consequently they are attempting to establish their own identity as both British and Muslim. So far they have been given little opportunity to influence the tariqas which are almost without exception led by first-generation migrants. The shaikhs that I interviewed all expressed concern about the future of the young but implicit in their attempts to promote their teachings to them is the assumption that the new generation of Muslims will continue traditions made sacred in the place of origin. The young, on the other hand, have not been brought up in an environment where the localised sacred space has such significance. They feel inclined to extend the barriers of ethnicity by promoting the universalism of Islam. It remains to be seen whether it is possible for the tariqas to continue in their present form as the new generation of leadership inherit them and use their structures to promote their own vision of Islam in Britain.

Köse has also noted the success of the charismatic Sufi leaders in gaining converts to Islam.[6] Although the achievement can generate considerable pride on the part of the original migrant minority, it can also produce tensions. The original community of migrants may not be conscious of age-old customs that infuse their practice of Islam whereas the new converts are likely to be more critical. Converts are sometimes implicitly opposed to perceived ethnic or cultural customs and this further opens up the divide between ethnicity and religion. These new communities of indigenous Muslims remain small in number but they can be significant in providing the migrant incomers with signals of success in their new location. The new converts are evidence that Islam is being successfully promoted in a non-Muslim environment and thus religion can provide a new sacred raison d'etre for existing in the new location even if the original reason for migration was economic or political. This is particularly true in Islam where Muslims can call upon the powerful symbol of the original Hijra or migration from Makkah to Medina.

Sufis and anti-Sufis

In addition to the dynamics of internal transformations taking place within the tariqas, the confrontation with the Muslim reform movements will also shape the future. The struggle between the opponents of Sufism and the tariqas has been dominating the Muslim world since the Wahhabis manifested their strong anti-Sufi rhetoric into an organised form in the eighteenth century. This struggle continues through most parts of the Muslim world and has been regenerated by the Salafi movements and the variety of religious/political organisations demanding an Islamic state in many parts of the Muslim world. In Britain, most of the Muslim communities have perpetuated these historical struggles originating in their homelands into the new environment.

When I undertook my field work for the monograph, *Sectarian Influences within Islam in Britain*, in the early 1990s, the predominantly South Asian

Muslim community were already beginning to question the wisdom of retaining the label 'Barelwi' to describe Sufi-laden traditional Islam, the major form of the religion found in Britain.[7] Barelwi, associated with the nineteenth-century reformer and activist, Muhammad Raza Khan of Rae Bareilly, who reorganised Sufi-laden Islam against the counter-attack of the various Wahhabi-influenced movements in the subcontinent, was not known to the rest of the Muslim world, and in the heterogeneous environment of Britain where Muslims had settled from all over the globe, it risked being labelled as sectarian. Instead, the Barelwis preferred to rally around the identity of Ahl as-Sunna wa-Jama'at.

The arrival of traditional Muslims from many parts of the Muslim world with allegiance to either a tariqa or to rural-based popular Islam with loyalties to the hierarchy of living and deceased holy men (and women) generated by Sufism stimulated dialogue and hastened a process already underway amongst subcontinent Muslims to lose the epithet of 'Barelwi', seen as open to criticism as sectarian and not accessible to Muslims from elsewhere, and introduce Ahl-as Sunna wa-Jama'at.[8] The title, referring to Sunni Muslims, is thus highly contested.[9] A number of movements and strands of Islam use it to define themselves, not in the neutral sense of signifying Sunni identity, but in a highly charged atmosphere of claiming legitimacy, authenticity and a sense of specialness. The appropriation of the title as a religious identity label also serves to fix rival movements as 'other', at best deviant or guilty of innovation, at worst, to be branded by the tool of fatwa as non-Muslim or even guilty of idolatry.

In spite of the attempt to claim legitimacy by contesting the right to be the Ahl-as Sunna wa-Jama'at, traditional Muslims in Britain were under threat from the better organised nineteenth- and twentieth-century reform movements whose rhetoric coincided with various needs of the younger generation British-born Muslims. The reform movements were far from presenting a united front as they were themselves divided between nineteenth-century movements such as Deoband, originating in the Indian subcontinent and historically the opponents of the Barelwis, who were inclined towards isolationism as the main tactic for dealing with Western culture and education; Jama'at-i Islami based organisations with their rhetoric of an Islamic state, and the new critics of traditional Islam represented by movements such as Hizb ut-Tahrir[10] and al-Muhajiroun who identify themselves as Salafi or neo-Wahhabi.

However, all these movements share a looking-back to an ideal Islamic past and reconstituting this past in the present as the means to ensure a utopian vision for an Islamic future. The ideal past may be found in the period of the Prophet in Medina as constituting a perfect Islamic state in which politics and religion merged seamlessly, or as in the case of the Salafis who call upon Muslims to return to a pure faith as practiced by the Salaf (the first three generations of Muslims cited in Hadith as the most devout and correct in their practice and belief). This idealisation of the past and the hope for its reconstruction at some future point is, by definition, critical of the period in between. Muslim history is judged to be a deviation from the truth of the revelation, either through harmful bida (innovation), contact with Western culture, or in the case of subcontinent

Muslims, influence of Hinduism. Thus all the movements are critical of Sufism and Sufi-influenced traditional Muslims who refer to tradition as their claim for authenticity. Many blame Sufism itself for the decline of the Muslim umma.

The call for a purified Islam freed from outside influences and various cultural accretions strikes a chord with British-born Muslims as they struggle with their own identity formation. Caught between British, ethnic and Muslim identities, many see their parent's version of Islam as completely compromised by local customs originating in the villages of the place of origin. Instead they attempt to construct an Islamic identity that is part of imagined international umma that seeks to locate itself in the universals of Islam as discovered in the Qur'an and Sunna. In recent years, new organisations have appeared urging participation in British democratic processes and the reconciliation of Islamic identity and British citizenship. Although such movements have their ideological roots in the activism of Sayyid Qutb and Maulana Mawdudi, the radical voice that called for an Islamic state has been toned down to a gradualist approach and the emergence of 'British Islam'. The success of these movements such as the MAB (Muslim Association of Britain), MCB (Muslim Council of Britain) and ISB (Islamic Society of Britain) to attract British-born generations of Muslims has led to Anthony McRoy claiming that 'the old traditional, subcontinental Islam, with its cultural accretions, has lost out to challenges from the contextualized radicalism of Mawdudism, Qutbism and Khomeinism'.[11]

The counterattack

Thus I have found myself previously pessimistic about the ability of customs and traditions located in the Barelwi tradition and often identified with places of origin being able to survive in the British context. The subcontinent Sufis, with their custom-laden version of Islam focused on the intercession of saints and the Prophet, shrines, baraka (the power to bless), powers, miracles and the performance of dhikr maintained within the shaikh/murid relationship, had never been able to organise themselves nationally in Britain in spite of their numerical superiority

The arrival of a number of charismatic Sufi pirs and shaikhs from the subcontinent provided the impetus for greater cohesion as they formed powerful groups of Sufis able to construct mosques and produce promotional literature to counter the reform movement's criticisms.[12] However, the traditional loyalty of each group of murids to their own shaikh counteracted this push towards a stronger and more assertive identity. In spite of these developments throughout the 1980s, there remained huge hurdles to overcome before traditional Islam could successfully compete with the reform movements' ability to organise themselves, promote their message and recruit from British-born Muslims. Unfortunately the shaikhs who had come to Britain continued to promote allegiances that were narrowly confined to ethnic identity. Although some shaikhs were aware of the need to create a national consciousness amongst traditional Muslims they were not able to succeed, because local organisations of Muslims duplicated loyalties formed over hundreds of years in a particular region of origin.

The ethnic and religious rivalries that dominate the Ahl as Sunna wa-Jama'at prevent the possibility of unity even amongst the Pakistani-origin Muslims let alone any kind of framework that brings together tariqas from other parts of the Muslim world. Several daunting problems need to be overcome in order for the Ahl-as-Sunna wa-Jama'at to successfully compete with the reform movements and ensure its survival at the heart of the British Muslim community. In an article published in 2005 I argued that the primary challenges are:

1   to win the loyalty of British-born Muslims who are alienated from the ethnic and religious divisions brought by their parents from the place of origin;
2   to develop a systematic doctrinal challenge based on Qur'an and Hadith that counteracts the teachings of the reform movements;
3   to develop an education system in Britain that rivals the Dar al-Ulums established by the reform movements, and;
4   develop organisational structures that compare with the tight-knit movements found amongst the reformers.[13]

In this article, and another published in 2006, I outlined a number of case studies that appeared to go beyond traditional practices to make innovations that were able to appeal to the young and provide an apparently more effective cement to bond the tradition and provide it with a national identity.[14]

Alongside the julus (processions) on the birthday of Muhammad, publicly held on carefully selected routes in British inner cities, introduced by Sufi Abdullah of the Namkholvia Naqshbandis and others; the introduction into Britain of relics believed to belong to Muhammad himself (a hair of the Prophet's beard is maintained in a terraced house in Nottingham and another in a mosque in Lancaster); dhikr groups congregating to chant the names of Allah in countless mosques across the country, and sacred journey made to shrines of Sufis in Pakistan and Bangladesh creating a global network of sacred space, other manifestations of Sufism in Britain attempted to engage directly with the Wahhabi and Salafi influences upon the young and to continue old hostilities with their traditional rivals.[15]

Shaikh Muhammad Hisham Kabbani, the North American Naqshbandi khalifa of Shaikh Nazim also came to Britain and began to organise a series of high-profile conferences in which international gatherings of shaikhs and their murids come together with each other to promote a sense of unity but, more significantly, Shaikh Kabbani had written a seven-volume *Encyclopaedia of Islamic Doctrine* that begins to develop a systematic doctrinal challenge based on Qur'an and Hadith that counteracts the teachings of the Wahhabi-influenced movements.[16] Sch developments consciously set out to promote a globalised Sufi identity as the normative form of Islam. To develop an education system in Britain that rivals the Dar al-Ulums established by the Deobandis, the subcontinent Barelwis opened a small college in Nottingham and recently (2005) in Manchester. The four sons of Pir Abdul Siddiqi, the founder of the Hijazi Naqshbandis, have also begun to fulfil their deceased father's dream of establishing a Muslim university in Britain at Nuneaton in the East Midlands. The four brothers are the first British-born Muslims to inherit leadership of a traditional subcontinent Sufi tariqa. They have combined innovative teaching, distance learning and summer camps to provide studies in tasawwuf, Islamic law and jurisprudence with traditional dars-i nizami curriculum all organised around the focal point of the first British shrine containing the body of a deceased Sufi leader.

The organisation of summer camps demonstrate the ability of the Sufi movements to imitate the successful strategies of their rival to recruit from the second- and third-generation British Muslims. Most of the initiatives described above were led by various branches of the Naqshbaniya but the Idara Minaj ul-Qur'an, a Qadiri-based movement has developed organisational structures that compare with the tight-knit movements found amongst the Wahhabi reformers. I have argued that these borrowed structures appearing in a Sufi movement require a reassessment of the traditional organisation of a tariqa and may provide a model for future movements that is more appealing to young Muslims. In addition, the Idara Minaj ul-Qur'an has not only borrowed the organizational form but also some of the rhetoric of the twentieth-century Islamic revivalist movements yet this has been achieved without compromising traditional Muslim Sufi-influenced belief and practice.[17]

Convergence and divergence

These developments suggest that the Sufi tariqas in Britain are beginning to respond belatedly to the challenges presented to them by their Wahhabi and Salafi critics and perhaps make up lost ground with regard to capturing the hearts and minds of the British-born generations. Although I have previously argued that most of the individual tariqas are still primarily engaged in reproducing localized cultural forms of Islam where religion is secondary to ethnicity, reinforcing ethnic identities and thus presenting a typology of 'cultural binary fission', the attempt to rally around a common identity of Ahl as-Sunna wa-Jama'at does present the possibility of a genuine transglobal Sufi counterattack, a kind of 'counter-reformation in the face of a "protestant" critique from Wahhabi and neo-Wahhabi movements'.[18] However, all of the above attempts to recover ground lost to the reformist movements have not been radical enough to transform the model of the transmigration of traditional Islam to Britain. Cultural binary fission remained essentially untouched. The problem is that each of the examples listed above, although attempting to take on the reform movements by adopting strategies borrowed from them, have only succeeded in continuing the ancient rivalries between Sufism and the reformers historically prevalent in the Indian subcontinent and elsewhere in the Muslim world. In continuing the old rivalries, nothing significant has been achieved that contributes to the development of a uniquely British or even Western form of Islam. Divergence of sects and cultural binary fission remains the norm but the groups that represent traditional Islam and the Sufi tariqas have become more effective. It probably has helped to maintain the loyalties of their British-born generations to some extent but it has not placed the tariqas or their memberships in the heart of new discourses taking place in the British context.

However there are signs that change is taking place. If, on one hand divergence has continued, on the other hand, there are indications of a shift towards convergence amongst young British Muslims and their leaders. Significantly this convergence refocuses awareness on the spirituality of Sufism as opposed to its role as a carrier of ethnic or cultural identity. The pioneering groundwork to forge a British Islamic identity was carried out by young British Muslims whose original thought and action was influenced by Maulana Mawdudi and Sayyid Qutb with their rhetoric of an Islamic state and the removal of all cultural accretions from Islam. The call for an Islamic state as an essential to practice the faith had more mileage as a tactic for change in Muslim majority nations. In Britain it seemed an impossible dream, at best a hope for a distant future, at worst a tactic that would antagonise the majority population and its official agencies of government and social control. However, the rhetoric of identifying and struggling against cultural accretions could be developed as a critique of ethnicity and an effective tool for carving out a uniquely British space for Muslims. The success of this strategy is apparent. First, the impetus for identity struggle has clearly shifted from ethnic origin to discourses around Muslim identity and citizenship issues. In addition several key organisations have developed which represent the voices of young British Muslims to government and other official agencies, completely bypassing the mosques which remained controlled by the older generation still operating under the model of cultural binary fission.

However, the old reformist argument of removing cultural accretions to find a 'pure Islam' can result in a loss of richness and diversity that generations of tradition have established as part of the religion. At worst it leads to forms of fundamentalism and primitivism, even aggressive radicalism that have plagued Islam in the last 20 years. On the whole, Sufis were not prone to such forms of primitive Islam but they were open to criticisms of cultural accretion as long as they were unable to discern where tradition and ethnicity separated. On the other hand, they retained an inner piety and aura of spirituality that appeared to be absent from the more politicised reform movements. Recent voices are emerging that appear to take account of these factors and are prepared to draw upon the new reform rhetoric of moderation, citizenship and participation in Western democracies but also realise the value of Muslim piety and spirituality. The exemplar for this kind of convergence is Tariq Ramadan. Whilst on one hand encouraging British Muslims to participate actively in British democratic institutions from a standpoint of Islamic values and to reassess their position as citizens of a non-Muslim society through creative reinterpretation of Qur'an and Hadith utilising the methodology of traditional Islamic sciences, on the other hand he is deeply aware of the lack of spirituality. Ramadan calls for 'the birth of a new and authentic Muslim identity, neither completely dissolved in the Western environment nor reacting against it but rather resting on its own foundation according to its own Islamic sources'.[19] In the process, British Muslims are called upon to be activist but to maintain spirituality and faith as the innermost circle of their Muslim identity.[20] He argues that many young Muslims are leaving Islamic associations because they feel that something is missing, a 'something' that he identifies as spirituality.[21] He argues that Islamic spirituality shares the 'demanding nature and in-depth work on the "I"' usually associated in the West with Far Eastern traditions[22] and calls upon Muslims to take care that their religious practice does not descend into 'mechanical ritual, lifeless and without spirituality … where the soul is absent'.[23] In the midst of an erudite and compelling political discourse on citizenship, Ramadan also calls upon Muslims to maintain their spirituality, defined in an Islamic sense as the 'way in which a believer keeps his faith alive and intensifies and reinforces it'.[24] Spirituality is defined as remembrance and he puts forward the Sufi position that all Islamic practices, particularly prayer, are means of recollection (dhikr).[25] In the first half of his book, *Western Muslim and the Future of Islam*, he provides an analysis and description of the beliefs and practices of Islam, asserting that according to Muslim tradition,

> God in His Oneness (*tawhid al-rububiyya*) put into the heart of each human being an original breath, a natural longing (*fitra*) for the Transcendent, for Him. Muslim spirituality is the work of the consciousness of the believer does on the self in order to be liberated from all forms of worship of things other than the Transcendent and to find a way to this original breath and its purity. This way towards the One (*tawhid al-uluhiyya*) is difficult and demanding because human nature also tends to be drawn to the contingent realities of the world.[26]

In Tariq Ramadan's exposition of the role of Western Muslims we hear a convergence of the new moderate political activism and its engagement with citizenship and identity issues but embedded in a spirituality which takes its inspiration from traditional Muslim piety with its foundations in tasawwuf. It would be difficult to assess Ramadan's influence on British Muslims. The older generation leadership of the Ahl as-Sunna wa-Jama'at based in the mosques are generally wary of his call to creatively interpret the primary textual sources of Islam even though he insists upon utilising traditional Islamic sciences. On the other hand, the more moderate of the British reformers, especially those influenced by the ISB (Islamic Society of Britain) seem to be excited by his call to discover the values of Islam within the processes of British democracy.

Ramadan is intensely aware of contemporary ethical issues such as environmental concerns and calls upon Muslims in the West to avoid 'binary vision' and turn to finding 'committed partners' who can 'select' from Western culture attributes that are positive and promote the human good and at the same time fight actively against the negative aspects of consumerism and the 'destructive by-products' of modern society.[27] This is a long way from the reproduction of culture that is exhibited in cultural binary fission described above. It is, on the contrary, an attempt to carve out a new cultural and religious space that creatively interacts with the new environment. There are others who utilise the language of tasawwuf and traditional Islamic sciences to articulate Islamic concerns for ecology. In the edited collection, *Islam and Ecology*, a number of voices can be heard, from Saadia Khawar Khan Chishti, who from a position of Islamic immanence embedded in the Divine Name al-Muhit, Allah's permeation of His attributes throughout all creation, argues the need for reverence and respect for the environment,[28] through to S. Nomanul Haq who utilises the discourse of khalifa to argue that the human being is essentially theomorphic, that is to say the innate ability to recognise God defines the natural state of the human being.[29]

Such figures are able to articulate the narratives of tasawwuf and traditional Islamic sciences in an intellectual environment, addressing both Muslims and non-Muslims, able to communicate fluently in English and are sometimes members of academia themselves. They by-pass the world of the mosque and do not demonstrate their loyalty to tariqa and shaikh even when they are themselves murids but nevertheless Sufism influences their worldview. They are not exponents of folk tradition or the Islam of local traditions but they are often fluent in their understanding and use of fiqh. The new Sufis are as scriptural as their old adversaries, able to utilise Qur'an and Hadith to great effect to put across their message on the issues that matter to them. Ethnicity is transcended to discover common cause in either a universal consciousness of umma or the ideological belonging to the Ahl as-Sunna wa-Jama'at. For the young British Muslims of South Asian origin the inspiration is as likely to come from their own generation of shaikhs originating in Damascus who travel a preaching circuit in Europe and North America or from high profile Western converts than it is from the South Asian elders in the tariqas who still pull up drawbridges of isolation in their respective spiritual fiefdoms of Coventry, Bimingham, Bradford or Manchester. Tasawwuf in Britain is beginning to go transglobal and escape the confines of ethnicity and locality.

The World Wide Web is an essential aspect of this globalisation. Epitomising the new Sufism are websites such as www.masud.co.uk and www.deenport. com.[30] The online presence of traditional Muslim tasawwuf does not advertise itself as Sufism or even rally behind the epithet of ahl as-Sunna wa Jama'at, but rather prefers to speak of itself as representing traditional Islam and the teachings of the four madhhabs. The websites originate in Spain, Britain and North America and address themselves specifically to Muslims in the West. There is an implicit but not explicit critique of Wahhabism and Salafism. For example, Imam Zaid Shakir, born in Berkeley, California states on his website 'it is our desire to see Muslims, especially here in the West, avoid the historical tendencies that have resulted in fragmentation and the loss of influence of our Ummah by benefiting from our wealthy heritage'.[31] The site is advertised as 'able to present you with a wealth of information mined from classical sources of our enduring tradition'.[32] The key to interpreting the allegiance of the site lies in the acknowledgement of tradition as an oblique critique of the Wahhabis and Salafis who are often critical of isnaad and ijaza, preferring direct interpretation of original sacred sources. Tradition refers to the four founders of the schools of law,

Al-Ghazali and various 'sober' Sufis such as Al-Muhasibi and Abu Talib Makki.[33]

The two websites selected above address themselves to British Muslims and are the vehicles of dissemination for the views of Shaikh Abdul-Hakim Murad and Shaikh Nuh Ha Nim Keller. The latter is a high-profile American convert educated in philosophy and Arabic at the University of California, UCLA and a shaikh in the Shadhili tariqa. He describes himself as a specialist in Islamic law, especially the traditional sciences of hadith and Shafi'i and Hanafi fiqh which he studied in Syria and Jordan.[34] He is the author of books on tasawwuf and classical jurisprudence.[35] Shaikh Abdul-Hakim Murad describes himself as a commentator on Islam in Britain. He is a British convert formerly known as Tim Winter and currently a lecturer at Cambridge University. He graduated with first-class honours in Arabic from Cambridge in 1983 and is well-known as a translator of classic Sufi texts.

The websites function as online information sources to resolve questions posed by young Muslims that arise from living in a non-Muslim environment. The answers provide erudite explanations based on classical fiqh. Most of the websites are owned by educated young Western Muslims with allegiance to traditional Islam and Sufism and skilled in the traditional Islamic sciences. A common feature of the websites is the emphasis on fiqh. This 'fiqhsation' echoes and competes with the scripturalist approach used so successfully by the Wahhabi and Salafi groups and manifests a more gentle but nonetheless equally conviction-orientated version of islamicisation that avoids politicisation.

In other respects, the websites demonstrate a continuity with the earlier strategies adopted by the tariqas and their supporters described above. The articles on the website, although written in a style that demonstrates both familiarity with English language and scholarly modes of writing echo well-trodden themes that could be heard in any sermon delivered by Barelvi imams in British mosques or delivered in conferences wherever such groups and their sympathisers gather. Typical articles in the genre are 'Who are the ahl al-Sunna?', a direct attack on Al-Albani, the renowned Salafi leader. The content is around the contested label of Ahl as-Sunna wa-Jama'at or the identity of the Firqatun-Najiyyah (the saved sect).[36] Other articles are on tasawwuf and shari'a by Shafiq ur-Rahman;[37] *The Meaning of Tasawwuf* by Shaikh Shahidullah Faridi;[38] an article on Abdul Qadir al-Jaylani (Gilani) considered by most tariqas to be the greatest of all Sufis, the *Qutb*, written by Abdul Aziz Ahmed.[39]

As mentioned above all of these themes are common themes in polemical writing aimed towards traditional Sufi opponents but on the websites they also function as pedagogical material for young supporters of tasawwuf and recruitment devices for the uncommitted. The websites provides a means for the traditional supporters of Sufi-orientated Islam to narrow the gap on their rivals who have been previously able to more effectively mobilise in Britain and elsewhere in the Muslim diaspora spaces, but more significantly they demonstrate the international or global identity now attached to the supporters of such forms of Muslim tradition. The online shaikhs are not guardians of tomb-shrines, successors to hereditary lineages descended from long-deceased awliya, first-generation pirs and shaikhs who have formed bastions of support around mosques built in various British cities and commandeered as territory, nor are they those that visit from places of origin to preach, collect funds and return home. Although commanding support of young British Muslims attracted to their teachings and seeking both tradition and spirituality, such support transcends regional or ethnic loyalties. Most of the online shaikhs are trained and educated in the Middle East, especially Damascus, and are unlikely to have connections with Pakistan, Bangladesh or the cultures of places from which the families of British Muslims originate. However, that does not stop young British-born Muslims of South Asian origin being influenced by them. In Britain, the Sufi shaikhs are beginning to successfully argue that it is their aqida (normative belief and practice) which is the norm of Islam, and it is the Wahhabi/Salafi critique that is the aberration from traditional belief and practice. This discovery of unity of belief and practice is able to provide an antidote to the traditional divisions within British Sufism based on ethnic loyalties. It also has the benefit of forging alliances with other British Muslim groups and individuals who are resistant to the radical movements and finding themselves sympathetic to the rich currents of spirituality within Islam but whose historic and ideological roots lie in Maulana Mawdudi and Sayyid Qutb. The influential presence of the online shaikhs may well lead to the demise of cultural binary fission and to the emergence of a transglobal Sufism that will differ from historic precedents in that it will not be tariqa-dominated around the influence of one significant charismatic figure but rather will find tariqa and shaikh/murid relations sublimated to serve the cause of 'traditional Islam'.

Notes

1 Werbner (2002: 3).
2 Werbner (1990: 28).
3 Ibid.
4 Sanyal (2005: xi).
5 Geaves (2000).
6 Köse (1996).
7 Geaves (1996a).
8 Elsewhere I have posited a categorisation of the Ahl as-Sunna wa Jama'at in Britain as follows:

> 1   an inner circle of *murids* around a living *shaikh* based in a mosque;
> 2   an outer circle of *murids* who extend the *tariqa* to other centres of Muslim population across the country;
> 3   a further outer circle of non-initiated Muslims who are drawn to the mosque because of the status presence of the *shaikh* whose advice they seek on religious and non-religious matters;
> 4   another outer circle that use the mosque to visit the *shaikh* because of his access to *karamat*. This group will looking for traditional sacred solutions to life problems and crises;
> 5   an outermost circle that uses the mosque because it is local to their homes but does not preach a Wahhabi or Salafi orthodoxy.

(Geaves, 2000)

9 The use of the term and its contestation are not a modern phenomenon. Shaikh al-Haytami (d. 1567) defined Sunni Muslims in the context of unanimity and dissent. He argues that the unanimity that defines the Ahl as-Sunna was transmitted by Imam Hasan al-Ashari (d. 936) and Abu Mansur al-Maturidi (d. 944). He states that scholars who follow their path are defined as Ahl as-Sunna. Bid'a is defined as those who dissent from this path (Al-Haytami, n.d., *al-Fatawa al-Hadithiyya*, Beirut: Dar al-Ma'rifa, p. 205). Imam an-Nablusi (d. 1143) links the ahl as-Sunna wa jama'at to the Firqatun-Naajiyyah (the Saved Sect), the group of salvation from amongst 73 sects of Islam (Imam Nablusi, 1920, *al-Hadiqat an-Nadiyya*, Vol. 2, Huseyn Hilmi Isik (trans), Istanbul: Hizmet Books, p. 103).

10 Hizb ut-Tahrir was founded in 1953 in Al-Quds (Jerusalem) by Taqiuddin al-Nabhani. According to its own literature, the organisation exists to revive the umma from a state of serious decline and to remove all traces of ideas, organisational structures and political formations that have originated from the West (Kufr) rather than from the Qur'an and Sunna. The final objective is the restoration of the Khilafah rather than the series of independent Muslim states that exist in the present time. It is this that marks them out from organisations such as Jama'at-Islami which seek to overthrow secular Muslim states and replace them with Islamic governments who firmly abide by the shari'a. In one vision there is a series of independent Islamic states to replace the existing Muslim nation states, in the other vision, nation states disappear to be replaced by a khilafah. Hizb ut-Tahrir defines itself as a political party whose ideology is Islam and which works with the Muslim umma to restore the khilafah (www.hizb-ut-tahrir.org/english/definition/messages.htm, p. 1).

11 McRoy (2006: 235).

12 For a detailed analysis of the impact of the arrival of pirs and shaikhs in Britain see Geaves (1996).

13 Geaves (2005: 7).

14 As well as the above article I also explored these issues in Geaves (2006: 142–160).

15 Geaves (2005: 7–8).

16 Kabbani (1998).

17 I have described these developments in Geaves (2005) and Geaves (2006).

18 Geaves (2005: 9).

19 Ramadan (2004: 83).

20 Ibid., p. 85.

21 Ibid., p. 125.

22 Ibid., p. 119.

23 Ibid., p. 121.

24 Ibid., p. 79.

25 Ibid., p. 79.

26 Ibid., p. 120.

27 Ibid., p. 76.

28 Chishti (2003: 73).

29 Haqq (2003: 129).

30 The two websites used as examples are typical of a genre that represent Sufi-orientated Islam. Others examples are the Deen-Intensive Foundation at www.deen-intensive.com; The Nawawi Foundation at www.nawawi.org; The Zaytuna Institute at www.zaytuna.org; Ibn Abbas Institute at www.ibnabbas.org; and representing various individuals, www.sunnipath.com and www.zaidshakir.com.

31 www.zaidshakir.com, p. 2.

32 www.zaidshakir.com, p. 2.

33 www.zaidshakir.com, p. 2.

34 The biographical information is contained in the website www.masud.co.uk/nuh, p. 1.

35 His English translation of *Umdat al-Salik* (The Reliance of the Traveller), 1991 by Sunna Books was certified by al-Azhar, the first book on Islamic jurisprudence in a

European language to achieve such a distinction. He is also the translator of *The Sunni Path: A Handbook of Islamic Belief* and *Tariqa Notes* (A Handbook of the Shadhilli path of tasawwuf), www.masud.co.uk/nuh, p. 1.

36 These vociferous debates take place around the meaning of the Hadith which attributes the Muhammad as prophesising that the umma would break into 73 sects of which only one would be Firqatun-Najiyyah (the saved sect or group). Obviously all the various factions claim to be Firqatun-Najiyyah, the genuine contender for the title ahl as-sunna wa-jama'at.

37 www.masud.co.uk/Islam/misc/shafiqur, pp. 1–14.

38 www.masud.co.uk/Islam/misc/faridi, pp. 1–6.

39 www.deenport.com/lessons.

References

Chishti, Saadia (2003) 'Fitra: An Islamic Model for Humans and the Environment', in *Islam and Ecology*, Richard Foltz, Frederick Denny and Azizan Baharuddin (eds). Cambridge: Harvard CSWR.

Geaves, R.A. (1996a) *Sectarian Influences within Islam in Britain*. University of Leeds: Monograph Series, Community Religions Project.

Geaves, R.A. (1996b) 'Cult, Charisma, Community: The Arrival of Sufi *Pirs* and their Impact on Muslims in Britain', *Journal of Muslim Minority Affairs*, vol. 16, no. 2, July, pp. 169–193.

Geaves, R.A. (2000) *Sufis of Britain: An Exploration of Muslim Identity*. Cardiff: Cardiff Academic Press.

Geaves, R.A. (2005) 'Tradition, Innovation, and Authentication: Replicating the "*Ahl as-Sunna wa Jama'at*" in Britain', *Journal of Comparative Islamic Studies*, vol. 1, no. 1.

Geaves, R.A. (2006) 'Learning the Lessons from the Neo-Revivalist and Wahhabi Movements: The Counter-attack of the New Sufi Movements in the UK', in *Sufism in the West*, Jamal Malik and John Hinnells (eds). London: Routledge, pp. 142–160.

Haqq, S. Nomanul (2003) 'Islam and Ecology: Toward Retrieval and Reconstruction' in *Islam and Ecology*, Richard Foltz, Frederick Denny, Azizan Baharuddin (eds). Cambridge: Harvard CSWR.

Haqq, S. Nomanul (2003) 'Islam and Ecology: Toward Retrieval and Reconstruction', in *Islam and Ecology*, Richard Foltz, Frederick Denny and Azizan Baharuddin (eds). Cambridge: Harvard CSWR, p. 129.

Kabbani, Hisham (1998), *The Encyclopaedia of Islamic Doctrine, Vol. 1–7*. As-Sunna Foundation of America, Chicago: Kazi Press.

Köse, Ali. 1996. *Conversion to Islam*. London: Kegan Paul International.

McRoy Anthony (2006) *From Rushdie to 7/7: The Radicalisation of Islam in Britain*. London: Social Affairs Unit.

Ramadan, Tariq (2004) *Western Muslims and the Future of Islam*. Oxford: Oxford University Press.

Sanyal, Usha (2005) *Ahmad Riza Khan Barelwi*. Oxford: Oneworld.

Werbner, Pnina (1990) *Stamping the Earth with the Name of Allah: Zikr and Sacralising of Space amongst British Muslims*. Unpublished paper, University of Manchester.

Werbner, Pnina (2002) *Imagined Diasporas among Manchester Muslims*. Oxford: James Currey.

7 Playing with numbers

Sufi calculations of a perfect divine universe in Manchester[1]

Pnina Werbner

Intimate relations in the modern world

Much of the discussion of traditional Sufi cults and orders in Pakistan has tended to assume that local Sufi orders are perpetuated through inherited traditional village and familial ties (see, for example, Lewis 1984: 12).[2] So too, discussions of Pakistani labour migration to Britain have tended to stress the continued embeddedness of migrants in pre-migration village, family and biradari (caste cum kinship) ties.[3] Whether as migrants or Sufi followers, the assumption is thus that Pakistani settlers remain locked in traditional, pre-modern forms of sociality. A break from these implies either a modernist quest for individual spirituality in western oriented Sufi meditation circules, or a move to modernist, reformist and often politically activist Islamic groups. The present chapter suggests, contrary to these assumptions, that Sufism in Britain has created the potential for a myriad of local and translocal elective relations of intimacy between prior strangers. It thus opens up new worlds of association and trust within the modern nation-state, which are governed neither by the state nor by kin relations.

Intimacy is always gendered. This is particularly evident in some Sufi groups which open up spaces for legitimate, relatively egalitarian relations between the sexes, in shared sociality, camaraderie and cooperation.[4] In the most reformist groups, by contrast, there is strict separation between men and women grounded in ethical assumptions about sinful contact, though intimacy with the (male) shaikh is for women a felt experience even in these groups.

Localism and transnationalism in modern Sufism

South Asian Sufism in Britain, as on the subcontinent, varies widely in size, form and content.[5] It encompasses all the major Sufi orders active on the subcontinent (Qadiriyya, Chistiyya, Suhawardiyya, Naqshbandiyya) and many smaller fraternities focused on more localized Pakistani saints, alive or dead. In Manchester, Sufi orders range from a very strict Naqshbandi Mujaddidiya order to more traditional Sufi orders at one end of the spectrum and, at the other extreme, somewhat eclectic Sufi fraternities. Despite this variability, all the different Sufi circles meeting in the city have developed translocal relations and mutual visiting throughout Britain, extending into Pakistan. Seen as voluntary organisations, Sufi groups have created new national and international networks that bridge towns and cities and link members of different kinship, regional and caste groups in relations of amity and quasi-kinship. At the same time, the majority of followers remain Pakistani, despite the fact that groups perceive themselves as inclusive and open to non-Muslims and non-Pakistani. In practice, however, cultural strangers rarely integrate into the Urdu and South Asian dominated cultural milieu in which Pakistani Sufism in Britain is practised.

Recognizing the variability of Sufi groups and practices in any single locality and, at the same time, the continuities across localities, is critical to comprehending Sufism as a global movement. First, because it refutes the counter-globalisation approach that argues that Islam is always locally unique since it is embedded in distinctive ways in different cultural systems. According to this view, Sufi Islam differs radically in different places, from Morocco to Indonesia, as Clifford Geertz (1968) famously proposed. Against Geertz I have argued (Werbner 1995, 2003) that Sufism as a discursive formation encapsulates an integrated set of assumptions about saintly world renunciation, spiritual authority and closeness to God, which travel globally and are widely shared across the Islamic world.

This is not to deny, however, the concrete rootedness of Sufi cults in local contexts, or indeed the positive ways in which Sufi disciples embrace modernity (on this see Werbner 1996a, 2003). It is to argue, nevertheless, that the deep structural logic of Sufism contains a determinative symbolic force which shapes the cultural environments where new saints settle. This is so even when – as in the case discussed here – Sufi cosmology and practice are inscribed through high-powered modern technologies.

If Sufi cults are translocal, the variability of Sufi shaikh–disciple relations they foster even in a single locality exposes the limitations of historical theories that posit the linear development of Sufism, from khanqah to Sufi order to tai'fa,[6] or from directing-shaikh to mediating-shaikh, as proposed by Buehler in a version of modernization theory (Buehler 1998: esp. 191 *passim*). This theory of historical phases – from the living, directing-shaikh to the mediating, dead shaikh or peripatetic, media-cum-mediating-shaikh – poses a false historicity: it fails to recognize the cyclical features of Sufi orders and regional cults, which are characterized by periodic waxing and waning, rise and fall, growth and decline (Trimingham 1971; Werbner 1977). At any historical period, only rare individuals rise to be new living saints and directing-shaikhs of real distinction. The cults they found seldom retain the same charismatic aura of the original founders under their successors.

Buehler's argument fails also to recognize that saints are perceived and experienced differently by different disciples, who make different demands on a living shaikh. Some followers approach a saint in the hope of obtaining intimacy with God via the saint; others regard him as the subject of love who mediates their mundane life desires with God. The very same saint can thus be both mediating and directing, depending on the situation, or on a disciple's expectations. In this sense it is the disciples who define and determine the nature of the connection between saint and follower, as much as the saint him or herself does. In practical terms, the result of these fluctuations in time and variations in perception gives rise to an apparently diverse range of Sufi circles, yet followers continue to recognize an affinity to one another and to share some basic assumptions in common.

Islam in Britain

Despite the wide acceptance of saints and their centrally focused orders or regional cults, most UK Punjabi Pakistanis are not active followers of a particular saint or pir locally. They see themselves as the people of the Prophet's Sunnah in general, are happy to host and attend the lectures of visiting pirs or Barelvi 'ulema, and to seek protective amulets or healing from local and subcontinental Pakistani pirs. They participate in processions on eid milad-un-Nabi and sometimes attend a local commemorative 'urs festival, but without being initiated to a particular saint, a step taken only by a few. Nevertheless, the performance of dhikr, the remembrance of God's name, is very popular. In the early days of immigration, I was told, the practice of dhikr was unknown, and in the rare instances when dhikr circles were held, condemned by orthodox 'ulema. Today some Barelvi mosques are reputed to have very large dhikr circles, and although in Manchester dhikr is still performed by a select few rather than the majority, there are many dhikr circles in the city.

Sufism crosses the boundary between Shi'a and Sunni in Pakistan as elsewhere in the Middle East and Muslim world. The present chapter discusses the particular circle clustered around a Sufi Shaikh who is a Shi'a from Pakistan, but there are other established Shi'a Sufi orders in Britain, mostly Iranian (see Spellman 2004a and 2004b, Geaves 2000: 138–139) or Turkish Alevi (Geaves 2000: 113–114).

Despite this, a major further feature of Islam in Britain, including Sufism, is that on the whole it remains nationally and ethnically divided. There are Pakistani, Bangladeshi and Arab mosques, as well as Turkish and Shi'a mosques, and the language of sermons and even supplicatory prayers in the Pakistani mosques, whatever their tendency, is Urdu rather than Arabic. At the same time, children are taught to read the Qur'an in Arabic, and few youngsters can read and write in Urdu unless studying it in school as an examination subject. Mosque attendance among the younger generation is also a matter of choice and by no means universal, even though most youngsters remain pious and stress their Islamic identity, which they feel to be beleaguered both locally and globally.

In this context, the Sufi groups I studied, with one important exception, were relatively small and intimate. The main source of recruitment in many of them remained the older generation of migrants, but membership was augmented by recent younger immigrants from Pakistan, mostly in-marrying spouses, and even more so in the group discussed below, by young Pakistanis, born or brought up in Britain, who were mostly well educated. One traditional order had, exceptionally, a young, working-class following.

Magic squares and the quest for cosmic knowledge

Whereas some of the larger Sufi fraternities were enmeshed in local mosque politics in Manchester (Werbner 2002), most Sufi groups were too small to be regarded as significant political actors. They did, however, in other respects, resemble other Sufi regional cults: they were inclusive, boundary crossing, centrally focused social formations. A key feature was their shared sense of intimacy generated not only with the Sufi saint or guide, but among the followers, with each other. Here I want to focus on one such group, but there were many others.

Shaikh Abidi's group of devoted followers is an extremely intimate one. Indeed, several core followers are siblings of a single family, a sister and three brothers and their spouses. Shaikh Abidi, addressed by his devoted followers as Sufi Sahib or simply Shahji, used to live in Manchester where, in addition to his healing activities he was also a businessman, before returning to his home in Karachi. He moves back and forth between his homes in Manchester and Karachi, unless anti-Shi'a violence makes this impossible. A Shi'a with broadly tolerant views on matters of gender, music and religious difference, during his prolonged return visits to Manchester he holds a communal meal at his home

Figure 7.1 Abidi with his followers.

every evening, starting at 8pm and going on sometimes until well after midnight. Followers sit on the floor in the company of the Shaikh and, as in some of the other Sufi groups in the city, the meal is laid on a giant plastic tablecloth spread over the carpet. Before the meal there is a prayer and sometimes a dhikr session. Followers are educated and many are successful firm managers, businessmen or professionals, both men and women. One follower is a (Sunni) psychiatrist in a local hospital. They all speak fluent English but the conversation usually flows in Urdu and Punjabi, as in Baji Saeeda's group.

Shaikh Abidi is clean shaven and dresses dramatically, Middle East style, in kaftans and turbans of varying colours, or a red Arab kefiye, over a pure white tunic. He is a true eccentric who refuses to fit into any mould. During most evenings he (and along with him the group) continue to watch television out of the corner of their eyes while they discuss his latest mystical projects. He took up playing the sitar some years ago, and among his followers are a couple of Sikhs. His enthusiasms and obsessions infect the whole group. He has cured people of all nationalities, including Hindus and Mancunian Jews.

Distinctively Shaikh Abidi has been working on a series of projects, all of which involve numerological or alphabetical computations of the Qur'an and other sacred texts. He uses a very powerful computer and laser printer, helped by some of his more technologically-minded followers. He also writes prophetic books which comment on and predict world events. His quest for esoteric knowledge is thus all-embracing. Altogether he has written four books, of which one,

Figure 7.2 Abidi with his books of Prophecy.

Divine Prophecy, has been translated into English. His followers help translate some of his writings into English, another all-consuming activity. He has also written a beautifully illustrated Qur'an in Urdu. His prophetic predictions of the outcome of world affairs, whether or not they come true, tend to point in most cases to a hopeful future – for example, in the case of the Israeli–Palestinian conflict. He had predicted the fall of the Soviet Union and the Berlin Wall, the Balkans war – all in 1980, long before they had happened. He said that he had predicted that Germany would rule the EU and then it would split up. He also predicted that London and the south of England would be flooded by the sea. He told me he just writes and does not know what he is writing. He only reads it afterwards. It is a sort of automatic writing, divinely inspired.

The regular group that meets daily is usually quite small, about ten people. Now and then, visitors come from elsewhere – London, Slough (near London), Peterborough, Southhampton, Leeds and Blackpool. Shahji used to have a house in the Slough area of London and he still has a large following there. The evenings pass in relaxed talk, joking and gossip or in discussions of the latest numerical project. Very often the group videos itself and later watches videos of past gatherings. Members of the group are also involved in translating some of their guide's prophetic books.

One of his most devout followers told me:

> You know, Shahji tells those of us who can't keep in tune to say dhikr quietly because it has to be said in harmony, all together. But at the Dar-ul-aloom (home to a rival Sufi group with a large following) the dhikr sounds just horrible, a cacophony of voices.

The harmony of group sociality and the harmony of the sound produced in dhikr are thus intimately linked in the eyes and experience of followers.

At the airport on the day of Shahji's departure for Karachi there are delegations from as far afield as London. He is showered with expensive gifts, including a diamond ring and a widescreen television set.

Abidi claimed that his knowledge was passed down to him from his father and forefathers. This includes his knowledge of hikmat, Greek or Unani medicine. His genealogy, shajara nasb, stretches all the way back to Ali, he claims, the original Caliph and companion of the Prophet. He was born in United Province, India, and arrived as a refugee to Karachi in 1948 when he was a child. The experience of Partition left him deeply unhappy. He sought a real pir (guide), a person whom he had heard lived near Muree. Finally, after some searching, he reached a mud hut where there was an old man with a long beard. He began to visit him daily. There was an elderly postman there who wrote down all the pir's words. He told Shahji that when he started as a young postman, the faqir was exactly the same age as he is now. One day Shahji tried to count the large number of stray dogs around the hut. He counted a particular number but the faqir said: you have forgotten that dog over there. And these dogs all have families (in other words, the pir had extramundane knowledge of a person's mind as well as a superhuman physique). The pir had come from the direction of Gilgit and was also a descendant of Ali. He finally died and, without even knowing where his grave was located, Shahji found it immediately, just where the wagon stopped, even though it was located in the wilderness and there were no signs leading to it.

This murshid visits him in visions. Once, Shahji told me, he started a new wazifa (a Sufi repetitive set prayer or liturgy) in England, a very powerful wazifa, and he had a vision of drowning. He was in a small boat, being tossed up and down by giant waves, and he could not swim. Then his murshid came along, the water reaching only up to his knees, and carried him safely to the shore. After that he promised not to read this particular wazifa in England, but rather to wait until he got back to Pakistan. What is the name of his silsila? Is it Naqsh-bandi or Chishti? Shahji dismisses this question with a wave of his hand. It is just Abidi.

Among followers in England, Sufism represents a form of esoteric knowledge of a hidden reality that may be mastered as objective fact. Some also stress med-itation, dhikr, dreams and visions as leading to such knowledge. Abidi, for example, spends a good deal of time interpreting the visions seen or experienced by disciples during the performance of dhikr. These are aired and discussed in public for all to hear during the nightly sessions at the Shaikh's home.

But the hallmark of Abidi's current project is the numerical and lexical manipulations of the Qur'an, using letter values as equivalent to numerical values, alif being one, beit two, yey ten, mim 40, and so forth, much like the numerical system used by Jewish kabbalists. Indeed, Shahji reads any kabbalist literature he can lay his hands on in English.

Abidi was described to me by his followers as the most knowledgeable person alive, and the last living Sufi in the world. On my first visit I was shown a giant, intricate chart of numbers hanging on the wall. The saint explained to me that the table represented the sum of the seven most important surahs of the Qur'an in numerical form. It consisted of 25×25 large squares (total 625), each of which was divided into 4×4 little squares (16). The total number of small squares is thus 10,000 (100×100). Each number in the chart is different. Despite this, each row and column of four little squares adds up to exactly the same number, and so too do all the larger squares. Each row and each column of 100 small squares also adds up to the same number. One can then multiply the sum of one row or one column by 100, or of a row of four by 625, to get the total numerical value of the seven surahs. Abidi proved all this to me, drawing out of his pocket a largish pocket calculator. The chart is called a 'naqash'. The very same table had also been copied by Shahji in Arabic numericals in his meticulously neat hand-writing on to a silk cloth. This silk cloth, followers told me, is totally unique. If I place it on my head, they said, I would have visions, and I would also get bless-ings and solutions to all my problems.

The chart, as it turned out, was only the most modest of all Abidi's projects. During his stay in Manchester in 1999–2000, he was working on a much more ambitious naqash, this time of the whole Qur'an as well as the Torah. This naqash consisted of a million squares (1,000 × 1,000 small squares or 250 × 250 large squares = 62,500). The same principles applied to the larger chart as to its smaller equivalent, but this time all the work had to be done using a powerful computer. He already knew the numerical value of the whole Qur'an and Torah (which had both been computed by others). To produce the chart, his computer printed out strips of tiny numbers, using a PC Excel program. The strips were then stuck together on an enormous sheet to be taken to the printer.

The Shaikh said that when he first started to write the Naqsh he was totally overwhelmed and wanted to give it up. But one of his followers came to see him at his home and persuaded him to go on. His hand used to tremble. The numbers came by vision – he would want to write one number and would end up writing another.

To his young and highly educated followers, mostly born or educated in England, the magic charts reveal a miraculous knowledge which is divinely inspired. This knowledge enabled their shaikh to unlock a hidden, deeper reality through highly scientific numerical computations. The charts proved the holiness and perfection of the Qur'an, one which their shaikh was able to demonstrate scientifically through his amazing mathematical genius. The chart revealed that a book which might seem on the surface arbitrary and complicated is, in reality, divinely constructed as a perfect order.

Hence, the awe inspiring numerical perfection of Shahji's magic squares reveals for followers the mysteries of divine universal perfection. This esoteric

Figure 7.3 The Naqash.

practice of numerical and alphabetical combinatorial manipulation, known in the Islamic world as 'djafr' and more common among Shia followers, is thought to contain 'the Universal intellect' (Fahd 1999a) so that, in the words of one anonymous author, 'to understand the mystery of numbers is to penetrate that of the Divine intelligence' (Fahd 1999b). It is based on the belief that, as Schimmel tells us, 'letters are a veil of otherness that the mystic must penetrate' (1975: 411).

In February 2000, several months after I first met him, Shahji announced that the million-square chart, referred to as the 'ark', was now complete. The reference to the ark was to the ark of the covenant housing the Ten Commandments that followed the Children of Israel through the desert, but Shahji sometimes conflated it with Noah's ark (an unintended and unconscious English pun). He stresses the legacy of this esoteric knowledge from the 'Bene Israel' and recognizes the affinities with the Kabbalah. He also has an enduring interest in biblical tales.

The Shaikh continued to perfect the chart. One day, for example, towards the end of the project, he realized that there were mistakes in two of the sheet strips, and it had taken his nephew 24 hours to locate them. The $1,000 \times 1,000$ squares of numbers, a million different numbers, each number different and unique, which added up together to the same number in all the columns and rows, was being printed out first on a high-powered laser printer. The numbers were tiny, almost microscopic, and were printed on 100 sheets of 100×100 squares, each about the size of an A3 sheet, before being taken to the printer to be produced as a single whole.

Two weeks later the ark arrived back from the printer and was unfolded for us to behold. A large, laminated scroll, some three by three metres in size, it was opened by one of the disciples on the living room floor with everyone present gazing at it in awe. The thousands of tiny numbers and squares merged at a distance into intricate patterns, almost like a Persian carpet. The chart was framed in dark gold and bore the title, 'The Eleven Commandments' (a reference to the original Ten Commandments plus the Qur'an). For the onlookers it was replete with mystery and power. Shahji explained to me that it was based around sacred numbers such as 19, 10, 11 and 2. The number one signifies the unity of God, and can be reached via 19 and 10. The number two stands for the Prophet and can be reached via 11. The number 19 is a holy number, the number of the Prophet, he said, and he had to recalculate the first table once he realized that fact.

He showed me a recently published American book in English which reported on how, through the use of modern technology, the Torah (the Pentateuch) was discovered to be based on a complex code which, once cracked, could be used to generate all kinds of prophecies (such as the assassination of Yitzhak Rabin, the Israeli prime minister). This discovery linked into one of Shahji's other major projects.

Hence, in addition to his numerical projects, Shahji had also written out a book which was said to replicate the Jaffar Jama'a, an esoteric book said to be authored by Ali. The book, of Imam Jafri, sixth descendent of the Prophet, was

Figure 7.4 Abidi, the Ark and his pocket calculators.

subsequently lost without a trace. A description of how this book had been constructed was discovered by Shahji in an Egyptian text in Arabic, and formed the
basis for his own project of reconstruction. Arabic has 28 sounds, he explained.
The Jaffar Jama'a was divided into 28 chapters, each with 28 pages. It was said
to weigh 28 kg. The whole book consisted of four-letter word combinations of
28 letters, which were never repeated twice, much like in the case of the Naqash.
Some combinatorial words make up known words or recognizable names. Each
book has a laminated plastic cover with a picture of a mosque in colour, bound
in a spiral binding. Then there is a page of highly reduced pages from another
book, given to Shahji in Egypt. After this there are pages and pages of squares,
each containing four letters. Each page is 28 × 28 and there are 28 pages and, as
mentioned, 28 volumes. This is likened to countries, cities, streets, rooms in a
house.

In February, as the ark was being completed, Shahji's version of the Jaffar
Jama'a was flown over to Manchester from Karachi on a Pakistan Airlines flight
and unveiled in front of the assembled disciples. It was treated with great veneration, covered with two cloths and raised above the floor on a table. The outer
cloth, a heavy brocade, was removed first, followed by the green and gold inner
cloth in which the scrolls were wrapped. I was told that the opening of the inner
cloth was a moment to make a wish. An aura of sanctity and awe prevailed
among the assembled congregation as the book was slowly unwrapped. Everyone stood around silently, the women with their heads covered.

Figure 7.5 The Jaffar Jama'a covered by a brocade.

Interpreting the Jaffar Jama'a (also sometimes referred as the ark) is the responsibility of an expert with divine inspiration since it is said to contain all the knowledge in existence, past, present and future. It is for this reason that the book is regarded as immensely powerful and opened with such great reverence. I was told that in the hands of the wrong person it could do immense harm since it was able to tell the future. Nevertheless, followers were still concerned with the meaning of the book. In the absence of a key to unlock the mostly meaningless alphabetical combinations the book remained for them a frustrating mystery which even Shahji's genius could not fathom.

After dhikr meditation, normally in a darkened room with the chanting loud and vigorous, Shahji asks each of the persons seated what visions they had, and interprets these.

The Shaikh also computes names. This is part of his divinatory and prophetic insight into the deeper truth of his followers and the supplicants who come to see him. Thus he took my original name at birth and worked out that it represented the number eight: 'bnynah'. He computed the total alphabetical number $(2+40+10+40+1+5)$, which he said came to a total of 98, and divided it by nine. This left a remainder of eight. He then read out in a book what nine meant, which was a sort of horoscope describing my various qualities, inclinations, life chances etc. He also did the same for my companion, although in his case the Shaikh also added his connections to the companions of the Prophet.

Figure 7.6 The Ark.

Curative powers

In addition to his alphabetical and numerical ventures, Shaikh Abidi is a well-known Sufi faith healer who, until his retirement, travelled widely in the Middle East and England. His miraculous healing was, in the past, regularly reported in the press, both in Britain and in Morocco, Tunisia and Egypt. He has in his possession a gift given to him, he says, by one of the Gulf Shaikhs whose wife he treated successfully. Sufism, he says, is his hobby. Abidi keeps the press reports on his healing activities in a giant, leather-bound folder of press cuttings, starting with two articles in English from the *Jewish Telegraph*, which reports on his healing of Jews in north Manchester, and in the *Manchester Evening News*. Other press cuttings are from North Africa and the Gulf.

One of his most devoted followers in Manchester told me: 'Shahji is the only one who, when someone sends an arrow, he can cause it to turn back' (i.e. he causes the aggressor to be harmed by his own aggression). She gave as an example her schoolfriend whose husband left her and attempted to take from her not only her six children but all her property. She met the schoolfriend by chance at the local grocery store and took her to see Shahji. At the time the friend was extremely depressed. But after meeting Shahji, the friend won her case and was awarded and the house and guardianship of the children. One of her friend's daughters is now married and has children of her own. Her ex-husband died recently. Now the friend helps her cook the evening langar for the gathering at Shahji's house.

She herself has been helped by the Shaikh in many ways – following a car accident – which he had predicted in advance – she had been in hospital for six months, was unble to walk and was in a wheelchair, but he cured her. It was a miracle that the children escaped unharmed. He had also helped her with serious family problems. Her family have known Shahji a very long time, since the early days when he lived in Longsight. She and her brothers, who are all followers, regard their connection to the Shaikh as a great blessing, she said. She also sees it as a special privilege that she alone is responsible for cooking the langar. This is a heavy duty, especially since the Shaikh has moved back to Manchester permanently. There are usually about a dozen people visiting the Shaikh every evening, but on the weekends, numbers may swell to 30 or more. She gets some help from female followers with some of the dishes but she is solely responsible. She usually cooks about six dishes, including pilau rice. When I asked her if this was not an onerous burden she told me, 'By now it is second nature'.

She told me she is very lucky to have been chosen to be the cook and provider. She is the Shaikh's chosen one. She said people can't approach close to him because he is surrounded by a protective shield of *muaqqil*, which she translated as angels, guardian angels. When people greet him, however, they come close to him and kiss his shoulder, including his nephew who was said to have been a follower in England from the age of 11 (he is now 42) and to have acquired some powers in his own right.

World-embracing tolerance

Abidi prides himself on his world-embracing tolerance, expressed by his wide range of non-Muslim followers and the range of guests he hosts periodically. On my last visit to his house, in May 2006, he was being filmed by a new Manchester-based, Asian satellite station (DSTV). Among his guests that evening were the Honourable Tony Lloyd, MP (one of his followers is an active member of the Labour Party and sometimes a city councillor), a Sikh follower (who had bought him his first sitar), myself (a Jewish Israeli university professor), a Christian English doctor and the head of the Indian Association in Manchester. All those interviewed stressed his tolerance, the open house he held, and the fact that he was a man of peace in troubled times for Muslims. Even secular visitors respond to his and his followers' warmth and generous hospitality, his wide smile and his evident enthusiasm for his projects. He has written treaties on why music is permissible in Islam, why there are no beautiful huras (women) in Paradise and why people don't drink alcohol there (since Paradise is totally different to worldly existence) why there are two ruhs (souls) rather than just one, and various other commentaries correcting Sufi and Islamic interpretations by other Muslim thinkers.

The husband of one of the followers had been, she told me, a very strict Muslim who forbade her or the children to listen to music. It was all haram. She was really suffering. She would wait until he left the house and turn on the radio or television. Once, when he came back home, his daughter ran up to him and said: 'Mummy was listening to haram'. He was spoiling the children, she realized. She loved him, but she could not agree to all these prohibitions. Shahji saved him. He taught him that music was good, to be tolerant of people from other religions. Her husband confirmed this story. He said that in the past, he would never shake hands with a Sikh or a Hindu, it was napak (unclean). He even refused to eat cheese, for example, because he said one didn't know where it came from. Shahji had saved their happiness.

He had healed a Hindu who came to him barely able to walk. He had injured his back and was bent over almost double. Shahji first healed him and then they went for an hour and a half walk in the Trafford Centre (a very large shopping mall, where the Shaikh often took his morning stroll), and the man was walking along briskly, quite straight. They came back to the house and now and then the Shaikh would say to him, 'You'd better practise your walking again'.

Another case he cured was of a man who had had a stroke and half his face was distorted. He simply massaged the face and lifted the muscles back into their healthy position.

The Shaikh explained that his knowledge of healing, herbalism, ayuvedic medicine and Unani medicine came from his father and ran through the family. In other words, he is also a hakim turned shaikh.

Conclusion

Sufi groups like Shahji's assembling regularly in Manchester highlight the complex conjunctures of tradition and modernity, universalism and particularism, community and voluntary association, scientific and esoteric knowledge, that typify Sufi practice in contemporary Britain. A familiar feature of Sufism is that the figure of the saint appears to be unique while at the same time exemplifying certain shared commonalities. The sense of uniqueness which the saint conveys in his or her manner, projects or style, prove to followers that he or she is an autonomous agent, able to think and act with integrity, in terms of inner truths known only to him or her. These truths are a gift from God, bestowed on the saint because of his or her extraordinary qualities. The uniqueness of saints is thus a key feature of their charisma. This uniqueness, seen across many groups, creates a sense of the heterogeneity of Sufism, with followers believing that it is only *their* saint who has disclosed the true path.

Against the singular stress on the Shaikh as a mediatory figure, it can thus be argued that in the case of living saints, they may also often be a source of inspiration. In addition, in Britain they are invariably the locus of national and transnational organisational relations. Hence, despite the apparent variety and heterogeneity of Sufi groups that co-exist in a single British city, they bear, at a deeper level, many similarities. It is significant, I think, that like other groups, Shahji's group also fosters national and transnational networks which connect Pakistani settlers from different places in new social configurations that are both voluntary and intellectually exploratory.

Despite the apparent variety and heterogeneity of Sufi groups that co-exist in a single British city, they bear, at a deeper level, many similarities. It is significant, I think, that all the groups foster national networks which connect Pakistani settlers from different places in new social configurations which are both voluntary and intellectually exploratory. In all the groups, the Shaikh is not merely a mediatory figure but a source of inspiration. In addition, he is the locus of national and international organisational relations.

Most Sufi groups in Britain are open and tolerant, but few are as openly and explicitly so as the one described here. Most groups also attempt to have contact with the state or its representatives, as highlighted in the meeting at Abidi's house that I attended, filmed for a local Pakistani TV station. But it is in the relations between disciples and the shaikh that similarities are most striking.

Some groups like the Abidi group are openly and explicitly tolerant but have no contact with the state or its representatives. It was in the relations between disciples and the shaikh that similarities were most striking. May we say, perhaps, that Pakistanis in Britain are returning to a khanqah style of Sufism? This, I think, would be to gloss over the complex mix of mediation and direct intimacy which marks all the groups, even where their leaders refuse the title of 'pir'. Even if some groups are larger and more organized than others, nevertheless shaikhs and khalifas – at present all still living shaikhs – do have direct contact with young disciples.

It is perhaps a mistake to focus exclusively on relations between saint and disciple. Above all, intimacy is a quality of social relations between disciples themselves. Seen in a broader sociological perspective, Sufi cults in Britain, like other forms of religious organization, create links between Pakistani communities which go beyond prior kinship or village relations. Such cross-cutting ties across British cities, extending into Pakistan, create a consciousness of a broader community which is at once actively chosen by individuals, and at the same time reinforces their sense of identity as Muslims.

Acknowledgements

The research on which this chapter is based was conducted in 1999–2000 with a grant from the Leverhulme Trust. I wish to thank the Trust for its generous support. An earlier version appeared as Werbner, Pnina (2004) 'Sufi Cults, Intimate Relations, and National Pakistani Networking in Britain', in Jamal Malik (ed.), *Muslims in Europe: From the Margins to the Centre.* Munster: LIT, pp. 227–246.

Notes

1 Versions of this chapter were first presented at the International Workshop on 'Muslim Minority Societies in Europe', in March 2001, at the Pakistan Workshop in May 2003, and at a conference in Jakarta. I am grateful to participants in these workshops, and particularly Jamal Malik, Julia Howell and Martin Bruinessan for their comments.
2 For a full discussion of this issue, see Werbner (2001, 2003: 129–133).

3 See, for example, the contributions by Ballard, Shaw and others in Ballard (1994).
4 On one group, with a woman leader shaikh, see Werbner (2007).
5 On this variability see Basu and Werbner (1998).
6 Eaton (1978), who argues for this view, cites Trimingham (1971). In actual fact,
   however, Trimingham recognizes that ta'ifas were the major vehicle for the spread of
   Sufi orders and not a separate phase.

Bibliography

Ballard, Roger (1994) (ed.) *Desh Pardesh: the South Asian Presence in Britain.* London:
   Hurst.
Basu, Helene and Pnina Werbner (1998) *Embodying Charisma.* London: Routledge.
Bayly, Susan (1989) *Saints, Goddesses and Kings: Muslims and Christians in South
   Indian Society 1700–1900.* Cambridge: Cambridge University Press.
Buehler, Arthur F. (1998) *Sufi Heirs of the Prophet: the Indian Naqshbaniyya and the
   Rise of the Mediating Sufi Shaykh.* Columbia: University of North Carolina Press.
Eade, John and Michael J. Sallnow (1991) 'Introduction', *Contesting the Sacred: The
   Anthropology of Christian Pilgrimage.* London: Routlege.
Eaton, Richard W. (1978) *Sufis of Bijapur, 1300–1700.* Princeton: Princeton University
   Press.
—— (1983) *The Rise of Islam and the Bengal Frontier, 1204–1760.* Berkeley: University
   of California Press.
—— (1984) 'The Political and Religious Authority of the Shrine of Baba Farid', in
   Barbara Daly Metcalf (ed.), *Moral Conduct and Authority: the Place of Adab in South
   Asian Islam.* Berkeley: University of California Press, pp. 333–356.
Eickelman, Dale F. (1976) *Moroccan Islam.* Austin: University of Texas Press.
——. (1977) 'Ideological Change and Regional Cults: Maraboutism and Ties of "Closeness" in Western Morocco', in Richard P. Werbner (ed.), *Regional Cults*, ASA Mono-
   graphs No. 16. London and New York: Academic Press.
Evans-Pritchard, E.E. (1937) *Witchcraft, Oracles and Magic amongst the Azande.* Oxford:
   Oxford University Press.
—— (1949) *The Sanusi of Cyrenaica.* Oxford: Clarendon Press.
Fahd, Tofic (1999a) 'Djafr', *Encyclopaedia of Islam.* Leiden: Brill.
—— (1999b) 'Huruf', *Encyclopaedia of Islam.* Leiden: Brill.
Geaves, Ron (2000) *The Sufis of Britain.* Cardiff: Cardiff Academic Press.
Geertz, Clifford (1968) *Islam Observed.* New Haven: Yale University Press.
Gilmartin, David (1984) 'Shrines, Succession, and Sources of Moral Authority', in
   Barbara Daly Metcalf (ed.), *Moral Conduct and Authority: the Place of Adab in South
   Asian Islam.* Berkeley: University of California Press, pp. 221–240.
—— (1988) *Empire and Islam.* Berkeley: University of California Press.
Gilsenan, Michael (1973) *Saint and Sufi in Modern Egypt.* Oxford: Clarendon Press.
Hetherington, Kevin (1994) 'The Contemporary Significance of Schmalenbach's Concept
   of the Bund', *The Sociological Review*, 42, 1: 1–25.
Lewis, Philip (1984) 'Pirs, Shrines and Pakistani Islam', *Al-Mushir*, XXVI: 1–22.
Liebeskind, Claudia (1998) *Piety on its Knees: Three Sufi Traditions in South Asia in
   Modern Times.* Delhi: Oxford University Press.
Malik, Jamal (2004) (ed.) *Muslims in Europe: from the Margins to the Centre.* Munster:
   LIT Verlag.

Mann, Elizabeth A. (1989) 'Religion, Money and Status: Competition for Resources at the Shrine of Shah Jamal, Aligarh', in Christian W. Troll (ed.), *Muslim Shrines in India: Their Character, History and Significance*. Delhi: Oxford University Press, pp. 145–171.

Schimmel, Annemarie (1975) *Mystical Dimensions of Islam*. Chapel Hill: North Carolina University Press.

Schmalenbach, H (1977) 'Communion – a Sociological Category', in *Herman Schmalenbach: Society and Experience*, trans. G. Luschen. Chicago: University of Chicago Press.

Spellman, Kathryn (2004a) *Religion and Nation: Iranian Local and Transnational Networks in Britain*. Oxford: Berghahn.

—— (2004b) 'A National Sufi Order with Transnational Dimensions: the Maktab Tarighat Oveyssi Shahmaghsoudi Sufi Order in London', *Journal of Ethnic and Migration Studies*, 30, 5: 945–960.

Trimingham, J.S. (1971) *The Sufi Orders in Islam*. Oxford: Oxford University Press at the Clarendon Press.

Turner, Victor (1974) *Dramas, Fields, and Metaphors*. Cornell: Cornell University Press, Chapter 5.

Werbner, Pnina (1995) 'Powerful Knowledge in a Global Sufi Cult: Reflections on the Poetics of Travelling Theories', in Wendy James (ed.), *The Pursuit of Certainty: Religious and Cultural Formulations*, ASA Dicennial Conference Seiries on 'The Uses of Knowledge: Global and Local Relations'. London: Routledge, pp. 134–160.

—— (1996a) 'The Making of Muslim Dissent: Hybridized Discourses, Lay Preachers and Radical Rhetoric among British Pakistanis', *American Ethnologist*, 23, 1: 102–122.

—— (1996b) 'Stamping the Earth with the Name of Allah: Zikr and the Sacralising of Space among British Muslims', *Cultural Anthropology*, 11, 3: 309–338. (Also published in Barbara Metcalf (ed.), *Making Muslim Space in North America and Europe*. Berkeley: University of California Press, pp. 167–185.)

—— (2001) 'Murids of the Saints: Migration, Diaspora and Redemptive Sociality in Sufi Regional and Global Cults', *International Journal of Punjab Studies*, 8, 1: 35–55. (Also appeared in *Muslim Traditions and Modern Techniques of Power*, Yearbook of the Sociology of Islam 3, Hamburg: LIT Verlag, pp. 265–291.)

—— (2002) *Imagined Diasporas among Manchester Muslims*. Oxford and Sante Fe: James Currey and School of American Research (SAR).

—— (2003) *Pilgrims of Love: the Anthropology of a Global Sufi Cult*. London and Bloomington: Hurst Publishers and Indiana University Press.

—— (2007) 'Intimate Disciples in the Modern World: The Creation of Translocal Amity among South Asian Sufis in Britain', in Martin van Bruinessen and Julia Howell (eds), *Sufism and the Modern in Islam*. London: I.B. Tauris.

Werbner, Richard P. (ed.) (1977) *Regional Cults*. London and New York: Academic Press.

8 The emergence of transethnic Sufism in Germany

From mysticism to authenticity

Gritt Klinkhammer

Sufism has been transregional for a long time. Sufis have always travelled to non-Muslim countries for missionary reasons, as we know from the histories of Indonesia, China and other countries. Thus, transethnic Sufism is neither a modern nor a Western phenomenon. The early establishment of Sufism in Europe at the beginning of the twentieth century by the Indian Chisti Shaikh Hazrat Inayat Khan, for example, could be perceived as missionary work, but transethnic Sufism in the West has not only been a matter of establishing traditional brotherhoods with a mixed ethnic clientele. It is also a story of individual travellers and 'converts' who have established and transformed Sufi ideas in non-Muslim lands by publishing literary works, performing Sufi music and dance, or opening centres of Sufi healing.

The earliest European writings on Sufism are examples dating from the fourteenth and fifteenth centuries,[1] but the first serious reception and assimilation of Sufi ideas in Europe – by Orientalists, artists and travellers to Muslim lands – only began in the eighteenth and nineteenth centuries.[2] The height of the early German reception was at the beginning of the nineteenth century at which time collections of oriental fiction were translated into German and travelogues were being written by German travellers.[3] Famous early examples of a fascination with Islam and Sufism are found in the writings of the German poet Johann-Wolfgang von Goethe[4] who praised the Qur'an and the Muslim poets Hafiz and Rumi. The same applies to the Orientalist Friedrich Rückert, who prepared the first poetic translation of the Qur'an, as well as to the German translation of *The Book of One Thousand and One Nights* at the beginning of the eighteenth century, which found immediate popularity in Germany and in the whole of the Occident.

The German view of Islam, and Sufism in particular, is in some respects different to that of the classical European Orientalist countries, such as Great Britain and France, because of its lack of colonial engagement in the Orient. In Germany, an aesthetic turn to the Orient, imagining the Orient as positive and ethical, can be observed during the eighteenth and early nineteenth century.[5] One example of the yearning and, at the same time, the unease that was provoked by images of the Orient becomes apparent in an entry in the German Brockhaus encyclopaedia from 1830:

Oriental: In the history of culture the word Orient is linked with the notion of a mysterious size, majesty and silence, which float over the grave of primeval times, out of which emerged, with priesthood and patriarchal dignity, the mental development of humankind in the middle of the most magnificent and tremendous phenomena of the life of man. At the same time the word is connected with the imagination of simplicity and marvel in persistency and steadiness, which designate likewise the character of the physical as well as the moral world of the East.[6]

In the following, I will argue that early German reception of Sufism was dominated by particular transformations of images and special readings of Sufism/Islam as a social, political, cultural or religious counter-power to Western societal developments. I will not focus on what Sufism essentially is, but on what it has been and how it has been viewed historically in Germany, from its early reception up to today. This perspective is based on the hypothesis that the perception and adoption of Sufism has been greatly affected by Germany's own societal crises, which took place between the eighteenth and twentieth centuries.[7] When German religious thinkers first began to invent themes such as 'mysticism' and 'hermeticism', the Sufi image as a counteractant or antidotal response to secularism and rationalism prevailed, whereas the current German transethnic Sufism is dominated by the theme of 'authenticity' as an answer to religious pluralism, post-modern global relativism and hybridism.

In all of these discussions of Sufism, Islam has been assigned several roles depending on the background of the recipient's ideas. Sufism has been seen as linked to or disconnected from the Sunni and Shi'ite mainstream, and the so-called 'Orthodox' or 'Shari'a Islam'. The relationship between Sufism and Islam has, of course, also been contested in Islamic countries.[8]

Sufism as the other side of civilization: Sufism as mysticism

Whereas the early formed notions and images of Islam by Orientalists were to a large extent negative, the European perception of Sufism was from the beginning more ambivalent. The manifold phenomena of Sufism in Islamic countries as mysticism, ecstasy, the worshiping of saints, folk religion, healing practice, brotherhood, philosophy (and others) generated the basis of European observations. Judgment of these phenomena depended on the prioritization and special perspective of the observers. The idea of Sufism and Islam as separate phenomena can be found in the eighteenth-century writings of those who travelled to the East and Orientalists of various countries. American travellers such as the diplomat John P. Brown (*Oriental Spiritualism*, 1868) as well as British scholars of the East India Company such as Sir William Jones (*On the Persians*, 1807), and Sir John Malcom (*Historia of Persia*, 1815) described the Sufis as wild and free thinkers and were seen as only superficially connected to the 'Mahometans'. Sufi practices such as dancing and drinking wine would surely have had nothing to do with the strict tenets of the Arabian Prophet. Rather, it was assumed that the Sufis' behaviour was of Indian origin.[9]

German Orientalists searched for the roots of Sufism outside of Islam until the beginning of the twentieth century. The German Orientalist Richard Hartmann (1881–1965), for instance, was convinced of the syncretistic and non-Islamic character of Sufi ideas and practices. He stated: 'Even if Sufism is not sufficiently understandable without considering the intellectual developments of Islam, this is no cause to exclude direct external influence. Indeed, the actual roots of the whole movement have nevertheless been found outside of Islam'.[10] He identified these roots in the spiritual thinking of Manichaeism and Indian Theosophy, and defined Sufism as a new syncretistic mystical phenomenon that only later on turned towards Islam.[11]

Subsequent German research on Sufism developed in two directions: on the one hand, a critical study of religion in the context of the social and cultural sciences emerged. The sociological criticism of Islam by Max Weber is a good example of this because Weber's evaluations were based on the most widely known studies of Islam at the end of the nineteenth century. Weber described Islam as an essentially religious and military force of warriors, incapable of achieving inner reforms that could lead to a modern secular society, and lacking an individual search for salvation and mysticism. He assessed Sufism as a mass movement with orgiastic and contemplative aspects that hindered the development of the religion and the inner-worldly acculturation of Shari'a Islam.[12] This critical sociological view of Sufism survived until the late twentieth century when Ernest Gellner called Sufism a primitive and superstitious religion of rural regions, 'the Opium of the People', the opposite to the intellectual and urban Shari'a Islam.[13]

On the other hand, a study of religion emerged at the end of the eighteenth century, which searched for the roots of religions in general, either in the idea of God, as the phenomenological study of religion did, or in predispositions of the human being as in psychological approaches. An overview of historical developments of the nineteenth century is important in order to understand these efforts.

Enlightenment, and therefore secularism, which restrained the influence on society of churches and religion in general, were strong forces. At the same time, advancements in the natural sciences were on the rise and industrial cities emerged. Poverty, a growing sense of isolation and the loosening of traditional morals, especially in the cities, were some of the consequences of the industrialization and secularization of society. In the scientific field, a positivistic, rational worldview prevailed and many intellectuals perceived these developments as a crisis of enlightenment. In this context the concept of religion as universal, and an essential disposition of human beings, emerged, which could not and indeed should not lose its value.[14]

One of the important masterminds of this new search for true religion was the Protestant theologian Friedrich Schleiermacher who proposed to find true religion in religions other than Christianity. This meant looking for the inner essence of each religion in order to find the general and infinite religion amongst all the finite religions.[15] In his quest to find the true religion, Schleiermacher emphasized the importance of religious feelings, for example, the feeling for an infinite transcendence instead of concentrating on metaphysical truth or moral dimensions of particular religions. He himself also spoke about mysticism in this context, though it was not a central theme in his discourse.

In the nineteenth century, research on foreign and exotic religions, initially based on philological work that made old, sacred texts accessible, was often conducted in the spirit of Schleiermacher's idea of looking for the essence of the true religion. In doing so, some scholars of religion were searching for archaic resources that would renew the 'spiritual emptiness' of their own society, and the waning religious piety of its citizens. Therefore, the sciences of history and philology of religion defended imagination and sensitivity in a century of prosaic thinking and increasing atheism.[16] Articles on 'mysticism' in diverse encyclopaedias from the nineteenth century give evidence of the acknowledgement of Indian, Persian, Turkish, Arabian and Greek sources.[17] Mysticism, which had initially been expressed by the Christian dogmatic term 'theologia mystica', started to turn into a positively connoted universal notion. It was then found in other religions and believed to reveal a type of primordial monotheism (Urmonotheismus). The degree of vivid mysticism, perceived as the awareness of the secrets of a religion, seemed to be a measure of the validity of a religion in general and sacred texts of foreign origin seemed to give evidence of this.[18]

The work of the Protestant theologian Friedrich August Gotttreu Tholuck, which was influenced by the writings of Schleiermacher, is a good example of what this means for research on Sufism. Tholuck translated Arabic, Persian and Turkish texts into Latin which were published in 1821[19] and again four years later in a short German edition as 'Blüthensammlung aus der morgenländischen Mystik'. He devoted his translations to the missionary goal of 'arousing sluggish and shallow minds in order to lead them to a truth higher than domestic morality and ordinary intellect'[20] and accordingly added an essay on mysticism and Sufism to the translated Sufi texts. Although Tholuck was aware of the problems regarding the origin of these sources,[21] he assures the reader that the texts would give a vivid account of Sufism. He also argues, against older images of Sufism as a pre-Islamic cult, that,

> in all probability ... Sufism has been the product of an inner-personal religious arousal of the followers of Muhammad. This arousal was soon after the introduction of Muhammedanism grasped the deeper minds of the Muhammedans and received over time a more definite character.[22]

At this point, I do not want to list more details about Tholuck's historical failures in his description and reconstruction of Sufism. Asking how Sufism was reinvented by its reception in Germany, it is interesting to note that Tholuck's essay focused on a comparison of the religious revitalization potential of Sufism and Christianity. He came to the conclusion that the Orient is primarily 'image and feeling' whereas Christianity and the Occident, respectively, are 'thought'. This would be the reason why only a few Occidentalists were consequent practitioners of mysticism as quietism, which Tholuck understands as the proper aim of all mysticism. Islamic mystics, to the contrary, endeavour to attain this goal often. To attain the state of peace and 'insensibility', they would apply extraneous means: 'They are whirling in circles so long that the bodily spiralling helps to dispatch the consciousness, or they are sitting on the floor and blocking all vents of the body and soul.'[23]

Tholuck bemoans the fact that, in his judgment, Christians would not be capable of such keen pursuit. However, based in the Islamic religion, Sufism could not develop its great potential, and 'today it often acts as though powerless and ignoble, because it is on the wrong track: Oriental mysticism always remains as Quietismus and ineffective contemplation and is open to mystical pantheism'.[24]

According to Schleiermacher, Tholuck holds mysticism as a peculiar but most sacred realm of life. Therefore, the extreme emotional states of Sufis should not be assessed as pathological as Sufism needs theoretical explanation by Occidental man because 'no Oriental man is able to do that. Oriental people usually implant mysticism magically and magnetically into their adepts, since each Oriental mystic recognizes the need for learners to be well led by an elder mystic (pir)'.[25] The central loss of the Oriental man would be that he is unaware of the actual aim of his afforded emotions. Mysticism could conjoin with every historical religion, but not every religion would suit mysticism. In Tholuck's opinion the Qur'an hardly seems to be a work of mysticism at all: 'The being of God in the world, its living in the human soul is there (in the Qur'an) less called for than in the Old and the New Testament.'[26] Therefore, he recommended reflecting on the goals and religious sense of Sufism from the rational view of the Christian. In general, Sufism served as a positive example of vivid piety that is not alienated by enlightenment and rationalism, but it requires Western reflection that if provided could allow it to contribute to religious revitalization.

This German interpretation and application of Sufism as a universal and positive mysticism, which helps to justify the existence of religion after the Enlightenment, can also be observed in writings of other German thinkers. Theologians like Rudolf Otto, who published the seventh edition of Schleiermacher's book in 1899, Friedrich Heiler, who translated and wrote the preface to Evelyn Underhill's[27] book, and others established the notion of mysticism as a universal religious notion of non-institutional, individual religious feeling.[28] Religion emerged as a phenomenon 'sui generis'. The German Orientalist Paul Klappstein (1919) wrote, in the preface of his translated Sufi texts, that Sufism should be understood as mysticism and hence as a 'psychic predisposition' of human beings. This interpretation is deeply rooted in the German search for societal renewal through a process of spiritual binding in the beginning of the twentieth century. The works of Massignon, Nicholson and other early European specialists on Sufism showed similar interests. Annemarie Schimmel, a student of Friedrich Heiler, was the most famous German scholar emerging from this school and she had become convinced that the real face of Sufism was the universal phenomenon of mysticism. She defended this perspective to such an extent that along with other scholars, she criticized some developments of Sufism as being non-Sufi-like.[29]

So far, I have focused on the early concepts of Sufism from a German point of view that was searching for a renewal of culture or religion through mysticism. If we turn our eyes to the early traces of Sufi practice in Europe, we find similarly rooted interests. The historian Mark Sedgwick exposed the genesis of the first personal network of men who were fascinated and already involved in Sufism by the end of the nineteenth and the beginning of the twentieth century.[30] Their efforts to learn from ideas and practices of strange religions were inspired by the ideas of a Perennial Philosophy,[31] which states that 'all religions shared a common origin in a single perennial, primeval or primordial religion that had subsequently taken a variety of forms, including the Zoroastrian, Pharaonic, Platonic, and Christian'.[32] The 'Perennials' also believed in a cultural and intellectual crisis in Occidental civilization because it had forgotten its link to these primeval truths. Therefore, they thought it was necessary to look for pure, old Hindu, Buddhist and also Muslim traditions.

Some of the Perennials found such primeval truths in Sufism, which they experienced by living among Muslims. In the end, they went back to their homelands and found some students, but did not establish a tariqa. Most of them, for example the Swede Agueli, the French Guenon, the German Fritjof Shuon and also their well-known students such as Titus Burkhardt and Martin Lings, were considered intellectuals rather than practitioners. Their books on Sufism are more widely known than their practice as Sufis of the Alawiyya Order, which they brought with them to Europe.

The success of the Indian Chisti Shaikh Hazrat Inayat Khan's journey in 1910 through America and Europe in order to bring his Sufi message to the West should also be seen in this historical context. Sufism's current image in the West as a universal spirituality separated from Islam became more widespread after the Second World War. This is the second phase of the reception of Sufism, which I will turn to now.

Sufism in the context of the New Age movement: Sufi spirituality as therapy[33]

After the Second World War, the German reception of Sufism entered a new phase as the post-war generation searched for new patterns of life. The churches' influence on society and citizens diminished and political and societal criticism grew as well as a search for freedom of individualist expression. The so-called 'students' revolt' and 'sexual revolution' were central expressions of this period.

Accordingly, by the late 1960s and early 1970s, a more experience-based form of Sufism was introduced in Germany by people who did not seek a new religion, but were searching for a spiritual self. There, in particular, the spread of mainstream Sufism was only minimally related to the immigration of labourers in the 1960s.[34] The presence of transethnic Sufism in Germany must be identified and investigated as a phenomenon within the scope of the 're-sacralization'[35] of Western society, which began in the early 1970s.

In Muslim countries, the institutionalization of Islam and folk tradition was deeply influenced by Sufism. In contrast to Germany it remains a rather separate phenomenon from orthodox Sunni Islam, even today. Sufi orders in which Germans play a significant role, have minimal contact with immigrant mosques. This can be explained by the fact that some of these groups do not require their members to become Muslim, for a time at least.[36] It is characteristic of the German reception and spread of Sufism that none of its representatives and publicists committed themselves exclusively and strictly to Islam until the 1980s.[37] Instead, the universality of Sufism's 'spiritual psychology' was stressed and mixed creatively with other doctrines. As experienced by 'seekers' between the 1960s and 1980s, Sufism had a close connection with psychotherapeutic techniques. During my survey on Sufism in Germany, Sufi followers told me that they had met their first shaikhs because of their interest in therapeutic and esoteric courses on physical and/or spiritual self-healing. Some of the younger members of different orders told me also that, even today, they came to the movement as a result of their voyage through the spiritual therapeutic market.

The dhikr ceremonies offered by the early shaikhs are reported to have worked well with the New-Age goal of 'self-transformation' via the discovery of the true self. Here it is worth mentioning Stanislav Grof, the co-founder of transpersonal psychology, who in 1978 developed the 'Holotrope Therapy' during which a trance is initiated through hyperventilation in an attempt to penetrate deeper spheres of consciousness and areas beyond individual identity. A cure is supposed to take place spontaneously as the body is reunited with these deep realms of consciousness.[38] Religion and spirituality are viewed as innate features of the body which need only to be activated. Today, some German Sufi followers from different orders combine their Sufi experiences with the East Asian healing methods of shiatsu and reiki or link Sufi doctrines with the therapeutic method of *Familienaufstellung* (family constellations) developed by Hellinger[39] and others.

Various individuals – some of whom were later to become khalifas and shaikhs of different orders – provided self-awareness seminars in the 1970s and 1980s based on humanist and transpersonal psychology combined with dhikr-exercises. Muhammad Salah Id, who later played a central role in the foundation of the German Burhaniyya Order, also integrated a (shortened) Sufi-khulwat[40] into his classes. Some of the early centres of these activities were the large, metropolitan cities of Berlin, Hamburg and Munich.

Having provided seminars combining Sufism and psychotherapy for several years, Abdul Halis Dornbrach,[41] Muhammad Salah Id[42] and Hussein Abdul Fattah,[43] three central figures of the emerging German Sufi scene, founded the 'Institute for Sufi Research' in Berlin in 1979.[44] The aim of the newly founded institute was

> to make the exterior doctrine accessible to a wider audience ... [T]he condition of the Sufi's path is that the seeker, as the Sufis say, becomes involved in the 'Greater Holy War', the war against one's own self. The Institute for Sufi research was founded to clarify these preconditions. ... If He, Allah subhana taala, has mercy on this institute, it will soon own a 'Sufi healing

school' in a rural location which could assume the responsibility for offering a little help to the vast number of spiritually sick people in the cities through genuine advice for life found in the last revelation.[45]

This quotation is derived from a typescript of interviews with 11 shaikhs from Germany, England, Turkey, Iraq and other countries compiled on behalf of the institute. The typescript was intended to act as a kind of advertising brochure to convey to readers that it is possible to get in touch with any of the shaikhs through the institute.[46] It was never published in this form, but it is of interest in terms of understanding the self-image of Sufis in Germany at that time. They offered Sufism as a market of shaikhs who worked with different techniques, but were potential leaders on the – generally – same path to spirituality. The authors presented the Western Sufis as an international network of individual 'Eastern' shaikhs and their Western muridun (disciples) who combined the wisdom of Sufism with new esoteric and scientific knowledge from thinkers like Fritjof Schuon, George Ivanovich Gurdjieff and René Guénon.[47] As with the cultural and institutional background of the 'Eastern' shaikhs, Islam appeared to be unimportant and went largely unmentioned. Of greater importance was the scientific authority these new Sufi practices were awarded by psychologists, philosophers and others. For example, in the introduction to the typescript, the authors also recommended Oscar Ichazo, who worked in the field of transpersonal psychology in connection with Sufism.[48]

One year later, the Sufi institute found a rural location in the Lüneburger Heide in Lower Saxony where it was able to open a 'Sufi healing school' known as House Schnede. Salah Id and Makowski rented a house,[49] lived there with a large community, and used it as a convention centre for spiritual seminars. Abdul Halis and other well-known Sufis such as Reshad Field,[50] the Turkish Halveti shaikh Muzzaffer Ozak[51] and Shaikh Nazim[52] offered dhikr, lectures and workshops. Yoga workshops, classes in humanist psychology, esoteric seminars on energy flow and similar classes were also provided.[53]

A few months after the house was opened in 1981, Salah Id died in a car crash. Despite the loss of such a central figure like Id, little changed in the workshops offered at the house. Indeed, this event may well have reinforced the open-minded nature of the courses offered in the house, because Id was the only Muslim of origin among the leaders in Schnede. In the following years, the convention centre concept proved insufficient to cover the costs of the house and finance became an increasing problem. The community lived in House Schnede until the mid-1980s, and then moved to a small neighbouring town where they lived and worked.

Up to the mid-1980s, the sympathizers and organizers of House Schnede institutionalized their spiritual and Sufi-like way of life – if at all – in communities of small autonomous groups, which celebrated dhikr together more or less regularly and sometimes recited wird (repeated recitation of short names or characteristics of Allah) while also continuing to study humanist and transpersonal psychology and practice esoteric forms of life support, e.g. I-Ching, Tarot etc. Their relationship with the shaikhs was more symbolic than actual, thus they did not feel entirely committed in one-way or the other.

The forms of 'seeking' or 'wandering' through the offerings of the spiritual market did not resemble those of a religious community that agreed on a doctrine or tradition. The views were very heterogeneous, the community members did not follow any single shaikh, only a few of them believed in Islam, and the visitors and tenants of House Schnede even included sympathizers of Baghwan.[54] The targeted group of House Schnede can best be described as 'spiritual individualists', for whom spirituality is supposed to lead to the recognition of something transcendent, extraordinary or even god-like as immanent in the life of the individual.[55] Miriam, a member of the Burhaniyya, clearly expressed this to be the valid attitude of the order even today when she remarked that she only joined the Burhaniyya because of the wird and the muraqaba (meditation directed towards the shaikh): "God does not mean anything to me." Sufism was understood less as a religious confession than as a way of experiencing oneself (*Selbsterfahrung*). If religion would need the belief in non human beings, it did not appear to be religion at all, but a new way of experience and relationship – and this is what they were seeking. For that purpose, new methods, including religious methods, were used.

In accordance with Thomas Luckmann's theory,[56] this development can be described as a double privatization of religion in a secular Christian society. First, the acquisition of Sufi practices and ideas was for the most part a personal matter. Hence, the degree of adaptation was up to the individual and was subject to a bare minimum of sanctions based on membership or belonging. Loose and sometimes short-lived networks were established. People broke away from Christian traditions and looked for answers and techniques for achieving self-awareness in diverse and mostly foreign traditions. They were convinced of the universal truth and power of self-healing available in various old and foreign traditions like Sufism. Moreover, religious traditions were mainly used as possibilities for the creation of self-awareness and self-knowledge (*Selbsterkenntnis*) with the aim of reaching a better understanding of one's own biographical and micro-social problems. The ego in its psychological, 'cosmic' and spiritual/energetic structure was the focus of study and tarot cards, horoscopes, the I-Ching and swinging, together with body-focused therapeutic and spiritual methods used for this purpose. It was also the time of the so-called sexual revolution and people were discovering their bodies, emotions and sex beyond marriage and family. Like the prophets, with a unique style of life, the shaikhs also stood for new forms of experience, authority and relationships.

German Sufism in global competition: traditionalizing mysticism as 'authentification'

In the mid-1980s, the German Sufi scene changed dramatically as the cultural aspects of Islam became more important. One of the several possible contributing factors to this change is that the Iranian revolution roused public discourse on the topic of Islam in West, as well as among the Western Muslim migrant community. The question of what had failed in the modern, secular political development of Iran arose and, in scholarly research, the field of 'Post-colonial Studies' emerged. Sensitivity for the cultural and interest bound perspectives of research became stronger, and in the 1990s the view of religion as a cultural and identifying force changed. Nevertheless, Islam was then, and is still, mostly not well received in the West.

At the same time, the Sufi-oriented groups started to settle themselves as different traditions or schools. The first group, which established itself as a Muslim Sufi Order, was the Haqqaniyya of the Turkish Cypriot Shaikh Nazim. Today this is the biggest Sufi group in Germany with approximately 500 members.

Nazim's early German followers were so-called 'dropouts' from mainstream society. Some of them had travelled in the Near and Far East and later lived together as Sufis in Berlin while others moved to Mecca and Medina for religious studies in 1978, and from there went to Damascus for a while[57] where Shaikh Nazim lived at that time. When they returned to Germany in the mid-1980s, they started to offer dhikr-groups in the name of the Naqshbandiyya-Haqqaniyya Sufi Order, named after Shaikh Nazim al-Haqqani who was by that time already known in Europe. Hussein Abdul Fattah, an elusive character of the German Sufi scene, offered many courses on Sufism in the name of Nazim, but with a very Western interpretation and made an important contribution to the spread of the Haqqaniyya in Germany. However, from the beginning the inner circle was troubled by having to comply with the rules of what Nazim called the Sunna of the Prophet Muhammad. These entailed wearing clothes such as jalabas and turbans, growing beards and getting married, to name but a few. Nazim's authority and charisma, as a spiritual leader from the Muslim world, made the reconnection to Islam perfectly natural because to follow him meant to follow Islam. Nazim, to this day, is also accepted by Turkish Muslims in Germany and, when he visits periodically, he speaks in Turkish mosques (in Turkish). The German Sufi centre also keeps contact with some Turkish adherents of Nazim, but they do not attend dhikr meetings of the German group; they prefer visits to the German Khalifa Hassan discreetly. A second transethnic group, which originated from a New Age background is the Mevleviyye, or what has sometimes been called the Halisiyye (the pure) led by the German Abdul Halis Dornbrach (born in 1945). He studied Arabic as teenager somewhere between the ages of 13 and 16, converted to Islam at the age of 20, travelled throughout Turkey for several years and studied in Aleppo, where he lived in a Mevlevi lodge and studied Islamic law. After several turns in his Sufi life, following and teaching different traditions of Sufism, he bought a house near Berlin in 1991 in order to establish a centre of Mevlevi Sufism. Until that time he had taught a mixture of several Sufi traditions, but then focused on the way of the Mevleviyye. He designed the centre in the style of a Turkish Sufi lodge (tekke) and offers home study courses via the Internet, weekly courses at the tekke on the Mevlevi way, and is looking for students who want to be part of the 1,001-day Mevlevi training.[58] He emphasizes the important rule of adab, the correct behaviour of a Sufi.

Since there is quite a lot of competition between Sufi Orders in the West, as a German shaikh, it is not easy to be acknowledged as authentic. There are various conditions for obtaining acknowledgement as an authentic, genuine Sufi leader: the ijaza, the certificate of a learned shaikh, and/or a revelation and calling by Muhammad through the medium of dream are possible prerequisites to initiation as a shaikh. In a non-Muslim environment, being a native Muslim embodying a Muslim-Sufi life helps to gain the acceptance of followers. Clearly, a crucial condition for getting acknowledgement as a genuine religious leader is the ability to get a large number of devotees.

Indeed, Abdul Halis has been a central figure from the very beginning in spreading and organizing Sufism in Germany and has had many students, but he has had little success in gathering many followers or murids (disciples) as a shaikh. Today he still seems to have good connections to Sufis in Turkey, enough money to have bought property and built the German tekke, and the practical knowledge and ability of an educated Muslim and Sufi shaikh. Nevertheless, he only has a few students, mostly German women – although it is safe to say that Mevlevi Sufism is the most widely known form of Sufism in Germany as well as in the West in general.

The question of authenticity is often a controversial subject among Sufis (and sometimes also of non-Sufis) and Halis's charisma, dreams and knowledge seem not to be enough proof of his authenticity. He has even tried to add some formal confirmation by seeking legal recognition as a religious order in Germany. He has also had dream visions of bringing the dead body of his Syrian Mevlevi murshid (teacher) Farhad Dede (1882–1977) to the German tekke in order to establish the centre as a place of pilgrimage for Muslims. Thus, to attract followers it seems to be better to have a dead, authentic shaikh present than to be merely a converted German shaikh.

There are some further small transethnic Sufi groups or orders in Germany and individuals who offer courses on Sufi music and healing etc. It is not possible to mention all of them here,[59] but I would like to mention a third important transethnic Sufi group in Germany, namely the Burhani Order.[60]

As mentioned earlier, the early Sufi followers and New Age adepts of House Schnede formed the basis for the later established Burhaniyya branch in Germany. In the late 1980s, Shaikh Nazim designated his khalifa for Germany. Many of the early members and visitors of Schnede House also followed Nazim and his community grew and opened new centres. The open market for Sufism was about to close its doors at this point, since Muzaffer Ozak, Salah Id and his murshid shaikh Osman in Karthoum (and some other important figures from the scene) had died and the old heroes, such as Reshad Feild and Abdul Fattah, had to withdraw after some time due to personal problems. Thus, the followers had to decide if they themselves wanted to leave or to stay, and which shaikh they wanted to follow.

These events were occurring at the same time as a conflict between the early Sufis in Germany emerged about the post of the khalifa of the Burhaniyya, after some of the German groups had begun to claim their independence as Burhanis.[61] One of the group leaders presented himself as the independent leader of the tariqa Burhaniyya. This did not meet with the approval of some German Sufis nor with that of Shaikh Ibrahim, the son and khalifa of Osman. Although Ibrahim did not speak German or English, he started to increase his presence in Germany.

Ibrahim removed the self-proclaimed khalifa from his tariqa and the rest of the group followed him establishing a Sudanese based branch of the order. They rented a room for a zawiya and organized regular meetings for dhikr. In 1991, this group and others set up the Burhaniyya Foundation to collect money for the purchase of Schnede House, which they finally purchased in 1992. Ibrahim soon reformed the autonomous structure into a centralized one. There is currently no khalifa in the German branch, only local leaders for the organization of zawiyas and for public relations. These leaders have neither spiritual power nor religious authority. All European branches of the Burhaniyya adopted this structure. It appears to be a defence mechanism against new single-handed efforts by local leaders to break from the main tradition.

The changes in the formal organization of the tariqa were accompanied by transformations in ritual and doctrinal action along more openly Islamic lines. The Burhanis began to refer to their dhikr of the assembly only as 'hadra' which means 'presence' or 'attendance' of the shaikh and, therefore, accepted that the way to God is only open through Shaikh Osman's presence.[62] They promoted a special myth, concerning the origin of their souls, to explain the character of the German branch.[63] The German Burhaniyya members now feel like a privileged group in possession of special knowledge and with proximity to the current ruler of cosmic and spiritual reality. One Burhani member proclaimed, 'we are the chosen ones for doomsday'.

Previously, new students almost always converted to Burhani-Sufism before converting to Islam. Although the German Burhanis still see Sufism as the basis of and a more authentic version of Islam, it is now taken for granted that an adept will soon convert to Islam.[64]

Today, the Germans are advised by the Sudanese on questions of Burhaniyya practices and every zawiya (community) includes some Sudanese members for leading the dhikr and singing Osman's qasa'id, songs that he post-mortally revealed to the Sudanese. The Sudanese are their experts on the rituals and they accompany the Germans in singing and dancing the dhikr. They are the 'native Muslims' who create authenticity for the German branch.

Every year, the Europeans have a meeting in Schnede House to celebrate the hauliya meeting, the annual feast for Osman.[65] Shaikh Ibrahim and other Sudanese join in the feast every year and give classes, to men only, on dhikr and qasa'id.[66] During the feast, the Sudanese also offer lessons on the shari'a, especially to the women. However, the Germans have a rather different approach in their behaviour and acceptance of Islamic rules. They interpret some of the rules in their own way, for example, the women use nail polish[67] and do not always wear a headscarf or pray five times a day. The most important change for the Sudanese Sufi order was the insistence by the German members that women should take part in the dhikr beside the men, although they now accept that the women are not allowed to sing. But in 2003, Ibrahim prohibited women to dance. Thus, even though the Germans are a very important and powerful group of the worldwide Burhani Order, some decisive Sudanese rules seem to prevail.

Declaring that they represent the best of Islamic traditions, the German Sufis attempt to spread Burhani-Sufism. In order to do this they have begun recording the songs by and about Osman, and have invested in revitalizing the infrastructure of Khartoum. While they were previously very reticent when it came to the publication of texts from Shaikh Osman, they are now translating the qasa'id for their German student community. They say that they are afraid of being misunderstood because the verses contain special comments on the Qur'an, which differ from the classical commentaries. The verses include, for example, the idea that the Burhanis may expect special gifts in the hereafter.[68] Thus far, they have publicized Burhani-Sufism through the music of their Sudanese 'mystic troubadours' and this seems to reflect their own fascination with Sudanese Sufism.

Conclusion

The parameters, within which the Western and particularly European reception and adoption of Sufism proceed, are multifaceted. First of all, the interest in Sufism emerged in times of an increasing development of secularism. This was the time when 'mysticism' entered a process of separation from 'church discipline' (*Kirchenzucht*) and began to stand for 'original religious experience'. In the meantime, Schleiermacher was one of the German masterminds arguing for the existence of a universal religious experience.[69] The reception of Sufism in Germany as mysticism has to be understood in this context.

The Perennials as well as the theologians and most German Orientalists searched for and found a new source of universal truth in Sufism, which seemed to be absent in the increasingly secularized Western Christian societies. That is why Richard King is correct when he claims that the separation of politics in the notion of mysticism is a central subject of Western Orientalism.[70]

The second phase of Sufism, in the context of the New Age, was more spirituality and therapy oriented, which means that the aspect of 'self-experience' within Sufi rituals was emphasized. This corresponded with the search for freedom and new, sometimes vague, orientations of the times. In this phase, Sufism was perceived as independent from Islam and, accordingly, mixed with other, often South-East Asian, forms of spiritual experience.

The third phase is marked by the formation of German branches of Sufis, such as the Naqshibandiyya, the Burhaniyya and the Mevleviyye. This I have called a turn to 'authenticity', because these Western Sufi groups stopped dealing with hybridization or alteration as previously common in the context of the New Age. On the contrary, it seems that the perception of uncertainty and relativity of the global and open plural market of religious and spiritual forms led to a more fundamental search for shaping 'authentic' forms of Sufi life.[71] Authenticity here means having a mixed form of Sufi practice: original traditions from the homeland, Islam as the real context of Sufism, and a real Sufi-shaikh – in general it seems that the new German Sufis were trying to imitate the Sufism of the shaikhs' homeland tradition.

Today, Sufism is received in Germany in all three forms in coexistence. We find a Sufi healing market, a Sufi-music market, a large variety of books on Sufi-mysticism and poems, which can be found among offerings of the New Age market. Then, there exists an understanding of Sufism much like that of the Perennialists: of one manifestation of an universal mysticism, which is the source of each current religion and is therefore more general, authentic and true than the 'orthodox' religion of Islam can be – as we have also seen in early German reception of Sufism according to the writings of Schleiermacher. This perennialist idea exists among the followers of the described groups[72] as well as among the customers of the Sufi-market. Finally, there are Sufi orders that try to be 'genuine' or 'authentic' Sufic, Islamic and culturally correct, according to their shaikhs' homeland tradition. The result is a colourful carpet of the most diverse forms of Sufism, sometimes adopted by the same people – even if the understanding of Sufism and of the different ways do not always seem to fit together.

Notes

1 See Georgius de Hungaria (*c*.1422–1502) who, while he was in captivity in Ottoman lands, studied Islam and especially Sufi orders and wrote the *Tractatus de Moribus, Condictionibus et Nequicia Turcorum*, published in 1481 (ed. R. Köhlau (1993), Cologne: Böhlau).
2 See Rana Kabbani (1986) and, for example, Barbara Hodgson (2006).
3 Ludwig Ammann (1989: 4).
4 J.-W. Goethe (1994); see also Katharina Mommsen (2001); on other German poets from the nineteenth century see Andrea Pollaschegg (2005).
5 Ludwig Ammann (1989: 1–3) and Pollaschegg (2005).
6 *Allgemeine deutsche Real-Encyclopädie für die gebildeten Stände*, Leipzig: F.A. Brockhaus, 7th edn, Vol. 8, 1827, 97f.:

> Orientalisch, morgenländisch. In der Geschichte der Cultur verknüpft man mit dem Worte Orient den Begriff von einer geheimnisvollen Größe, Majestät und Ruhe, welche über dem Grabe der Urzeit schweben, aus welcher mit dem Priestertume und der Patriarchenwürde die geistige Entwicklung des Menschen mitten unter den erhabensten und furchtbarsten Erscheinungen des Völkerlebens hervorging. Zugleich verbindet sich mit jenem Worte die Vorstellung von dem Einfachen und Wunderbaren im Beharrlichen und Steten, welche ebenso den Charakter der physischen wie der moralischen Welt im Osten bezeichnet.
>
> (quoted by Ludwig Ammann, 1989: 37–38)

7 This follows the general agreement that identity is established through self-construction and difference; see Niklas Luhmann (1993). Exotic and strange phenomena are predestined to become the model for shaping new self-identities.
8 See Rüdiger Sesemann (2004), Elisabeth Sirriyeh (1999), Carl W. Ernst (1997: 10–18).
9 See Carl W. Ernst (1997: 8–14).
10 Richard Hartmann (1916). In this article he also refers to Goldziher and Nicholson and others who thought in the same way.
11 Ibid.
12 Max Weber (1972: 375–376).

13 Ernest Gellner (1981: 127).
14 Compare Hans G. Kippenberg (1997).
15 Friedrich Schleiermacher (1799: 248).
16 Hans G. Kippenberg (1997: 69).
17 It starts in the Catholic Kirchen-Lexikon (1893) and the Protestant Real-Encyclopädie (1862). In older German encyclopaedias on religion neither foreign religions nor the notion of mysticism were positively connoted.
18 Real-Encyclopädie (1862): 'Mystik im religiösen Sinne ist demnach die Religion, sofern sie ein Leben des Menschen in dem Geheimnis d. i. in Gott und Gottes in uns ist. Denn Gott ist das Geheimnis'.
19 Tholuck published this first long edition under the title: *Sufismus sine Theosophia Persarum Pantheistica* (1821).
20 In its preface he wrote: 'dass diese Auszüge die Frucht tragen mögen, träge flache Geister zu erregen und zu etwas Höherem hinzuführen als Hausmoral und Brauchverstand'.
21 He criticizes the historical sources collected and translated by Silvester de Sacy (Tholuck 1825: 6).
22 Ibid., p. 36: 'daß der Sufismus das Erzeugnis einer innerlichen religiösen Erregung der Muhammedaner ist, welche schon bald nach der Einführung des Muhammedanismus die tieferen Gemüther ergriff, und nachher eine bestimmtere Gestaltung gewann'.
23 Ibid., p. 39.
24 Ibid., p. 40.
25 Ibid., p. 43.
26 Ibid., p. 47: 'Das Seyn Gottes in der Welt, sein Einwohnen in der menschlichen Seele wird dort weniger als im Alten und Neuen Testament gelehrt'.
27 Evelyn Underhill (1928). For further details about earlier history of the European discovery of mysticism see Louis Bouyer (1974), Gebhardt Löhr (2005).
29 According to Muhammad Iqbal, she criticizes an excessive veneration of shaikhs as saints and abuses of the shaikh's power, like the selling of healing amulets as 'Pirism' (Schimmel 1995: 43 and 338).
30 Mark Sedgwick (2003).
31 The notion stems from Agostino Steuco, *De perenni philosophia* (1540); he was a Christian Platonist.
32 Mark Sedgwick (2003: 24).
33 The following chapter is based in parts on Gritt Klinkhammer (2005).
34 There is a significant difference in regard to the sources of the development of Sufism between European countries open to immigrants based on the different situations in the countries of origin of the Muslim immigrants. Given that 80 per cent of the immigrants in Germany are from Turkey, Sufi tradition was not very widely represented or at least not publicly visible. The ban on Sufi Orders in Turkey in 1925 strongly limited the public practice of Sufism and led to new forms of Sufism such as the tradition of the Suleymancis.
35 Daniel Bell (1980).
36 Mosques were even more open for dhikr groups and visits by different shaikhs in the 1960s and 1970s than today, because most of the mosques are now bound to a particular Islamic association.
37 This observation is based on various conversations with members of the Burhaniyya and disciples of Shaikh Nazim and Abdul Halis. See Chapter 3.
38 Stanislav Grof (1987).
39 Regarding their reception of Hellinger, they remark that 'psychologists know how it functions, but we know why it functions'. What is meant is the Sufi's belief in the creation or existence of souls prior to the beginning of the world. The 'healing of the soul' can only occur when the soul finds its true position in the world.
40 Khulwat is a 40-day retreat during which one fasts and recites names of Allah and the Qur'an.

41 Abdul Halis Dornbrach is of German decent and currently shaikh of the Mevlevi branch with his own Tekke (zawiya) in Trebbus. See Chapter 3.

42 Muhammad Salah Id (or in German transcription 'Eid') was an Egyptian (1945–1981) who studied politics in Germany and did his doctorate at the University of Heidelberg. He was involved in the Christian–Jewish–Islamic dialogue of the Evangelic Academy of Berlin (Id 1981).

43 Abdul Fattah is the author of many books on Sufism and goes by different names: Steff Steffan, Abdul Fattah, Stefan Makowski. He lives in Austria and holds seminars on meditation.

44 A publishing house that produced books on Sufism and related topics was established at the same time. For further information on the central role of publishing houses in the development of the New Age phenomenon, see, for example, Bochinger (1995).

45 Stefan Makowski (likely date 1979: 24).

46 Ibid., p. 24.

47 They were inspired by 'perennial philosophy', which supports the idea that there is a 'primal truth' in all religions and a treasure of old esoteric knowledge in traditions like the mythical Corpus Hermeticum; see, for example, Sedgwick (2004).

48 His therapeutic school (ARICA institute) was founded in Chile and later moved to the USA and Europe (Munich, London); see, for example, Oscar Ichazo (1976).

49 As a result of which the registered association 'Sufi-turuq-community' was founded.

50 Author of *The Last Barrier* (London 1976). Reading this book inspired some interviewees to learn more about Sufism.

51 He died in 1985 and was well-known in Germany and the USA for his numerous journeys and books (e.g. *The Unveiling Love*, 1984).

52 Shaikh of one of the largest orders in the West. See Chapter 3.

53 I was allowed to view flyers from this period in Abdullah Halis' 'Sufi-Archive' in Trebbus (near Berlin) which impressively documented this colourful mixture of seminars.

54 Western Sanyasins were very interested in Sufi practices as Baghwan encouraged his Western students to meet with masters of Sufism.

55 On the etymology of the term 'spirituality' and its connotation in the New-Age context, see Christoph Bochinger (1995: 377–398 and 477–480).

56 Thomas Luckmann (1967).

57 For details, see Ludwig Schleßmann (2003).

58 See www.mevlevi.de.

59 See for an overview Markus Dreßler and Ludwig Schleßmann (2006).

60 For a more detailed analysis of the development of the Burhaniyya see Gritt Klinkhammer (2005).

61 In Britain, the organizing process of the Nazim group seemed to develop in the same way, so that Hisham Kabbani, the son-in-law and successor of Nazim, declared his unique position as the Nazim khalifa. But some of the followers in London seem to have ignored his statement. See Jorgen Nielsen *et al.* (2006).

62 About the changes of the ritual in Egypt one year after the death of Osman, see Earle Waugh (1991).

63 See Klinkhammer (2005: 278).

64 During my field visit to the hauliya (the annual feast of the shaikh's birthday), in 2002, they requested that I take the bayat (the vow of fidelity to the shaikh), though they did not ask me to first convert to Islam.

65 The feast is celebrated in Khartoum in spring and repeated in Germany in summer.

66 Shaikh Ibrahim died in 2003. His son Muhamed became his successor. This was proclaimed by Ibrahim some years before his death. It remains to be seen whether any changes will occur. On Muhamed see Klinkhammer (2005: 280f.).

67 This is discussed as a problem of the validity of wudu (the ritual washing for the five-time-prayer).

146   G. Klinkhammer

68 I had the opportunity to attend a lecture at the hauliya in 2002 where they presented
    and discussed a translation of qasida five (one of the 95 poems, respectively songs,
    which are said to have been written by the first Burhaniyya shaikh Osman).
69 For the Anglo-Saxon hemisphere, Eric Leigh Schmidt (2003) has shown a similar
    development.
70 Richard King (1999: 10f.).
71 On 'Authenticity and Globalization' see Stauth (1999).
72 Especially the followers of the German Alawiyya of shaikh Bashir Dultz, do not need
    to convert to Islam.

Bibliography

Ammann, L. (1989) *Östliche Spiegel. Ansichten vom Orient im Zeitalter seiner Entdeck-
    ung durch den deutschen Leser 1800–1850*, Hildesheim: Georg Olms Verlag.
Bell, D. (1980) 'The Return of the Sacred', in Daniel Bell (ed.), *The Winding Passage:
    Essays and Sociological Journeys 1960–1980*, Cambridge: Cambridge University
    Press.
Bochinger, Ch. (1995) *"New Age" und moderne Religion*, Gütersloh: Gütersloher Verlag-
    shaus.
Bouyer, Louis (1974) ' "Mystisch" – zur Geschichte eines Wortes', in Josef Sudbrack
    (ed.), *Das Mysterium und die Mystik*, Würzburg: Echter, pp. 57–76.
Dreßler, M. and Schleßmann, L. (2006) 'Sufismus in Deutschland', in Michael Klöcker
    and Udo Tworuschka (eds), *Handbuch der Religionen. Kirchen und andere Glaubens-
    gemeinschaften in Deutschland*, Munich: Olzog, pp. IV–2.
Ernst, C.W. (1997) *Sufism. An Essential Introduction to the Philosophy and Practice of
    the Mystical Tradition of Islam*, Boston: Shambala Publications.
Feild, R. (1976) *The Last Barrier. A Journey through the World of Sufi Teaching*, New
    York: Harper&Row.
Gellner, E. (1981) *Muslim Society*, Cambridge: Cambridge University Press.
Goethe, J.-W. (1994) *West-Östlicher Diwan*, Frankfurt am Main: Deutscher Klassiker
    Verlag.
Grof, S. (1987) 'Zwischen Spiritualität und Religion unterscheiden' (Interview with Stan-
    islav Grof leaded by Sebastian Murken) in M. Pilger and S. Rink (eds), *Zwischen den
    Zeiten. Das New Age in der Diskussion*, Marburg: diagonal, pp. 174–179.
Hartmann, R. (1916) 'Zur Frage nach der Herkunft und den Anfängen des Sufitums', *Der
    Islam*, Vol. 6: 31–70.
Hodgson, B. (2006) *Die Wüste atmet Freiheit. Reisende Frauen im Orient 1717 bis 1930*,
    Hildesheim: Gerstenberg Publisher.
Ichazo, O. (1976) *Arica Psychocalisthenics*, New York: Simon and Schuster.
Id, S. (1981) 'Innerlichkeit und Mystik im Islam', in Missionswerk der Evangelischen
    Kirche in Bayern (ed.), *Theologia mundi*, München: Missio, pp. 54–80.
Kabbani, R. (1986) *Europe's Myth of Orient*, London: Longman.
King, R. (1999) *Orientalism and Religion. Postcolonial Theory, India and 'The Mystic
    East'*, New York: Routledge.
Kippenberg, H.G. (1997) *Die Entdeckung der Religionsgeschichte. Religionswissenschaft
    und Moderne*, München: Beck.
*Kirchen-Lexikon oder Encyklopädie der katholischen Theologie und ihrer Hilfswissen-
    schaften* (1893), Band 8, Freiburg, 2. Auflage (1882–1903).
Klappstein, P. (1919) *Vier turkestanische Heilige: ein Beitrag zum Verständnis der islam-
    ischen Mystik*, Berlin: Mayer & Müller.

Klinkhammer, G. (2005) 'Traditionalizing Spirituality: The Burhaniyya Sufi Order in Germany', in S. Nökel and L. Tezcan (eds), *Islam and the New Europe. Continuities, Changes, Confrontations* (Yearbook of the Sociology of Islam, 6), pp. 263–282.

Knoblauch, H. (2000) ' "Jeder sich selbst sein Gott in der Welt". Subjektivierung, Spiritualisierung und der Markt der Religion', in R. Hettlage and L. Vogt (eds), *Identitäten in der modernen Welt*, Wiesbaden: Westdeutscher Verlag, pp. 201–216.

Löhr, G. (2005) 'Mystik in den Religionen: Überlegungen zu einer allgemein gültigen Definition des Mystikbegriffes', in *Glaube und Lernen*, Vol. 17: 165–177.

Luckmann, T. (1967) *The Invisible Religion*, New York: Collier Mac.

Luhmann, N. (1993) *Soziale Systeme*, Frankfurt am Main: Suhrkamp.

Makowski, S. (likely date 1979) *Antworten der Sufi. Gespräche mit den Sufi der Gegenwart*, co-editor El-Hagg Scheich Abdullah Halis Dornbrach, unpublished typescript, Berlin.

Mommsen, K. (2001) *Goethe und der Islam*, Leipzig: Insel Publisher.

Nielsen, J., Draper, M. and Yemelianova, G. (2006) 'Transnational Sufism: the Haqqaniyya', in J. Malik and J. Hinnells (eds), *Sufism in the West*, London and New York: Routledge, pp. 103–114.

Ozak, M. (1984) *The Unveiling of Love. Sufism and the Remembrance of God*, New York: Inner Traditions Intern.

Pollaschegg, A. (2005) *Der andere Orientalismus. Regeln deutsch-morgenländischer Imagination im 19. Jahrhundert*, Berlin: de Gruyter.

Real-Encyklopädie für protestantische Theologie und Kirche (1862), Band 15, Leipzig, 1. Auflage (1854–1868).

Schimmel, A. (1995) *Mystische Dimensionen des Islam. Die Geschicte des Sufismus*, Munich: Insel Taschenbuch.

Schleiermacher, Friedrich (1799 original, 2001) *Über die Religion. Reden an die Gebildeten unter ihren Verächtern*, ed. G. Meckenstock, Berlin and New York: de Gruyter.

Schleßman, L. (2003) *Sufismus in Deutschland*, Cologne: Böhlau.

Schmidt, Leigh Eric (2003) 'The Making of Modern "Mysticism" ', *Journal of the American Academy of Religion*, Vol. 71, No. 2: 273–302.

Sedgwick, M. (2003) *Sufism. The Essentials*, American University in Cairo Press.

Sesemann, R. (2004) 'Verfall des Sufismus?', in A. Hartmann (ed.), *Geschichte und Erinnerung im Islam*, Göttingen: Vandenhoeck & Ruprecht, pp. 171–193.

Shah, I. (1964) *The Sufis*, London: WH Allen.

Sirriyeh, E. (1999) *Sufis and Anti-Sufis*, Richmond: Curzon Press.

Stauth, G. (1999) *Authentizität und kulturelle Globalisierung. Paradoxien kulturübergreifender Gesellschaft*, Bielefeld: transcript.

Tholuck, F.A.G. (1825) *Blütensammlung aus der Morgenländischen Mystik nebst einer Einleitung über Mystik überhaupt und Morgenländische insbesondere*, Berlin: F. Dümmler.

Underhill, E. (1928) *Mystik: eine Studie über die Natur und Entwicklung des religiösen Bewußtseins*, Munich: Reinhard.

Waugh, E. (1991) 'Saintly Death: Coping with Grief through Human Transformation', in David R. Counts (ed.), *Coping with the Final Tragedy*, Amityville: Baywood, pp. 69–89.

Weber, M. (1972) 'Religionssoziologie', in *Wirtschaft und Gesellschaft*, Tübingen: J.C.B.Mohr (1922 original).

9 Growing up as a Sufi

Generational change in the Burhaniya Sufi order

Søren Christian Lassen

Introduction

Since the Second World War the general movement of migration from Muslim countries to Western Europe has included the translocation of Sufi orders, which, being in the shape of movements, stand in contrast to earlier receptions of Sufism in Europe that were primarily individually based. In recent years these Sufi movements have been the topic of several academic studies that corroborate the contention that the orders in the West take various forms in terms of membership and recruitment. A rough categorization could be the following:

1   Some orders are 'diaspora phenomena' in that they mainly attract migrants from Asian or African countries who are Muslims by birth. Many of these migrants actually carry the order's practice with them to their new country of residence, or they may be drawn into the organization as it offers a kind of attachment to their homeland.[1] One could say that such orders basically expand their sphere of activity in accordance with the movements of their adherents. As the disciples move to the West, so does the Sufi environment.

2   Another type is orders that have more success in attracting converts to Islam, to the extent that some of them mainly consist of converts. These can in turn be labelled 'convert phenomena'. This somewhat rigid classification says nothing about the respective orders' degree of 'orthodoxy', or whether orders that primarily attract converts are more or less orthodox.[2]

3   A third group is formed by movements that have been awkwardly labelled 'new age Sufis', i.e. groups that do not insist on the disciples' affiliation to Islam and typically attract spiritual seekers looking for personal religious experience from across several traditions. Among such groups, both members and leaders may be non-Muslims by birth.

This movement of Sufi orders from the Islamic world to a minority position in Western Europe may have introduced a number of changes in organization and practice. The present chapter will focus on one crucial issue for any religious movement – the generational change. This issue has two aspects, first the question of succession to hierarchical positions, second the recruitment of new adherents or members. Obviously, these issues are vital to the continuity of a movement, but not all religious groups are able to cope with such challenges. Recent history shows numerous examples of movements that for one reason or the other did not survive the founder's demise or decline – a striking example is the highly personalized Bhagwan movement which still exists, but is a shadow of its former self during the time of its founder Bhagwan Shree Rajneesh, later Osho (1931–1990). Sufi orders are not 'new religious movements' but they are new in the West, and as such face similar challenges; an important one being generational change. As several of the orders now flourishing in the West have ageing leaders, some transitions can be expected in the near future and, with that, the possibility of new forms of authority. As already mentioned, two challenges are crucial:

1   the question of authority – whether authority and power will remain in the hands of leaders from the order's homeland after it has established itself in the West; whether the power to interpret will remain in the hands of the traditional leaders; and
2   the recruitment of new members and the retention of existing members in the movement. This will impact most significantly where there are second-generation offspring and the ability of the movement to keep these young people involved and engage them in leadership positions. Most importantly, insofar the movement by offspring develops a second generation: keeping these young people in the order so that they in time can take over positions of responsibility.

The Sufi order Burhaniya, which has its homeland in Sudan and is now well established in Germany, throws light on the issues outlined above. In its own way, it combines all three of the 'types' outlined in the first paragraph: the early history of Burhaniya in the West shows strong resemblances with 'new age Sufism', but after some years it evolved into a movement that attracted converts to Islam, while preserving the connection to its homeland, partly through the agency of migrated North Africans residing in Europe. The connection to Sudan is also adopted by the converted members who do not seem to be in a position of conflict with the members who are born Muslims.[3] The generational change results in the creation of a new group of German-born Muslims – children of the first generation. These young people similarly have close connections with the Sudanese members and an attachment to the order's source in Sudan.

This chapter will first outline the history of Burhaniya in the West and briefly touch on the question of leadership succession, which is related to the movement's process of globalization. Second, it will treat the question of continuity of the movement through generational change. The account will be concentrated on Germany as this constitutes the dynamic centre of Burhaniya in Europe and is the country where the Burhaniya has by far the greatest presence in the West. The research builds on fieldwork carried out in Denmark and Germany since 2003, and information about the Burhaniya derives unless otherwise stated from observations, interviews and conversations with a large number of Burhanis. This chapter would never have been written without the friendly and generous cooperation of Burhanis in Germany and Denmark. In this respect I wish to thank the Tariqa Burhaniya for its unqualified acceptance of my curiosity.

Burhaniya – a regional Sufi movement comes to Europe

The full name of the Burhaniya order is Tariqa Burhaniya Disuqiya Shadhuliya. In its present form it originated in the 1930s in Sudan. It was founded by the Sudanese Shaikh Mohammad Osman Abduh al-Burhani, also known as Sidi Fakhruddin,[4] who is believed to have received instructions on a spiritual level from the thirteenth-century Egyptian Sufi Sidi Ibrahim Disuqi. As the order's official website explains:

> He held long nightly vigils in prayer during which he had visions wherein he was visited by some of the great saints. During these visions and in his dreams he learned some parts of the awrad – the special prayers of the Burhaniya. After many years had passed, he finally found a teacher, a blind stranger who had been sent to him by Sayyidi Ibrahim Disuqi, the original founder of the order. ... In a long vision taking over forty days he learned that his task was to revitalize the order of Sayyidi Ibrahim Desuqi.[5]

The present Tariqa Burhaniya is thus seen as a revival of Sidi Ibrahim Disuqi's original order, adjusted to the changed conditions of the twentieth century. These adjustments are said to be relaxations of certain more austere rules in order to make the requirements suitable to people of today: 'Mohamed Osman posed many conditions, including the condition that his followers are not allowed to go mad (*majzûb*) and that they need not perform the spiritual retreat (*khalwa*). Sayyidi Ibrahim and Sayyidina Husain signed a contract including 60 conditions.'[6]

The adjustments requested by the shaikh give an authorization for the Burhaniya's focus on living a normal life in society – instead of certain practices such as entering into seclusion and celibacy for a period of two weeks or more.[7] Sufi practice in the Burhaniya follows the guidelines laid down by the founder, Shaikh Mohammad Osman, who is believed to have been instructed by Sidi Ibrahim Disuqi in this respect as well. The practice requires a good amount of time and is divided into individual readings that the members do on their own, and collective rituals, usually performed in the order's meeting houses, zawiya. The individual practices are mainly reading the aurad,[8] prayer formulas and reciting the names of God, and can easily take up several hours each day. Each member has an aurad booklet that is used for the daily readings insofar as they are not learnt by heart. The readings are seen as the foundation of the individual's spiritual development and a precondition for the weekly collective hadra ritual. Hadra is a ritual sequence that combines dhikr, bodily movements and the singing of religious songs.[9] The male participants are divided between munshidin (singers), bust (hand-clappers who keep the rhythm of the ritual) and dhakirin (dhikr performers who stand in two rows while swinging the body from side to side). The participants chose which activity suits them best and then remain in the selected role. Hadra is performed by all Burhaniya groups every Thursday evening and on certain special occasions such as the birthday of the Prophet. In the Burhaniya dhikr is practiced only as part of the hadra ritual.

The order expanded during Shaikh Mohammad Osman's lifetime in Sudan and Egypt, where it acquired a large following. The history of the movement took a new turn when a small number of young Germans came into contact with the order and its shaikh in the late 1970s. These people formed an original core group, and several of the initial followers are still active in the movement today.[10] Shaikh Mohammad Osman, the founder of the (modern) order, passed away in 1983 and was succeeded by his son, Shaikh Ibrahim. During the tenure of this second leader Burhaniya expanded to several countries in Europe, America and Asia, and a number of organizational changes were accordingly carried out. Shaikh Ibrahim passed away in 2003 and was succeeded by his son, Shaikh Mohammad, who to this day is the leader of the order. All three heads of the modern tariqa have carried the honorific title Maulana, 'our master' – a title frequently given to Sufi leaders. During the last 25 years Burhaniya has undergone a process of transformation from a regional North African Sufi order to a dynamic transnational movement with an important presence in the West. To a great extent, the centre of gravity has moved to Germany, creating an alternative centre in Europe. The movement is represented in several German cities with groups of various sizes; the biggest being located in Hamburg, Berlin and Munich. In most cities the group has furnished a meeting place – a zawiya – in a building or a flat, and an organizational structure. Furthermore, the tariqa owns a large estate roughly 40 kilometres south of Hamburg, Schnede House, that is used for annual gatherings and otherwise rented out to groups outside the tariqa. Its total number of members in the country can not be given precisely, but would probably not add up to much more than a thousand, the great majority of whom are ethnic Germans. The movement has a common identity and many strong personal ties between cities and to Burhaniya groups in other countries, but it is somewhat isolated from the Muslim migrant populations in Germany and various other Western countries.[11]

This translocation of Burhaniya is reflected in the level of leadership: the founder, Shaikh Mohammad Osman, was a traditional Sudanese Sufi shaikh who spoke only Sudanese and who never visited Europe. These traits form part of the 'mythology' surrounding the founder: he is considered to have received deep insight and spiritual knowledge without any academic or scholarly learning, and he is seen as a pure source of wisdom and authenticity that the Burhanis still draw from and utilize daily.[12] This developing myth echoes that of Muhammad who is considered by Muslims to be a pure vessel that transmitted the revelations from God in an unchanged and undiluted form, although he was considered to have been illiterate. The second head of Burhaniya, Shaikh Ibrahim, travelled extensively and frequently visited the Burhaniya groups in Europe, spoke some English and oversaw the movement's expansion. The third and present head, Shaikh Mohammad, was raised and educated in Germany,[13] speaks fluent German and English and divides his time between Europe and North Africa. A recent development has further reinforced the order's transnational character: in April 2006 Shaikh Mohammad married a young German woman murid, born and raised in Hamburg. This came as a big surprise to the majority of the Burhanis who may have had reasons to expect that he would marry a Sudanese girl. Thus, the list of leaders reflects three consecutive stages of globalization: Shaikh Mohammad Osman remained in Khartoum and people came to him, whereas the son, Shaikh Ibrahim, travelled to the countries where the new disciples lived, and the grandson, the present leader, Shaikh Mohammad, is himself established in Germany.

The leadership structure of the Burhaniya was previously very traditional – the head of the order, Maulana, had in principle unlimited powers. This system was at first copied in Europe: each German city group was 'governed' by a murshid who had considerable authority, and all matters should in principle go through him. When it became clear that this system was too impractical, Shaikh Ibrahim introduced a global reform that created an organizational structure and at the same time opened the way for the intake of more members to powerful institutional positions. The structure was implemented in Germany in 1998, and each city unit now has a president and four sub-committees, responsible for finances, external relations, 'service' (practical matters) and religious guidance, respectively. Each of the sub-committees is chaired by a person responsible for that field. The same structure is found on a national level, with a president of the German national committee, and national committee chairmen responsible for the four areas. The committee for finance is obviously of great importance. The scope of external relations ('Öffentlichkeitsarbeit') is in principle unlimited and depends on the time and energy of the incumbent in this area. Several of the committees for external relations make great efforts for dialogue and cooperation with representatives of other religious groups. The committees for practical matters take care of the maintenance of the zawiya, among other things, but of special interest is the committee for spiritual guidance, irshad. The chairman of this committee is called murshid (guide),[14] but is authorized only to carry out practical guidance on how to read the daily aurad and other formulas. Maulana is said to be the only teacher in the Tariqa Burhaniya.

The Burhaniya now has a double identity with a spiritual centre and 'homeland' in North Africa and a new dynamic centre in Germany. In North Africa, Sufism is a strong force in society, and the Sufi tariqas, or 'orders', are important organizations commanding a substantial percentage of the population as members. The Tariqa Burhaniya is one of these significant organizations in Sudan and Egypt, but Sufi orders do not generally have a great following in Western Europe and remain more or less on the margins with regard to their size and influence. This is true both among Muslim migrants as well as among European converts with the possible exception of Britain where the dominant South

Asian communities have a close allegiance with Sufism. The Burhaniya, however, has only a small following among Muslims with migrant backgrounds and is largely isolated from the large Turkish presence in Germany. The movement remains dominated by German converts to Islam, although they are still a small minority among Muslim converts in the country.[15] In spite of the limited number of members, the Tariqa Burhaniya in Germany is a dynamic movement with considerable resources, human as well as material.

In general, the Burhaniya stresses that Sufism is a path that can and should be integrated into modern society; the members try to practise Sufism as part of their daily life, and prefer to avoid special clothing or outward manifestations of difference.[16] The movement in Western Europe comprises both men, women and children, and all are integrated into the order's structure. On the one hand Islamic norms concerning gender separation is practiced in the ritual sphere where women seem to take a secondary role – prayers are performed separately, and women do not actively participate in the weekly hadra rituals, but sit listening behind a curtain. On the other hand, however, women have a strong voice in the European movement and have an important place in the power structure. As yet women have not to my knowledge reached positions such as administrative head or chief murshid on city or national level. The important position that children and young people assume in the movement is the topic of the rest of this chapter.

First generation of spiritual seekers

The core group of German 'veterans' who were attracted to the Burhaniya Sufi practice in the 1970s and 1980s form the backbone of the tariqa in Germany, and they still hold most of the positions in the religious and administrative hierarchy. To a great extent these members are married and have children inside the movement and thus constitute the first-generation Muslim convert German Burhanis. During the period in question there was considerable interest in Eastern spirituality among German urban middle-class youth, and Tariqa Burhaniya emerged as a religious option among others.[17] Several of the German Burhaniya veterans had earlier been in contact with yoga, tantra, shamanism, the Bhagwan movement, and with various other spiritual teachers, including other Sufi leaders. A substantial part of the Burhaniya veterans had tried one or more religious or semi-religious groups, but had not formed a lasting attachment with any of them. For these people, the Burhaniya had appeared as one option among others, but finally selected as a place to commit themselves in preference to other possibilities.

The conversion of these veterans did not take place through reading Islamic literature or Muslim missionary activity, and most of them previously had no contact with Islam. Many of them were formerly practising Christians, but not all. Of considerable influence was a book that achieved wide readership in several European countries since it first appeared in 1976: *Ich ging den Weg des Derwisch*[18] or in the original English, *The Last Barrier*, written by the British author and Sufi teacher Reshad Feild. Several Burhaniya veterans stated that this book inspired them to seek out Sufism. The book is composed like a modern Sufi legend where the spiritually interested Feild meets a Turkish Sufi master in London and later travels to Turkey in order to undergo further training. With empathy and a large degree of self-reflection, the book recounts the author's struggles and gradual progress on the Sufi way of annihilating the ego. As one Burhaniya veteran relates:

> I liked the book so much, actually it was the only book of this kind that I had read, and I said to my friend: – I would like to meet a master like him, that would be wonderful. And my friend had said: – Such a one can be found, and I said: – Where? Then she said: – in Khartoum, in Sudan. And I said: – I want to meet him! But I didn't know anything, I had never had anything to do with Islam, and I had never heard anything about Sufism. It was just this condition that I read about, that someone from our world goes into another world, so to speak, and there reactivates his roots, from a wholly new perspective.[19]

This person later travelled to Sudan in order to meet the shaikh and is still an active member of the Tariqa Burhaniya. Her account seems to resemble Feild's spiritual quest in the Middle East and is in many ways typical of the German veterans: they were looking for a spiritual way, but knew little or nothing about Islam or Sufism. They were drawn into Sufism through meeting with the master or hearing about him. They started practising the Burhaniya rituals in small groups, and only gradually did it become clear to them that their attachment to Sufism would also imply becoming a Muslim. In retrospect they will explain that it came as a natural development and that after learning about the spiritual side of Islam they started longing for shari'a, to perform the Islamic rituals, and at some point they embraced Islam. They express the importance of being Germans as well as Muslims and whilst in Germany never wear Muslim dress in public. Conversion for these individuals came gradually, most of them embraced Sufism and took the pledge to the shaikh, and only later converted to Islam. The initial impulse to enter into the movement very often seems to have been meeting with the shaikh or hearing about him. Typically, when I asked one veteran if she could confirm that first came Sufism, then later Islam, she corrected me: 'first came the shaikh'.

Second-generation Muslims, but first-generation indigenous Sufis

The Burhaniya saw a substantial influx in the early years, but since the 1980s the recruitment has definitely slowed down and comes now primarily from the second generation. Whereas in some religious groups the transition to the next generation has proved to be a serious problem, this is so far not the case in the Tariqa Burhaniya. The children of the first generation German Burhanis are now coming of age, the oldest of them being in their early twenties, and it seems that most of these youngsters remain in the Sufi movement, and not just out of conformity to their parents' religious choice, although socialization has certainly taken place since birth. The young Burhanis are in general very self-reflective and take part in the activities of the order in addition to attending school or higher education. Their background is totally different from their parents – they are Burhanis and Muslims by birth and have never been inclined towards 'spiritual shopping' as many of their parents. One 16-year-old boy expressed it like this:

> I am inside from birth, so to speak. It was all a normal thing in daily life and so on. See, I don't know any other thing. ... There is no entry, it is just a decision on your part that now I want to start performing prayers. At some point I have said to myself, okay, this is my way and this is what I do. ... We were the first generation of young people, there were no real examples for us who have done it before.[20]

It is interesting that this young man speaks of his generation as the first generation. It is of course true in the sense that they are the first indigenous German Burhanis, and they will have to find their place in the tariqa and in German society as Sufi Muslims.

The young people do not need to convert to Islam, as they are born into it, but at some point about the age of 14 they will have to consciously start performing the Islamic rituals, basically the five daily ritual prayers. Participation in Sufi activities comes about much more gradually from early childhood. They will participate in hadra from a tender age, and several youngsters have turned out to be very good singers of Burhaniya songs in Arabic. Others are skilled in bust, the handclapping and rhythm-making. Seen in this light the process is similar to that of their parents: first comes Sufism, later Islam, at least regarding the formal aspects of the religion. The boys join in the hadra from a young age, learn the movements and become socialized into this way of practising, and only at a later point will they start doing their ritual prayers. Unlike their parents, they will not have to say the shahada, the confession of faith and sign of converting to Islam, as they are born Muslims. The young Burhanis to a great extent live like any ordinary German youth but with some differences that become noticeable with age. When their classmates start partying and drinking alcohol, they will abstain, and the separation of the sexes becomes apparent when they reach puberty. There is no such thing as dating or sexual relations before marriage, and this, coupled with other features of their lifestyle, sets them apart from their non-Muslim friends in school and elsewhere. Nevertheless, the young Burhanis maintain that they have a number of non-Muslim friends from school or university. However, similar to their parents they have little contact with non-Sufi Muslims.

The rest of the chapter will look more closely into three areas of the communal life of the tariqa in order to illustrate the promotion of solidarity in the new generation created through the collective ritual of hadra; regular social meetings and activities; and finally theatre performances regularly undertaken by young Burhanis.

Young people in Sufi practice

The young Burhanis are born Muslims and Sufis, and as they need not say the shahada, neither do they need to make the pledge of allegiance, baya, to prove their attachment, otherwise required for persons who want to enter a Sufi tariqa. Nevertheless, some feel the need to assert their Sufi identity through the performance of a small ritual. The weekly hadra ritual serves, among other things, to initiate children and young people into Sufi practice and integrate them in the roles that will be expected of them as adults. In the early period of Burhaniya in Germany the hadra would be carried out as a common activity with men and women mixing freely. It was later arranged that the Burhanis performed hadra separated into two gender groups, and finally, a few years back Maulana Shaikh Ibrahim decreed that the women could no longer play a physically active part in hadra, that is, they were no longer allowed to make the bodily movements and perform the dhikr as the men do. Instead they should sit silently and take part mentally, separated by a curtain from the men. This change was discussed, but accepted – the members had taken Maulana as their spiritual teacher and guide and this implied that they must obey his orders in ritual matters. Since then the ritual has been carried out with gender separation in all countries. No Burhani would say that the decision was wrong, but it is possible to sense some resentment among some of the women who suddenly were cut off from active participation in the order's most essential ritual.

Children are present at hadra with their parents almost from birth; as babies they obviously remain passive, but early on the different roles that men and women assume in the ritual are inculcated in the children, so the separation of the sexes is perpetuated among the new generation. Young boys are trained in performing the three different 'roles' in the hadra after their preferences are identified: some learn singing the qasa'id of the founder which form the poetic and melodious background to the ritual. The young singers are skilled to the same degree as many of their parents, even though they don't speak Arabic. Some have become proficient in bust, the handclapping and rhythm-making, whilst others stand in rows performing dhikr. In at least one city group young men frequently take full responsibility for the first part of ritual – they not only sing and perform bust, but know the whole sequence of prayers and invocations that are recited in order to open the ritual. From birth girls remain with their mothers behind the curtain that cuts them off from physical participation in the hadra, and thus gender division is internalized in the new generation.

Social meetings and activities

If the Burhaniya as an organization had only stressed the religious and ritual observances, it could have been expected that many young people would turn their backs on it in the process of finding their identity as adults. But the opposite is the case: young people find a number of interesting options within the order. The structure that the recruitment has gone through is the reason behind the somewhat biased age distribution. The first generation is roughly in the same age group, now between 40 and 60, and their children form the second generation. There is thus a large group of youngsters between 15 and 25, but far fewer small children and young teenagers. Similarly, there are few members between 25 and 40, and it is thus justified to speak of the second generation as a group. The young people – most of whom attend school or higher education – will go out to the cinema, bowling, sports and other leisure activities, sometimes accompanied by an older person. The group of youngsters in Munich has the benefit of a Sudanese in his late twenties who is resident there and takes special care of the young people. This person, who is a long-term member of the tariqa, takes them for various social outings, or reads aurad with them in the zawiya. In Berlin, the young people and many of their parents meet every Friday evening in the zawiya for 'youth night' with food prepared by the young people. In general, the order provides for so much social activity that it may fulfil the needs of the young people.

Apart from these local activities, the group of young Burhanis meet frequently across cities. Individuals will travel to visit friends in other cities or even in other countries, and regular meetings are organized for the young people. Every year during the Whitsun holidays the young Burhanis meet in the order's house in Schnede, North Germany, for a few days together with no specific programme. They organize the stay themselves and cook and clean and in other ways assume various responsibilities. Young Burhanis describe those meetings with enthusiasm, as gatherings where they enjoy each other's company and no one is excluded. The meet is, however, 'supervised' by the person who is responsible for maintaining the house, and in general the meetings are on the one hand organized almost entirely by the youngsters, but on the other hand could also be seen as a clear policy of the first generation to promote solidarity among the next generation.

In 2004 the first two weddings were celebrated between young people raised in the order. Since then, a few more young Burhanis have married, and this can be expected to be a regular feature in the coming years. Some of these marriages are between Germans, other are mixed, that is one German girl and one Egyptian or Sudanese boy. The existence of inner-group marriages is a significant sign of consolidation of the group. These mixed marriages reflect the significance of the union of the Shaikh and the young German murid. Its symbolic importance is profound, as it corroborates the close and lasting connection between Sudanese and Germans in the tariqa.

The Burhani youth theatre

Finally, the Burhaniya youth theatre is one activity which proves to be popular among the youngsters and the parents' generation alike, and which combines religious and social activities. This activity was started a few years back and is becoming a popular tradition. The youth theatre is performed on occasions such as the annual gathering in August at the Order's estate in Schnede, near Hamburg. A group of young Burhanis, aged around 15 to 20, play a sequence of small sketches that besides providing edifying entertainment serve to confirm and reinforce the Sufi and Burhani teachings among the actors themselves. The plays or performances are written and instructed by two adult Burhanis of the first generation and the content is mainly taken from the discourses of the founder, Shaikh Mohammad Osman. Small dialogues and typical Sufi teaching stories are staged and performed with dedication from the youngsters and great applause from the audience. The staged setting is usually a traditional oriental-looking location in what seems to be a pre-modern age, constructed by the youngsters. The archaic language used reinforces the traditional pre-modern setting. The plays invariably put forward a mixture of Sufi and general Islamic teachings mediated by parables from daily life. In the following I will briefly relate a typical excerpt from one of these plays.

The setting is somewhat like a traditional Sufi teaching session:[21] one young man plays the role of Maulana Shaikh Mohammad Osman dressed in a long gown and a white turban and surrounded by a few disciples. 'Maulana' behaves with dignity, speaks slowly and instructively, and the others show respect and devotion to him. He is seated on a chair whereas the others sit on the floor around him. The play consists of shorter sequences that are bound together by Maulana's teachings. One typical episode shows two religious scholars and a shepherd. 'Maulana' introduces the sequence and we see two formally dressed men on the stage gesticulating and purporting to be discussing serious matters. They are passed by a shepherd (played by a girl) dressed simply and carrying a long stick. 'Look brother, a shepherd', one of them exclaims, 'Let us go and make fun of him!'. 'No, let him be', the other says, 'I can see that he is a Sufi. Such people are not as simple as they appear'. 'It doesn't matter', the first one continues, 'we will just show and explain a little about the religion to him. That can not be bad. I can easily see that he is both uneducated and illiterate'. He turns to the shepherd and says 'Salaam alaykum, shepherd, we will impart the religion to you. Are you ready for that?'. To this the shepherd replies: 'Yes, but first tell me, which religion do you mean? Yours or ours?'. The scholar laughs: 'What do you mean, are there then two religions?'. The shepherd simply replies: 'The religion has several stages'. The second scholar tries to persuade his friend to end the matter here: 'See, brother, I told you that he is a Sufi, and you still want to teach him. Now be careful what you say to him!'. The first scholar poses a question to the shepherd: 'Tell me, what do you know of the alms tax (*zakat*)?'. The shepherd-Sufi replies again: 'Which one do you mean, yours or ours?'. The scholar says, 'If you think there are more than one, then tell me about both'. The shepherd: 'You people used to give 2.5 percent'. 'Yes of course, why should it be different?' the scholar exclaims, and goes on: 'Then tell me how you people do it'. The shepherd: 'You know that Allah is the Lord and we are His servants. Therefore we think that everything the servant owns in reality belongs to the

Lord. And all that he can collect of worldly goods should be in his hands only, not possessed in his heart'. The second scholar again steps in and explains that he also wants to pose a question to the shepherd: 'We thought that we should teach an uneducated shepherd. But now it is you who are explaining the religion to us'. He then asks the shepherd-Sufi: 'How is it when one is unattentive or unconcentrated during the prayer?'. Again the shepherd gives two types of answer: 'You people will make up for the unattentiveness by continuing after the end of the prayer. But believe me, we think that all the prayers in our whole life become worthless if we are unattentive just one moment'. After this the two scholars bow their heads in respect for the Sufi and leave the stage.

This sequence is typical for the youth theatre, in that it integrates the attachment to the general Islamic ritual duties and the Sufi understanding of a 'deeper', more spiritual meaning behind outer phenomena. The youth theatre serves to create a sense of belonging among the young people and demonstrates that Sufi life is clearly superior, the most pure and most meaningful way to live. At the same time it stresses the authority of the teachings of Shaikh Mohammad Osman. Further, the theatre combines the religious and the 'worldly' activities of the young Burhanis and in this way constitutes a model for the right way of life. It also brings them together on a common project that further promotes their cohesion as a group. It should be mentioned here that in 2006 there was talk of dividing the youngsters into two age groups: as more children come of age, the span between the young and the older becomes too wide, and it is thought better to have groups of younger and older second-generation Burhanis, respectively. Finally, the youth theatre – like the social meetings – includes the girls who here can participate in important and respected activites within the Tariqa, even though they are not allowed to take active part in the hadra ritual.

Conclusion

After a presence in Germany for a quarter of a century, some developments are clear in the Tariqa Burhaniya. The question of the supreme leadership in the order has not until now created serious problems, and the question of generational change has been treated in some detail. The members of the Tariqa Burhaniya in Germany can be clearly divided into a middle-aged first generation and a second generation which is now coming of age. The author's fieldwork suggests that young Burhanis in general tend to remain in the movement and are getting ready to take over certain key posts in the future. It has been shown that the organization – understood as the first-generation German Burhanis plus the Sudanese leaders – consciously follows a policy of including the young generation as much as possible in the movement's life and activities. The reason why this to a large extent succeeds may be that the order is able to fulfil almost all the social needs of the youngsters. In Germany, the Tariqa Burhaniya has achieved a size that amounts to a real environment able to maintain a community. Thus, indications are that the Burhaniya will succeed in perpetuating itself through its second generation; the generational change has begun and seems so far to be successful.

Another question to be considered concerns the situation of the young Burhanis which is totally different from that of their parents. Given that they were born into the movement and did not take a conscious decision that set them apart from their family and friends, one could be tempted to believe that they will be more 'orthodox'. Tendencies in this direction can be perceived – several of the young people are learning Arabic of their own accord, they fulfil their ritual obligations to the letter, and so on. On the other hand, the informal and joyful lifestyle and gatherings that the young people have, could point in the opposite direction. Gritt Klinkhammer has contended that the Burhanis have moved from a syncretistic search for spirituality to become a more orthodox Islamic movement, supervised by Sudanese shaikhs.[22] I will suggest that this move may become more clear in the next generation. The great internal comradeship and solidarity among the young Burhanis gives reasons to believe that the new generation may have an even greater cohesion than the present one. This may lead to an increased withdrawal from wider society. In my view there is a contradiction or dilemma in Burhaniya between forces that want to integrate as much as possible with the wider society, and forces that want to define themselves in contra-distinction to it. It remains to be seen which tendency will be uppermost, but I think this material illustrates some problems and difficulties involved in practising Sufism in mainstream Western society and in implementing a culturally rooted Islam in the secularized countries of modern Europe.

Notes

1 Werbner (2003) gives a detailed account of a typical diaspora order in Britain.
2 Geaves (2000: 145ff.) And Schleßmann (2003: 43ff.) Present the Naqshbandiya-Haqqaniya, a typical example of this type of movement that attracts both Muslims with migrant background and (a few) Western converts.
3 This is the topic of a recent article by Gritt Klinkhammer (2005).
4 Certain Arabic words, such as the names of the Burhaniya leaders, are transcribed as is usually done by Tariqa Burhaniya, reflecting the Sudanese-Egyptian pronunciation.
5 Taken from the tariqa's website, www.burhaniya.info/intranet/I_welc_e.htm (last accessed 20 August 2006).
6 Taken from the tariqa's website: www.burhaniya.info/intranet/I_welc_e.htm (last accessed 20 August 2006).
7 One explanation is that the Burhanis use to meditate one hour a day, and in a year that amounts to about two weeks. Thus, they fulfil the requirements, or put another way, the spirit behind the outer rules. (Interview, Copenhagen, January 2004).
8 Aurad is plural of the Arabic wird, and can be translated as 'special prayers of a certain order' (Trimingham 1971: 214ff.). In Burhaniya aurad refers to a definite body of prayers and recitations laid down by the order's founder and utilized as personal practice for each member. Could also be translatled as 'litany'.
9 This is not the place to discuss hadra in detail. A precise description of a typical hadra in Munich is found in Glasbrenner (2001).
10 The prehistory and early history of the European Burhaniya is related in Klinkhammer (2005: 264ff.) and Schleßmann (2003: 140ff.).
11 An exception is Denmark, where the majority of Burhanis have a migrant background.
12 Religious hymns or poems, qasa'id, written by Shaikh Mohammad Osman, have been

printed by Burhaniya and are utilized in the weekly hadra rituals. The discourses that he used to hold every night were recorded on tape, and Burhanis in Germany are working in collaroration with Sudanese on transcription and translation of them.

13 Maulana Shaikh Mohammad had, before assuming office, all but completed a study of medicine in Hanover.

14 Properly speaking, this person should be called 'chief murshid', as the other members of the irshad committee also are murshids, since they are authorized by Maulana to teach. The understanding of the concept murshid in Burhaniya differs from the more general use of the term as restricted to 'Sufi master' or shaikh.

15 The number of Germans who have converted to Islam is not known precisely. Spuler-Stegemann quotes a figure of 40,000 German *women* having converted due to marriage with Muslims, but more precise figures are not to be found (Spuler-Stegemann 2002: 309). In any case, the number of adult Burhanis with German ethnic background may be counted in hundreds, rather than in thousands, and therefore doubtless constitute a tiny minority among converts to Islam in the country.

16 As seen on the website:

> In Sufism, daily life is a challenge to develop the heart and the soul. The follower seeks to recognize and praise God in all aspects of His creation – while interacting with humans and with nature, in the family as well as in business. Since most of the Sufi orders spreading out in the West strive for integration in society, their members are not noticable by special clothing or behaviour.
>
> (www.burhaniya.info/intranet/I_welc_e.htm, last accessed 20 August 2006)

17 Klinkhammer (2005: 267ff.).

18 Feild (1997).

19 Interview with woman, Hamburg, 22 June 2005.

20 Interview with young man, Hamburg, 23 June 2005.

21 The following is transcribed and translated from my own video recording of a play, performed by the Burhaniya youth group in Hamburg, 26 May 2006.

22 Klinkhammer (2005).

References

Feild, Reshad (1997) *Ich ging den Weg des Derwisch. Das Abenteuer der Selbstfindung*, (translated from original: *The Last Barrier*), Rowohlt Taschenbuch Verlag.

Geaves, Ron (2000) *The Sufis of Britain. An Exploration of Muslim Identity*, Cardiff Academic Press, Cardiff.

Glasbrenner, Eva-Maria (2001) 'Tanz in der sudanesischen Bruderschaft Tariqa Burhaniya – Beschreibung einer Hadra', *Acta Orientalia*, 2001 (62), 81–91.

Klinkhammer, Gritt (2005) 'Traditionalizing Spirituality: the Burhaniya Sufi Order in Germany', in Sigrid Nökel and Levent Tezcan (eds) *Islam and the New Europe. Continuities, Changes, Confrontations* (Yearbook of the Sociology of Islam, 6), transcript Verlag, Bielefeld.

Schleßmann, Ludwig (2003) *Sufismus in Deutschland. Deutsche auf dem Weg des mystischen Islam*, Boehlau, Köln.

Spuler-Stegemann, Ursula (2002) *Muslime in Deutschland. Informationen und Klärungen*, Freiburg, Herder spektrum.

Trimingham, J. Spencer (1971) *The Sufi Orders in Islam*, Oxford University Press, Oxford.

Werbner, Pnina (2003) *Pilgrims of Love: The Anthropology of a Global Sufi Cult*, Hurst, London.

10 Home, nation and global Islam

Sufi oriented activities and community building among Bosnian Muslims in Southern Sweden

Catharina Raudvere and Ašk Gaši

Ja Kerimu, ja Allah	*O Noble, O Allah*
Ja Rahimu illallah	*O Merciful only God*
Subhanallah Hakk Allah	*praise upon the True God*
Bosni našoj selam daj	*Give our Bosnia peace.*
Ja Allah, Hu, Allah	*O Allah, Hu, Allah*
Bosni našoj selam daj.	*Give our Bosnia peace.*
Bosna teče dan i noć	*River Bosna flows day and night*
tekbir daje borcu moć	*Tekbir gives the fighter strength*
jer je poziv od Boga	*Because the call is from Allah*
da sačuva svakoga.	*to protect us all.*[1]

These verses are the initial stanzas from a hymn (ilahija)[2] with a classical Ottoman melody, but it had a new Bosnian text composed in the early 1990s during the war in former Yugoslavia. The original Turkish hymn that served as a matrix, "Ey Allahım", is in its turn a paraphrasing of classical Ottoman hymn tradition, with the Sufi master Yunus Emre's work as its supreme ideal. The refashioning of the poem emphasises Bosnia as a vulnerable nation at war and in the need of Allah's protection against strong enemies. The River Bosna flows like a vein through the country and as the pulse of the poem. It formulates an imperative to arouse Bosnia's fighters in trust of Allah. This forceful ilahija followed Bosnian Muslims (Bosniaks) into exile and was often sung at those stations in Sweden where refugees waited in the mid-1990s for residence permits. The popularity of this particular song illustrates the renewed interest in what was defined as distinctively Bosnian in terms of national and cultural heritage – until then an unknown history for many who were raised in the Yugoslav federation.[3] The obvious Sufi character of the adaptation, with its references to Allah's many names, the repetitive rhythmical chorus and the stylistic link to Yunus Emre added to the view of Bosnian Islam as something particular. This was a view embraced by some among the Bosnian Muslims who arrived in southern Sweden at the peak of the Balkan conflict, 1992–1995. Despite strong feelings for their homeland and for Bosnia-Herzegovina's new status as a nation, many of the refugees stayed on, and some built stable local communities. To some of them Sufism was a national legacy to fall back on, Sufi rituals forming an evident part of familiar community life; others had little or no knowledge of the impact of Sufism on Islam in Bosnia, or no interest in religion at all. Cherished, unfamiliar or rejected – attitudes toward Sufism are seldom neutral.[4]

The aim of this chapter is to focus on the process of community building and indicate how Sufi traditions could play such an important role in the national self-understanding of "Bosnian Islam" in a local Muslim congregation in Sweden. Sufism (tesavvuf), with its theological conceptions and ritual life, has apparently served as a means by which the Bosnian group has defined its heritage in times of national awakening, and also as a way of coping with life in new circumstances. The study derives its materials from a specific case study.[5] Malmö, Sweden's third city located in the far south, has perhaps the most active Bosniak communities in the country. There is a rich variety of Muslim, cultural and sport associations, engaging a large part of Malmö's Bosniak population. These various groups have been successful in organising Bosnian Muslims; besides, they have been able to negotiate between defenders of the Sufi heritage and a recent puristic wahabi (Bos. *vehabi*) mission. This chapter is not concerned with the individual or personal aspects of forced migration in wartime; it focuses on how a cultural and religious heritage like Sufism can play an essential role in community building – not in terms of abstraction or determination, but as a tool for cultural interpretation.

The mosque and meeting place of the Bosniak Islamic Community (Bošnjačka islamska zajednica Malmö) is located in an old industrial building on the fringe of central Malmö (Raudvere 2009). The five-storey complex has a private owner, but it is rented by the municipality in order to offer meeting points for various immigrant associations. The neighbourhood illustrates Malmö's industrial history, its heyday as well as its fall. Today most of the old factories have closed down, but a new commercial life has taken over. There are many small shops and businesses, almost without exception run by immigrants, a large proportion of them Muslims. In several buildings nearby there are other mosques and prayer rooms located in former factories and in basements of apartment buildings. Malmö has 15 official Muslim congregations, of which five are ethnically defined, but many more groups meet on a private or semi-public basis. It is hard to draw definitive lines demarcating the respective status of the various groups: many of them are unstable and highly dependent on the enthusiasm of a few individuals, and they are apt to attract people of specific ethnical backgrounds. Theological disagreements are also sometimes a reason for division.

The Bosniak community uses two floors in a part of the building. In daytime the place serves as a mosque, mostly frequented by elderly men, and during evenings and weekends it hosts family and youth activities organised by the association. A weekly dhikr prayer is also held here, without formal links to any order (tarikat) or association (cemat). It is performed as part of the ordinary programme and without any restrictions in regard to who is allowed to attend. During holidays mevlud gatherings are organised on the same conditions, conducted by the local imam.

Bosnian Muslims in Sweden

The history of Bosnians in Sweden goes back to the decades after the Second World War, when labour migrants were invited to come to Sweden.[6] Initially, during the 1950s and 1960s, migrants were often single men who settled in the major industrial areas. In many cases these immigrating men were later joined by their families, and before the Balkan war there were about 20,000 persons from Yugoslavia in Sweden, plus their children. Communist rule in Tito's Yugoslavia was another reason for leaving, although it was rarely as freely articulated among Bosnians as among Serbs and (especially) Croats. The workers from Bosnia were identified as "Yugoslavs" in official records as well as in the popular mind. Religious and ethnic diversities may not have been unknown, but they were certainly not emphasised in descriptions of the Yugoslavs as a minority group. Of the approximately 5,000 Bosnians among the Yugoslavs, 1,500–3,000 were of Muslim background. They seldom participated in or organised Muslim activities. When they did so, it was often in alliance with Turks and Albanians. Most of the early Bosnian migration settled in western and southern Sweden, a condition which goes some way towards accounting for the present-day intensity in the activities in this particular area of Sweden.

During and after the war in the Balkans, over 55,000 Bosnians were granted permanent residence in Sweden as refugees, with a peak in 1992–1995.[7] Today almost 80,000 Bosnians live in Sweden. They constitute a substantial part of Sweden's 275,000 Muslims (Stenberg 2002), though far from all are Muslims according to their self-understanding or for that matter connected to any Muslim association. Though numerous, the Bosnian Muslims are still not very visible as a religious group. As Europeans, they do not fit into the Swedish stereotyped image of Muslims, and the strong Sufi element in their way of practising Islam makes them different in relation both to the populist stereotype and to the cultural praxis of other Muslim immigrants in Sweden. Most of them are comfortable with the spaces on offer for religious activities and identities in a secular environment where the majority do not participate in public religious life.

In the mid-1990s many Bosnians lived in refugee stations for long periods while waiting for residence permits. Life in the stations was in many respects affected by the war, and many activities were organised at the stations by the more well-educated refugees. There was humanitarian aid directed towards fellow Bosnians in Sweden as well as provisions sent to Bosnia. Psychiatric aid to traumatised war victims was among the first things to be organised. A network among the refugees in Sweden was organised, "Bosnians help Bosnians", which operated in close collaboration with the Swedish public health administration. This help focused on psychological and spiritual needs, but not necessarily religious.

The scene in Figure 10.1 shows some of the teachers at "The Bosnian School" at a refugee station in Landskrona, organised by the Bosnians themselves and situated on the outskirts of a small town on Sweden's south-west coast. The school gave good-quality education to children and youngsters, as there were several teachers among the refugees; but owing to the situation in the Balkans, teaching with a specific national angle was also offered. The modules were defined by the teachers as "national themes", such as the Bosnian language, history and geography, as well as art and literature. The school at the Landskrona refugee station was an early initiative, and a successful one. The rapid organisation of fundamental education has remained a vital part of the narratives of the first period in Sweden, of decisive mobilisation and "Gemeinschaft". An important addition in comparison to the Yugoslav curriculum familiar to pupils and teachers alike was religious education. Islamic education took the conventional forms of Quran classes and teachings in basic theology, but was also in many respects present in various cultural activities. A pursuit quite unique to the Bosniaks, in relation to other Muslim communities, is choir-singing, and a particularly noteworthy feature is the prominent role of young women in choirs. In the particular Landskrona environment, the gatherings and performances with the choir "Muhacir" (lit. immigrant, alluding to those who followed Muhammed to Medina, but of course also to the diasporic situation) had a distinct Sufi angle in that many of the songs and ilahije incorporated Sufi themes. However, it is debatable to what extent singers or audiences were aware of this theological component, as the peak of the performances occurred in a tense period with national overtones. Success was undeniable, in any case, and the young people engaged in the choral group even produced a CD and made tours to other parts of Sweden. The school initiative was continued for a long time, as a Saturday school on a voluntary basis, even after many of the refugees had settled in Malmö and a new choir had been established under the name "Vatan",

Figure 10.1 Some of the teachers at "The Bosnian school" in Landskrona, *c.*1994. The school was organised by the Bosnians themselves during the long wait for residence permits.

Fatherland. In the early years in Malmö, the school functioned as a nexus for the community. Ilahija performances by the choirs are still talked about as a significant link to Bosnia's legacy, and the choral singers and their repertoire have a decisive role when Muslim holidays are celebrated. Members of the choir proudly emphasise the bridge-building character of their repertoire, as they sing in five languages: Bosnian, Turkish, Arabic, Persian and Swedish.

Islam and Sufism in Bosnia

The early history of Islam in the Balkans is largely the history of the Ottoman conquest in 1463 (Malcolm 1994: 51ff.; Heywood 1996). The coming of the Turks forms the historical background of Bosnian Sufism as well (Algar 1971). Visions of the Ottoman past as a Golden Age are very much alive in contemporary oral narratives; names of people and places are common knowledge. Sarajevo, from its foundation in 1463, was the Islamic centre for the area and also the site of the headquarters of several dervish tarikats. Written records from this period are scarce, but even in the early times there are references to foundation charters (sing. *vakufnama*) and meeting places for dervishes (sing. *zavija* or *tekija*). Travellers in the seventeenth century noted a number of Sufi-related institutions and buildings in the area. Sufism soon had a large impact on rural folk religion, and the orders developed quickly as a vital part of the urban networks. The dominant orders in Bosnia were the Nakšibendi, Kaderi and Halveti. In rural areas in Bosnia and Albania, the Bektašis had substantial influence,[8] while the Mevlevi order seems to have attracted urban strata.

Ottoman society was characterised by de facto plurality and organised by the structure of the millet system. In religious matters and in terms of civil law, the various religious communities lived separate lives. Nevertheless, there was a certain blend between Muslim (Sufi) and Christian traditions, especially when it came to the veneration of saints and the reception of healing blessings at holy mausoleums – a fact now usually deliberately forgotten by both parties.

After 400 years of Ottoman rule, the Balkans had a dramatic history in the first part of the twentieth century. Yugoslavia was deeply torn during and after the Second World War, but the worst blow against the Muslims came with Communist rule (Malcolm 1994: 51ff.). In 1952 all Sufi activities were forbidden by law, and the five active tekije of the time were obliged to close down – some locked up, others converted into local mosques (sing. *mesdžid*). The authorities were especially critical of the destructive and conservative influence of the šejhs – that is to say, their criticism was directed against the social impact of the Sufi-related institutions and their networks, rather than against the teachings or rituals connected to the tarikats. The first Mevlevi tekija in Sarajevo, from 1462, was torn down in 1957. It was a deed interpreted by Bosniaks as a clear indication of the government's agenda to eradicate Muslim monuments from the cultural landscape. Even today, the 1957 destruction remains a recurring theme when the systematic demolition of cultural landmarks during the 1990s war is mentioned. The Communist government was hostile to religion in general, but especially against

Islam. As a result Sufism went underground and dhikr, mevlud and tevhid became rituals of the private sphere, practised in secret. (It was a situation which created its own corpus of legendary narratives, where the saying goes "Islam survived thanks to women and mevlud".) Yet, even in the 1980s, before the war and the fall of Communism in the area, a certain renewed interest in Islam could be noted, not least an interest in Sufism. Many urban intellectuals who were part of this wave later became influential in diaspora communities, and their understanding of the relation between Sufism and cultural heritage proved to be of particular significance.

The revival of Islam and Sufism prospered in Bosnia after the war and was further increased by globalisation at large, especially in terms of transnational migration and travel (Mandaville 2001: 108ff.; Schaebler and Stenberg 2004). After the war, many Bosniaks in exile have frequently been travelling back and forth (Resic and Törnquist-Plewa 2002; Raudvere 2004). This mobility had its effects on local Sufism in the diaspora, as people can go on pilgrimages to türbes, visit famous šejhs and participate in major ritual events; they come back with religious souvenirs and mementoes with bereket and, perhaps especially, important publications. The last decade has seen a steadily increasing stream of books, booklets and pamphlets in circulation between Bosnia and the many diaspora communities worldwide. In Bosnia a number of titles have been translated from Turkish, Arabic, Persian and English in addition to the works in Bosnian. The communities in exile have likewise published extensively, and exports/imports go in all directions.

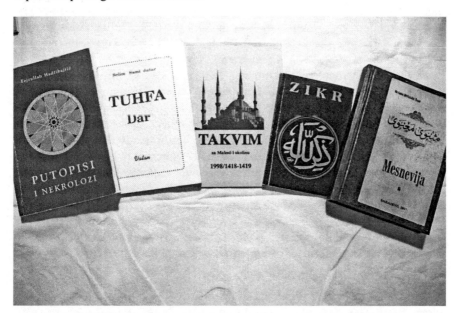

Figure 10.2 A selection of publications with a pronounced Sufi angle produced by Malmö Bosniaks. All these examples are private prints and were informally distributed through personal networks.[9]

Sufism has always been transnational, and the age of globalisation has seen new tendencies in Sufi missions geared towards awakening Muslims as well as towards attempting to convert non-Muslims. There are international Sufi centres today which attract people thanks to their charismatic shaikhs, who have become international superstars on a global arena. Three of the best known of these neo-Sufis, who have also had an impact in Bosnia and on the Bosniak diaspora, are the Hakkani shaikh Nazim al-Kibrisi (as well as his leading representative in the US, Hisham Muhammad Kabbani), Abdul Baki of the Halidi-Naqshbandi at Menzil in Turkey, and Fethullah Gülen's many educational institutions and pious associations originating from Turkey – but the master himself is now in self-imposed exile. There are significant differences between these groups (and their many sub-branches) in respect of teaching, style and audience. Yet, their respective success have points in common with regard to the use of new media and adaptation to the living conditions of today. These men can be termed neo-Sufis as they have gained a substantial global visibility, far beyond the traditional Muslim world, and attracted many non-Muslims to convert. Not least the latter fact has invested them with considerable prestige. It seems as if Nakshibendi-linked groups, with their more pronounced strictness, are more easily connected to more puritan Islamic groups. Their teachings and rituals can serve as an important tool at grassroots level, facilitating negotiation between traditional Bosnian Sufism and more Islamist trends. But there is also another aspect of the increased interest in Sufism. Since the war, several new Sufi groups have arisen in Bosnia. Many Sufi-oriented prayer meetings are organised as informal gatherings, either in private homes or in closed circles at mosque establishments. This may be explained as a result of the tearing down of tarikat structures during the Communist era, but also as a more individualistic mode of expressing religiosity, a mode more in tune with late-modern living conditions.

New media, particularly the Internet, have provided an international web of contacts along with the increased transnational travel. This cultural globalisation leads to new hierarchies, far away from local social structures, and to new modes of claiming authority and legitimacy. The importance of the Sufi šejhs proper has decreased with the many informal groups. Traditionally they had important positions as local community leaders, and šejhs exercised a significant influence on individuals' lives as they offered advice and guidance. The most important role for the šejhs today seems to be serving as dhikr leaders during ceremonies. This is not necessarily based on a strict division between separate Sufi orders – and in many cases the šejh is replaced by a vekil (a šejh's appointed deputy), or the repetitive prayer has become a more or less private event, without an initiated leader, regarded as an individual mode of prayer among others.

Bosnian Muslims in Malmö

There are several reasons for selecting the Malmö Bosniak congregation as a case study when focusing on contemporary Sufism in Scandinavian diaspora. With Bosniak refugees as main agents, Sufi-oriented rituals cannot be ignored, and the conditions and possibilities for them to practise their form of Sufism are deeply embedded in the events of contemporary history.

Bosnians constitute a large group of immigrants in Sweden today, as well as a substantial portion of Sweden's Muslim population. Sufism plays an important part in Bosnian Islam, historically and in the present – not necessarily in terms of Sufi orders or institutionalised activities, but as a vital factor in a national religious self-understanding and everyday religiosity. There are several agents involved here: the Swedish state, the municipality, the formal congregation (with its direct links to the Islamic Directorate in Sarajevo) and local Muslim authorities. What seems at first glance to be embedded in various horizontal networks (based on religious authority and/or national fellowship) is also part of vertical hierarchies encompassing both Swedish and Bosnian governmental administration. It is not only a matter of relations between Bosnia and Sweden, though: cultural globalisation is clearly manifest in both formal and informal ways. The tendencies of new global Sufism (with its charismatic teachers, attractive websites and successful image management) as well as the living conditions of the diaspora have had an impact on local Sufism, as practised in Malmö. Here strong cultural patterns meet with forms of Sufism that has travelled around the globe.

In Malmö 42 per cent of the population are defined as immigrants,[10] and it is known to be one of Sweden's most segregated cities. Despite the many problems, the municipality has played a very active role in the organisation of the Bosniak community, especially when it comes to housing. The Bosniak Islamic Community has its mosque and other facilities in a building rented by the municipality in order to offer adequate premises to immigrant associations which run activities for youth. The building is known in public records as "The House of Associations" ("Föreningarnas hus") or, more informally, just "the Brewery", as this large industrial building (10,000 m²) is an old brewery which now hosts 20 immigrant associations and clubs with very different activities. Initially, in 2004, this backing had governmental support through the Swedish National Board for Youth Affairs.[11] The explicit aim was to create coordination and democratic structure based on the conviction that club activities are the best way to integration, or even "natural integration", as it says on the Board's website. The place and space offered to Bosnian Muslims in Malmö is part of the government's and the municipality's actions to promote strategic pluralism. This support has unquestionably been a key factor for the Bosniak activities. Scandinavian trust in the boon of coordinated clubs and associations definitely works well with ways in which community life was organised in federal Yugoslavia. But support from the municipality also generates a rift between on the one hand Muslim life under public auspices and on the other private/semi-public groups; some the latter nowadays often developing a pronounced underground self-image in conscious contrast to the former.

Over the last 15 years, Bosniaks in Malmö/southern Sweden have been comparatively well organised in a large variety of associations and communities, not only in consequence of municipality strategies. Community life among Bosniaks in Malmö may be regarded as a symptom of what happens when people migrate and bring their religious traditions and customs to a new environment.

Figure 10.3 "The House of Associations" in Malmö, Sweden. Facilities arranged by the municipality at the disposal of about 20 immigrant clubs with youth activities. In the Bosniaks' part the rooms are flexibly arranged and the nexus is of course the large room that is used as a mosque, among other things. The floors between two storeys are removed, and at one long side a women's gallery is constructed.

Four phases of this process can be schematically outlined: break-up, arrival, community building and integration. However, integration is not the happy ending for all groups and communities, and the road to community building can be both bumpy and long; neither is it a definitive move from A to B. Unemployment is, as among most immigrants, still high. Owing to transnational mobility, with frequent travel between the two homelands, the phases do not represent a simple chronological line. The conquest of space in the new environment may, in line with Barbara Metcalf's argument, be divided into social, cultural and physical space, which are far from always possible to separate (Metcalf 1996: 2ff.). Proper premises, which entail a possibility to offer regularity in ritual life – all in compliance with the ambitions of the municipality – are part of what is presented as an image of success, inside and outside the group. At present the association is served by two imams, but only one of them works full-time. They serve southern Sweden at funerals, organise tours for Bosnian lecturers and preachers and have administrative and moral responsibility for what is done in the name of the community.

However, the story of the Bosniak congregation in Malmö, and of the process from refugee stations to a mosque of their own, would not be complete without a mention of the role played by strong and strong-minded persons. There have been several important individuals among the Bosniaks who have shouldered heavy responsibilities for their community over a long period of time. The combination of hard work and conscious strategies has been fruitful indeed; and the importance of Sufi theology for authority and responsibility as established forms of community building, in combination with the social and affective aspects of Sufi rituals, cannot be overestimated. Both old and young have shown the ability to transform established local traditions (far from always congruent) and make them take root under radically altered circumstances. Two individuals have been of special importance to the Bosniak group in Malmö in terms of how Sufi practices have developed in the diaspora, although they differ in age, formal education, affiliation to Sufism and in position and rank when it comes to ritual leadership.

Asim Ibrišević (b. 1940) served as imam among the Bosnian refugees in southern Sweden during the 1990s. As an appointed vekil this legendary person organised Friday prayers and dhikr gatherings already at the refugee stations, and he continued to do so in a private apartment in Malmö. These meetings, with their informal and open character, laid the foundation for the meetings now conducted on a regular basis within the association. As interest in these gatherings grew, dhikr was organised within the Bosniak association in its simple premises at the time. Asim Ibrišević comes from a well-known Sufi family and was a source of inspiration for younger people who wanted to establish Sufi rituals in the diaspora. He later returned to Bosnia. Ibrišević drew his authority from his direct connections to Sufi environments in Bosnia, and in view of his age he could be trusted to have the experience attributed to a dhikr leader. The more these ritual gatherings were included in the social web of the congregations, the less any tarikat structures were visible.

Figure 10.4 Asim Ibrišević (b. 1940) led the Friday prayers and organised dhikr gatherings already at the refugee stations in the 1990s. He later returned to Bosnia.

Figure 10.5 Idriz Karaman (b. 1960) is imam of the Bosniak community in Malmö and southern Sweden and currently head imam for all Swedish Bosniak congregations.

Even at the very beginning, younger people took the lead when organising religious education and prayers. Idriz Karaman (b. 1960) is imam of the Bosniak community in Malmö and southern Sweden. He is also at present head imam for all Swedish Bosniak congregations connected to the Islamic Directorate in Sarajevo (Islamska zajednica u Bosni i Hercegovini).[12] Karaman continues a family tradition from Bosnia as an imam, but he has also shown an ability to deal with changes and a completely new environment. He is leading a community which has a long tradition of acting in environments dominated by secularisation, but is also in the middle of a comparatively new encounter with globalisation. As the religious head of his community, Karaman is the leader of the weekly dhikr and Quran recitations, as well as of the larger mevlud recitations. He was comparatively young during the formative years of the congregation and not in a position to draw authority from any Sufi lineage or experience. Yet, Karaman is well-educated in Sunni theology and comes from a family with many imams and scholarly traditions. When he leads dhikr, it is with a legitimacy founded in the ritual traditions within Bosnian Islam. Today the ceremonies he is in charge of take place in the mosque of the congregation and as a part of the weekly programme. It is conducted in a mode which is easily interpreted as traditional by the participants. Both these influential individuals had a fundamental authority as they can easily be identified through their family background and established pious networks in Bosnia. The shifting conditions of their activities mirror the development of the congregation.

Sufi traditions in this particular community are not primarily tied to the conventional aspects of Sufism – the orders, initiations and šejhs – but to the specific forms and modes of prayer connected to Sufism: tevhid and dhikr, and to mevlud performances and ilahija singing. Tone Bringa has painted a vivid picture of everyday religiosity in a central Bosnian village before the war (Bringa 1995: 197ff.). Her analyses show how deeply rooted many Sufi traditions are (or were) in Bosnian Islam and agree with the observations made in Malmö 15 years later. Rituals and modes of prayer which would have been regarded as exclusively Sufi in other milieus are integrated in the present diaspora community in its cultural and social web as simply "Muslim". Bringa has also rightly pointed out that the terms Sufi and Sufism are not to any great extent part of the local religious vocabulary, which uses a rich variety of vernacular names for specific rituals, prayers, places and leaders of ceremonies. This also holds true for the Malmö diaspora. Avoiding talking about and relating to the various tarikats is also a way of underlining unity. Spiritual authority is rather drawn from charisma and family alliances.

The dhikr gatherings among the Bosnians in Malmö can be characterised as quiet moments and opportunities for recovery. These events also offer a certain quality of "home", with emotional links to Bosnia. The atmosphere does not stress exclusiveness; rather, the emphasis is on a sense of belonging, founded on the ritual and textual world of Sufism with its intense and affective rituals, its legends and its hymns.

There are two regular dhikr meetings open to members of the Bosnian community, as the ritual activities have developed with a notable division in terms of gender and age, agency and ritual authority. Within the framework of their own congregation, there are dhikr gatherings in the mosque premises on Sunday afternoons where both men and women participate.[13] Initially, dhikr gatherings were arranged twice a week by the Bosniak association, on Thursday and Sunday nights (Friday being the holy day and Monday held to be the birthday of the Prophet). Today the dhikr has developed into a part of a general women's meeting on Sunday afternoons. The average age is quite high, and few men participate. The ritual is led by the imam of the congregation, who is himself not an initiated dervish of any order. The mode of performing the dhikr is sanctioned by a shared conception of Muslim cultural heritage. As a dhikr leader, the young imam serves more as a responsible teacher and counsellor with ritual authority. No circle is formed, and participants sit in rows facing the imam but use rosaries for the repetition itself. The repetition of the names of Allah is preceded by Quran recitation (kiraet), repentance (istigfar) and praise of the prophet Muhammed (salavat). The repetition is pronounced aloud (but not loudly) and collectively; all participants join in, but the rhythm of the repetitive prayer is not accompanied by any pronounced bodily movements. Most participants follow the repetition with rosaries in their hands. The session is concluded by prayer (dova) and recitation of al-Fatiha. If there is a special reason (commemorating, rejoicing or celebrating), an additional tevhid may be read.

A second option, and one favoured by some younger men, is to attend an informal tekke in the basement of an apartment building close by, where a Turkish Nakşibendi vekil offers silent dhikr (hatm-i hacegan) every night.[14] On

Thursday nights in particular the event is well attended, though by men only and mostly Turks and Bosnians. This is in principle a meeting for initiated male Nakşibendi members only, but arrangements are made to accommodate other visitors, of whom there are quite a few. The non-initiated guests sit in an additional room and follow the dhikr in individual modes. The initiated dervishes sit in a circle (halka) and use – in the typical Nakşibendi manner – small stones (sing. *taş*) instead of the rosary when quietly repeating "the names of Allah". The hatm-i hacegan is concluded with Quran recitation and some short prayers. Hereby the strict division is concluded. All participants are then united to listen to the Turkish vekil's didactic conversation (sohbet), in which he comments on matters of current interest – usually in Turkish, but sometimes in Swedish. The participants are mostly Turks, Kurds and Bosnians, but men from Arabic groups also attend.

The vekil's meetings in the basement premises have established new contacts between individuals and also formed new schemes for dhikr meetings, based on Ottoman structures but very much a consequence of present diasporic circumstances. The group around the Turkish Nakşibendi vekil is stable, going back some 20 years, but there is no formalised union or registered association. The loosely defined Nakşibendi fellowship, in combination with trust in the vekil's ritual authority, is enough. He is an initiated Nakşibendi Halidi dervish and has received permission to lead dhikr ceremonies from his şeyh in Turkey. This ensures that the classical lineage is established and maintained. Still, his individual commitment is the most powerful driving force when it comes to keeping the dhikr fellowship together. Not only do participants represent different ethnic groups (and languages), but also very varying local ritual traditions and perceptions about ritual authority. Instead of the conventional connection between family tradition (and to some extent profession) and order affiliation, these new constellations mirror the conditions of life in the diaspora. Members of the group regularly go over to Copenhagen for larger Turkish Nakşibendi meetings; but the vekil's capability seems to be what invests the weekly meetings with a combination of what the participants experience as traditional and what comes across as a valuable ability to adjust to the problems and challenges of the present.

Martyrs, heroes and everyday life

Bosna, bedem avlija
u svakoj je gazija.
Svakom ime Alija
sad je vrijeme mehdija.

Bosnia's walled gardens
are in every hero.
All of them are named Alija
Now is the time for the mehdija.

Svi pod „Ehad" stanimo
s mehdijom da branimo.
Svima nam je jedan din
s narodima istočnim.

Let us all stand under The Only
in defence together with the mehdija
We have all one belief
together with the peoples from the east.

Bosni našoj selam daj...

Give our Bosnia peace...

The final stanzas of the ilahija quoted at the beginning of this chapter continue to focus on Bosnia as a Muslim nation. These last two verses link the heroic and Shia-influenced Ali paradigm with modern history, as they hint at the leadership of Alija Izetbegović (who died in 2003). Izetbegović was, and still is, a controversial person among the Bosniaks for many reasons (Malcolm 1994: 208ff.; Kepel 2003: 239ff.). His rejection of Sufism in his Islamic Declaration was based on his more puristic view of Islam, which was to a high degree influenced by the Muslim Brotherhood. Nevertheless, in a turbulent period he stood out as leader of the Bosnian nation. The future president was already looked upon as a hero and a martyr by this followers from the days of the Young Muslims (Mladi Muslimani) in the late 1940s, and that status was reinforced by the 1983 trials in Sarajevo against leading Muslim intellectuals, at the time when the Bosnian version of the present hymn was written. The final stanzas are less Sufi-oriented, but the melody, the intense rhythm and the repetitive choruses are of course still there. Instead the last stanzas offer a pattern where present-day problems are mirrored in the legacy of the past, which provides a model for interpretation of current conflicts and hope for the future. The "Alija" is not only a reference to a questioned contemporary politician; it opens up Shia associations, which are most certainly a facet of Bosnian Islam and not only in terms of Bektašism. The Ali paradigm bestows religious meaning on suffering and heroic resistance. The force of the tune and the words are inspirational whether understood as Sufi-oriented or Shia-influenced: everybody's contribution could matter despite whether the conflict is situated at cosmic, political or cultural levels.

The ending of this much-loved ilahija emphasises Bosnia as a nation united by Islam. It provided comfort in dark times, and songs like this one had a mobilising effect for the future with lines like: "All of them are named Alija/Now is the time for the mehdija." The term mehdija, in the plural, draws singers and listeners into the struggle, and a wartime flavour lingers. Rather than a returning Mehdi of salvationist character, it gives an apocalyptic aspect of war to the hymn. At the manifest text level, the end of the ilahija is more nationalistic than Sufi-oriented. It has a bearing on unity and an emphasis on the need for sacrifice from everyone. The eschatological touch of the twice-mentioned mehdija balances the more national-romantic tone in the image of Bosnia and its walled gardens.

The ilahija was frequently sung during the war as well as in the refugee stations in Sweden (Eastmond 1998). The well-known Turkish Sufi singer Sami Savni Özer recorded the hymn, with a text close in form to Yunus' classic poems, on a popular CD, *Ey Allahım*, in the early 1990s. The wide circulation of Özer's CD is an example in its own right of the strengthened links between Turkey and Bosnia at all societal levels, including religious ones. In their public activities in Bosnia and among Bosniaks abroad, Sufi groups (tarikats and cemats) from Turkey, like some Nakşibendis branches, like Halidi, and Gülen, and other Nurcu societies, have drawn on popular conceptions of the Ottoman heritage. Özer, perhaps the most renowned of the current Halveti-Cerrahi musicians in Istanbul, ensured that the tune was circulated and thereby imparting legitimacy to the new text and its message to the present: "Now is the time for the mehdija." Ten years after the end of the war in former Yugoslavia, a more spiritual interpretation of the struggle is an obvious option; but to most Bosniaks – even those who are too young to have personal experiences of the war – the war is present in the wording.

The war and the terror in the abandoned homeland remain a cultural background to most Bosnians. This is expressed in personal memories and as narratives within families, and it has a distinct impact on younger people, born or raised after the war. "The Bosnian tragedy" is part of most people's self-understanding. Many informants have emphasised the importance of ethnic fellowship as a reason for their commitment to the group. In their lives between nations, with frequent transnational travel, conceptions of distinctive national and ethnic character play a substantial role in their relations, not so much with other ethnic groups from former Yugoslavia as with other Muslim groups.

In the Malmö case, the Sufi gatherings are also part of a network of well-organised general religious activities. The result of the hard work of many individuals must be characterised as a success in terms of stable community building. A concrete example is provided by the way in which the groups have come to terms with defending the ideals of Sufism from severe *vehabi* criticism.[15] What used to be self-evident forms of prayer and celebration have become matters of choice.

For some members of this Bosniak congregation, the Sufi-oriented activities are the core of the fellowship in everyday life. The weekly *dhikr* gatherings, as well as the mevluds and tehvids in the community and in closely related groups, serve as a spiritual centre and supply moments of quiet in demanding lives. Interpersonal bonding is emphasised by the halka, and the surrounding oral genres (ilahije and legends) connect to a shared cultural legacy. The refashioning of classical texts in order to include recent cultural memory opens the traditions to new generations.

In many respects, these Sufi-oriented activities have traditional structures and established forms. There is an apparent emphasis on ritual, and even if it is downplayed leadership plays a substantial part. A ritual like dhikr would be unthinkable without a formal leader (an imam or vekil). There are also links, more or less formal, to Sufi orders and associations, especially with regard to transnational contacts.

As Sufism seems inseparable from the national heritage and distinctive national features to many Bosniaks, most forms of global Islam are, if not threatening, an obvious challenge. The preservation, reconstruction and defence of what was demolished by the war, materially or otherwise, have top priority on most Bosnian Muslim agendas. The very existence of a vital diaspora has changed Bosnian Islam and Bosnian Sufism as much as the war itself did. The fast exchange of information and possibilities for communication lead to a constant influence of ideas and arguments. This has helped Bosnian Sufi groups to strengthen their fellowship; but it has also made them a target for unifying – and smoothing-out local particularities – tendencies.

A particular form of this unifying global Islam is wahabism. It is global in its form of mission and in its unifying theological concepts, and it has been present in Bosnian Muslim milieus since the 1980s (Al-Ali 2002: 257ff.). From time to time, the tension between "the purists" or "the reformed" and the Bosniak congregation is increased. Vehabi-oriented persons with links to the congregation often criticise mevlud gatherings, dhikr prayers, the choirs and many other things that they regard as folk religion or lacking approval from the salafi sources. In response to this, the imam has forbidden the vehabis, as they are called, to sell or otherwise distribute their pamphlets, tapes and CDs inside the premises of the community. This more direct confrontation is appreciated by some as an honest way of defining a limit, whereas others would have preferred the older strategy of ignoring the vehabis.

With their background in a secular society the Bosnians are in many ways well integrated in Swedish society, although the unemployment rate is still high and many carry traumatic memories from the war. As a Muslim minority group, their way of organising themselves in associations and communities has helped them find a balance between integration and retaining identities and traditions. To many Bosniaks, Sufism is not a theological stance in relation to contemporary Islamic puritanism and radicalism, but rather conceived as a part of their national heritage. This does not, however, prevent vehabi-oriented persons in the local community from taking a firm stand against Sufism in general and its rituals in particular, and this conflict affects in the long run the stability of the group as a whole.

Notes

1 The text, well spread in Europe among Bosnian Muslims, is from a collection of hymns and songs, *Ilahije i Kaside*, published by the Bosniak Islamic Association in Wiesbaden, Germany, and printed in Sarajevo in 1998. The collection is dedicated in commemoration of a young šejh, Mehmed Hafizović, who died in battle during the war on the Balkans and is held in great esteem as a martyr. At the end of his essay on the history of the Nakšibendi tarikat in Bosnia Hamid Algar has translated four examples of ilahije, from both Turkish and Bosnian, which convey a more aesthetic and literary flavour of the genre than the present rough translation (Algar 1971: 199ff.).

2 Bosnian vernacular forms are used in this article when referring to Bosnian contexts, and Turkish when referring to Turkish milieus.

3 A CD with the Turkish version is still in wide circulation in Bosnia and in Bosniak diaspora. The cover of the CD recognises Sefer Dal as the author of the text and Cüneyt Koşal as the composer. Sefer Dal was the charismatic şeyh of the Halveti-Cerrahi tarikat in Istanbul until his death in 1999. The Cerrahis of Istanbul were deeply involved in aid to Bosnia during the war in former Yugoslavia, 1992–1995, and the Halvetis in general have been successful in winning new disciples in Bosnia-Herzegovina over the last 15 years. It is therefore far from surprising that the CD reached a wide audience and that many informants perceived the Turkish original as a "Yunus classic". The author of the Bosnian text is, as far as we know, anonymous.

4 It must be remembered that the majority of the Bosnians in Sweden with a Muslim background are not active in or connected to any Muslim congregation. Representatives of the national Swedish Bosniak Community estimate that approximately 12 per cent of the Swedish Bosniaks are connected to a Bosniak congregation, and far from always as active members or participants in services and activities.

5 This chapter is a result of cooperation between two independent academic projects studying Bosnian Muslims in Sweden. Ašk Gaši is currently finishing his PhD thesis in Islamology on Melami Sufism in contemporary Bosnia. Catharina Raudvere is conducting fieldwork among a group of Bosnian Muslims in southern Sweden, with an emphasis on their ritual life; she is Professor of the History of Religions at Copenhagen University. Ašk Gaši is a key informant in her project and an active member of the community described. The chapter is the initial outcome of a mutual interest in documenting Bosnian religious life in Sweden over the last 15 years. The eventual aim of the cooperation is to produce a proper documentation of prayer-rooms and mosques, associations and communities, publications, ritual life and personal memories connected to the Swedish Bosnian Muslim community at large.

6 In 1972 labour migration to Sweden was discontinued.

7 Between 1992 and 2005 almost 93,000 people from Former Yugoslavia obtained residence permits in Sweden, according to statistics from the Swedish Migration Board (www.migrationsverket.se). From 1980 to 2005, residence permits were given to convention refugees, war refugees, de facto refugees in need of protection and refugees on humanitarian grounds. There has been a certain re-migration, and many Bosniaks lead a somewhat translocal life with frequent visits to their hometowns and with many social, economic and religious links.

8 The emphasis on the Bektaşi order as paradigmatic for Balkan Sufism is largely due to John Kingsley Birge's monograph from 1937, which is based on interviews with refugees from the Balkans in Istanbul after the First World War. For a long time, Birge's book was one of very few with a focus on the ritual aspects of Sufism. Today Kosovo and Albania are the main areas for the Bektaşi-groups in the region.

9 From left to right: Fejzullah Hadžibajrić (1913–1990) was a Kaderi šejh and an important person in the efforts to legalise Sufism in Yugoslavia during the 1960s and 1970s. The volume with a selection of his travel accounts and obituaries of deceased Sufi masters, *Putopisi i Nekrolozi* ("Travels and Necrologies"), is the original book publication of the texts from 2002.

   Tuhfa ("Gift") by Selim Sami Jašar (d. 1951), who was Fejzullah Hadžibajrić's own šejh. The text is a poem with 796 two-line verses that offers spiritual instructions to disciples. The poem was originally composed in Turkish during the first half of the twentieth century and later translated into Bosnian by Hadžibajrić. After a period of oral transmission the translation was published in 1984, a second edition appearing in Malmö in 1996.

   Takvim, a calendar for the year 1998 indicating the hours of prayer, along with some texts for reflection.

   A dhikr manual printed before the war, in Sarajevo, by the national Islamic Association of Bosnia and Herzegovina. This reprint from 1996 had a certain circulation in Sweden and the European diaspora. The manual does not represent any specific tarikat tradition for dhikr. Readers and users interpreted the initiative as a way of propagating dhikr and tevhid as Bosnian customs, rather than as an expression a Sufi heritage.

   Fejzullah Hadžibajrić's translation and interpretations of Rumi's *Mesnevi* were originally published in two volumes in Sarajevo in 1985 and 1987. This copy is one of 17 printed in Malmö by followers of Hadžibajrić for circulation in Sweden in 1994.

10 I.e. born, or one or both parents born, outside Sweden; a quarter of the population is born abroad.

11 www.ungdomsstyrelsen.se.

12 The Bosnian term for community and congregation *zajednica* may be used in reference to the extended family and to larger communities and fellowships (Bringa 1995: 42), but the term can also imply an administrative body like the Directorate. The connotation is worth observing.

13 For a discussion on informal dhikr gatherings see Raudvere (2002: 171ff.).

14 A vocal Nakšibendi dhikr at the Visoko tekja during Ramazan is described at length

by Hamid Algar (1971). The ritual was conducted by the legendary šejh Sulhi Hadžimejlić during Ramazan in December 1969. The Hadžimejlićs are a well-known family in Bosnian Sufi circles and still very active. It should also be noted that Bosnian Nakšibendis conventionally say their dhikr aloud which is not the case among the Turks.
15 Cornelia Sorabji gives an interesting overview over criticism presented by "reformed Muslims" in Bosnia against popular ritual traditions, especially those involving music and songs (1994: 116ff., 126, n.1).

References

Al-Ali, N. (2002) "Gender Relations, Transnational Ties and Rituals Among Bosnian Refugees", *Global Networks*, 2: 249–262.

Algar, H. (1971) "Some Notes on the Naqshbandi Tarkiqat in Bosnia", *Die Welt des Islams*, 13: 168–203.

Birge, J.K. (1937) *The Bektashi Order of Dervishes*, London: Luzac's.

Bringa, T. (1995) *Being Muslim the Bosnian Way*, Princeton: Princeton University Press.

Eastmond, M. (1998) "Nationalist Discourses and the Construction of Difference. Bosnian Muslim Refugees in Sweden", *Journal of Refugee Studies*, 11: 161–181.

Kepel, G. (2003) *Jihad. The Trail of Political Islam*, London: I.B. Tauris.

Heywood, C. (1996) "Bosnia under Ottoman Rule, 1463–1800", in M. Pinson (ed.), *The Muslims of Bosnia-Herzegovina. Their Historic Development from the Middle Ages to the Dissolution of Yugoslavia*, Cambridge: Harvard University Press.

Malcolm, N. (1994) *Bosnia. A Short History*, London: Macmillan.

Mandaville, P. (2001) *Transnational Muslim Politics. Reimagining the Umma*, London: Routledge.

Metcalf, B. (ed.) (1996) *Making Muslim Space in North America and Europe*, Berkeley: University of California Press.

Raudvere, C. (2002) *The Book and the Roses. Sufi Women, Visibility, and Zikir in Contemporary Istanbul*, Stockholm/London: Swedish Research Institute in Istanbul/I.B. Tauris.

—— (2004) "Where Does Globalization Take Place? Opportunities and Limitations for Female Activists in Turkish Islamist Non-Governmental Organizations", in B. Schaebler and L. Stenberg (eds), *Globalization and the Muslim World. Culture, Religion, and Modernity*, Syracuse: Syracuse University Press.

—— (2009) "Between Home and Home. Sufi Heritage in Bosniak Diaspora", in C. Raudvere and L. Stenberg (eds), *Sufism Today. Heritage and Tradition in the Global Community*, London: I.B. Tauris.

Resic, S. and B. Törnquist-Plewa (eds) (2002) *The Balkans in Focus. Cultural Boundaries in Europe*, Lund: Nordic Academic Press.

Schaebler, B. and L. Stenberg (2004) *Globalization and the Muslim World. Culture, Religion, and Modernity*, Syracuse: Syracuse University Press.

Sorabji, C. (1994) "Mixed Motives. Islam, Nationalism and *Mevluds* in an Unstable Yugoslavia", in C. Fawzi El-Sohl and J. Mabro (eds), *Muslim Women's Choices. Religious Belief and Social Reality*, Oxford: Berg.

Stenberg, L. (2002) "Islam in Scandinavia: Notes on History, Organization and Present Situation", in S.T. Hunter (ed.), *Islam, Europe's Second Religion. The New Social, Cultural, and Political Landscape*, Westport: Praeger.

11 The reception of Sufi and neo-Sufi literature[1]

Mark Sedgwick

"Islamic Publishing is Poised for Growth," announced the headline of an article in *Publishers' Weekly*, the main US book-trade journal, in 2000. "Books on Sufi Poet Rumi and Sufism Abound."[2] Sufi literature is indeed popular in the West, and this chapter examines the extent, origins and nature of that popularity. It confirms that Sufi literature is now read in the West by millions, traces this phenomenon back to 1812, and argues that Sufi literature in the West is mostly read in distinctively Western ways.

Sufi literature in the West falls into the same four broad categories as it does in the Muslim world, but with important differences and with one significant sub-division. Most popular in the Muslim world are hagiographies of Sufi *walis* (saints). This is a genre found only rarely in the West, where the single widely read example is Martin Lings' *A Sufi Saint in the Twentieth Century*,[3] and so will not be considered in this chapter. Second most popular in the Muslim world is poetry, still recited in public, generally written in Arabic or Urdu, and often of recent composition. This is a major genre in the West as well, though the poets favored are not recent ones, but rather the great Persian-language classics, Jalal al-Din Rumi (1207–1273) and Muhammad Shams al-Din Hafiz (1325–1389). Next in order of popularity in the Muslim world come relatively easily accessible writings by modern Sufis, usually shaikhs. Recent writings by modern Sufis are also found in the West, with the crucial difference that the works in question were almost always written in Western languages, usually English, for Western audiences. Here there is a sub-division unknown in the Muslim world, between more or less overtly didactical works written by self-proclaimed Sufi teachers, and Sufi-inspired novels. Sufi-inspired novels are unknown in the Muslim world, where novel reading is far less popular than it is in the West. Finally, least popular in both the Muslim world and the West, come more difficult classic theoretical works, such as those of Muhyi al-Din ibn al-Arabi (1165–1240), simultaneously the best known (at least in the Sunni world) and the least accessible. Some of these are also found in Western languages, but the reading of such works by members of the public (rather than just by scholars) is a relatively recent development connected to trends that require a separate article. Classic theoretical works, then, are not considered in this chapter either.

As will be shown, when Westerners are reading the same texts as Muslims, as in the case of Rumi and Hafiz, they are generally reading them differently, because they are reading them in a different context. When Westerners are reading different texts – those written in Western languages for Western audiences, and Sufi-inspired novels – the differences are so great that the term neo-Sufi will be used rather than the term Sufi.[4]

Data

Two distinct sources of data are used in this chapter. The origins of the popularity of Sufi literature in the West are investigated using standard historical methodology. The extent and nature of that popularity is investigated with the help of sales data from the online bookseller Amazon. Amazon is not an ideal source, if only because the basis on which its sales data is calculated is not known, since Amazon (understandably) regards this as confidential commercial information. It is, however, the only available source of statistically meaningful data.[5]

Amazon has websites aimed at a number of markets, but only in the United States and the United Kingdom is Amazon's market share large enough for its data to be useful.[6] For this reason, this chapter concentrates on readership in the two major Anglophone countries. It also ignores the Internet, even though the Internet is probably increasingly important.[7] Separate studies using different data would be required for countries such as France and Germany, and also for areas such as Latin America. These other areas may well be of great importance. One major neo-Sufi author, for example, is probably now more popular in Latin America than in Europe,[8] and Rumi may be more popular in Argentina than anywhere else.[9] The readership of neo-Sufi works in the Muslim world is a major topic in its own right which will not be discussed in this chapter.[10]

Classic Sufi poetry

The top ten best-selling poets in America include Rumi and Hafiz, and in Britain include Rumi, though not Hafiz.[11] Historical sales data is not available, but the early publishing history of both poets in the West strongly suggests that this striking popularity is long established.

Hafiz first came to the attention of a significant section of the Western public in the early nineteenth century, with the publication of a German translation by Joseph von Hammer-Purgstall (1774–1856)[12] in 1812–1813. This was not the first translation into a European language,[13] but it was the first to reach a wide public, and inspired Goethe's *West-östlichen Diwan* of 1819. Noting the death of Hammer-Purgstall (as of someone "simultaneously eminent and almost dilettantish") in the *Zeitschrift der Deutschen morgenländischen Gesellschaft* in 1860, Professor Richard Gosche commented that "one can assert without fear of contradiction that no-one save Goethe with his *Diwan* and [Friedrich] Rückert has had such an enduring impact on the lay masses with regard to Oriental literature."[14] All three undoubtedly had an enduring impact, not only with regard to Persian, Arabic and Hindu literature, but specifically with regard to Sufi poetry.

Hammer-Purgstall's translation of Hafiz was in itself popular, and Goethe's *Diwan* was even more popular. It consisted partly of Goethe's own verse, and partly of an essay of 300 pages[15] on Oriental poetry, complete with entries on all the main poets, including not only Hafiz but also Rumi. Rumi had first been translated into German in 1819 by Friedrich Rückert (1788–1866), the other figure referred to by Gosche in the *ZDMG*, a former pupil of Hammer-Purgstall and a poet in his own right.[16] Rückert, however, was best known for his phenomenally successful verse work, *Die Weisheit des Brahmanen*,[17] and for his translations of the Quran and of the enduringly popular comic tales of Abu Muhammad al-Qasim ibn 'Ali al-Hariri (1054–1122).[18] The point of origin of the popularity of Rumi is less clear than that of the popularity of Hafiz.

As has been said, no data is available to measure the extent of the popularity of Rumi and Hafiz in the nineteenth century, but one indication of this that has recently come to my attention is that G.W.F. Hegel quoted Rumi at some length in his *Enzyklopädie der philosophischen Wissenschaften im Grundrisse* (1830).[19] The nature of the nineteenth-century reception, however, can be established, and has been discussed elsewhere. In summary, two crucial contexts are Deism and the Romantic Movement. Deism is no longer relevant, except in that it was one reason why Sufism came to be generally seen as an ancient and mysterious mystical tradition, probably older and greater than Islam.[20] The Romantic Movement, with its emphasis on subjective experience and individual self-discovery, remains very relevant, as will be seen.

The nature of the contemporary reception of these poets may be understood in two contexts, the first of which is purely aesthetic: Rumi and Hafiz wrote poetry that is, by any standards, superb, and have benefitted from talented translators. The same context exists in the Persian-speaking Muslim world, where both poets are read for their literary value as well as their religious message. This context has nothing to do with religion or spirituality, however, and so will not be further examined in this chapter.

The second context in which the continuing reception of Rumi and Hafiz may be understood is that of the popularity of spiritual works in general, not just of poetic works. Spirituality is one of four main categories of religious work recognized by the American book trade, the other three being "inspiration, prayer and Christian living." Spirituality is further subdivided between "tradition-based" and "cafeteria,"[21] the first being what scholars would generally call denominational or religious, and the second being non- or supra-denominational, sometimes called "supermarket" by scholars. In either case, the image is the same: of individuals constructing their own individual religious worlds out of disparate elements, often drawn from more than one religious tradition. The book trade's "tradition-based spirituality," then, is part of the scholar's religious category, and the book trade's "cafeteria spirituality" is the scholar's spiritual category. This chapter will follow general scholarly usage.

The distinction between religion and spirituality applies to both individuals and texts. When applied to texts, a distinction must be made between production and consumption. Rumi, probably a religious person (though we do not know), wrote within a denominational context, and can therefore be said to have produced religious texts. Mary Oliver, a popular contemporary American whose poems were described in *Publishers' Weekly* as "optimistic, clear and lyrical explorations of varying ecosystems ... mingled with rapt self-questioning, consolation and spiritual claims some might call prayers,"[22] is not writing within a denominational context, and can therefore be said to be producing spiritual texts. Rumi's poems can be said to be being consumed as religious texts if read within their original denominational context. When read outside that denominational context, as they almost always are in the West, they can be said to be being consumed as spiritual texts. Mary Oliver, who has no denominational context, can only be read as a spiritual text.

A person who reads spiritual texts need not necessarily be themselves non-denominational. Non-denominational spirituality, it is thought, also appeals to readers who belong to denominations, but want to "explore the depth dimension of the various religious traditions, not ignoring the fact there are significant differences or syncretizing them, but providing the richness of the various traditions," in the words of the editorial director of Ave Maria Press, a Catholic publisher.[23]

The second context for understanding the popularity of Rumi and Hafiz in the West, then, is the general popularity of religious and spiritual poetry. Two other best selling poets are Dante, whose *Divine Comedy* was in the top three best-selling poets in both markets, and Milton, whose *Paradise Lost* was in the top ten in both markets in 2007.[24] The single best-selling work of poetry in both America and Britain was Kahlil Gibran's *The Prophet*, once called "America's favorite birthday present."[25] Another popular poet in America is Mary Oliver, whose collection *Thirst* was in the American top five for much of 2007, and whose poems are, as we have seen, also spiritual texts. More than half of the top ten of America's best-selling poetry, then, is religious or spiritual.[26] The rest consists mostly of classic works such as *Beowolf* and the *Odyssey* which, given the periods in which they were composed, also have religious elements, and perhaps spiritual ones, but should probably be regarded as neither religious nor spiritual.

The popularity of Rumi and Hafiz, then, is long established in the West, and is related to the general popularity of spiritual texts, especially poetic ones.

Neo-Sufism

As has been said, the nineteenth century established Sufism in the Western consciousness as an ancient and mysterious mystical tradition, probably older and greater than Islam. The details of this tradition were not very clear to the general public, however. This allowed a number of religious leaders of the early twentieth century to legitimize their own teaching by reference to Sufism, sometimes with little real justification, as in the case of Georges Gurdjieff (1866–1949),[27] one of the most influential spiritual teachers of the century. Even when teachings and practice were closer to Sufism as found in the Muslim world, as in the case of Frithjof Schuon (1907–1998), there were still significant differences, as will be seen. It is for this reason that both varieties of Western Sufism – that represented by Schuon as well as that represented by Gurdjieff – are referred to as neo-Sufism.

This chapter limits itself to consideration of neo-Sufi groups that were most influential in the formation of the Western public's understanding of Sufism during the second half of the twentieth century.[28] The most important of these were the followers of Gurdjieff and Schuon, already mentioned, the "Sufi Order" established by Inayat Khan (1882–1927), the followers of Meher Baba (1894–1969), and the followers of Idries Shah (1924–1996). During the second part of the twentieth century, several further groups of neo-Sufis came into existence.[29] Some of these shared the main characteristics of the neo-Sufi groups already mentioned, but some did not. Those that did not will be labeled for convenience as "neo-orthodox," but will not be further discussed, as they are a topic in their own right that requires further research. The neo-orthodox groups are connected with the recent increase in availability in Western languages of classic theoretical Sufi works.

Although the teachings of these neo-Sufi groups varied widely, almost all had certain important points in common, as I have argued elsewhere.[30] These points have no equivalent in Sufism as found in the Muslim world, and derive from Western religiosity and spirituality. In summary, one common point, found everywhere save in Schuon's Maryamiyya and especially present in the Gurdjieff groups, was an emphasis on the individual spiritual search. Sufism in the Muslim world commonly emphasizes not the individual search, but the guided journey. Another common point was that all provided an answer to the problem of the plurality of religions, or – as some would put it – the plurality of religious forms. In very general terms, all presented Sufism as somehow above and beyond religions such as Christianity, Islam and Hinduism, building on the understanding of Sufism that had been established during the nineteenth century. It was an understanding that could be, and has been, supported by certain interpretations of Sufi teachings as found in the Muslim world, but the understanding as found in neo-Sufism is not found anywhere in the Muslim world itself.[31] One final point, more important in the interwar period than in the postwar period, was the provision of an explanation of the *Angst* and *anomie* felt by the interwar generation. This continued to play an important part in the Maryamiyya, but was less emphasized by other groups in the postwar period, and was never much present in the teachings of the one neo-Sufi of postwar origin, Idries Shah. *Angst* and *anomie* are not found in the same forms in the Muslim world, where their place is generally taken by a perception of being under attack from the West.

Of all the neo-Sufi groups that were well established in 1975, Schuon's Maryamiyya was closest to Sufism as found in the Muslim world. Its practice was almost identical with the latter, differing only in its approach to the Sharia. While Sufis in the Muslim world are mostly scrupulous in their attention to the Sharia, Maryamis were, on certain points, somewhat relaxed. Maryami teachings, however, differed from Sufism in the Muslim world by incorporating

Schuon's version of the Traditionalist philosophy of René Guénon, which included both an anti-modernist philosophy of history of part-Theosophical and part-Hindu origin, and a development of the European concept of the *philosophia perennis*, further developed by Schuon into the concept of the "transcendent unity of religions." According to this, all religions share a common primordial esoteric core, separate from the variety of exoteric forms. Sufism was, for the Maryamis, a way of accessing this primordial esoteric core.[32]

The teachings of Inayat Khan's "Sufi Order" were superficially quite distinct from those of Sufis as found in the Muslim world, presenting Sufism as something older than and separate from Islam, as "the essence of all religions and philosophies." Khan's early works are more likely to quote the Bible than the Quran. The *content* of his teachings, however, is far closer to Sufism as found in the Muslim world than is the *form* of his teachings. In a sense, Khan took Sufism and dressed it up as something other than Sufism in order to make it more palatable to modern Westerners. He is an example of a religious writer producing spiritual texts. The practice of his followers, however, included elements unknown in the Muslim world, notably the so-called "Universal Worship" of the "Church of All." There was also no suggestion that it was necessary to become Muslim or follow the Sharia. After Khan's death, that part of his following led by his son Vilayet became closer to Islamic norms.

The teachings and practices of Meher Baba at first had almost nothing to do with Sufism or Islam, except that he claimed a partly Sufi origin for his initial enlightenment in 1913. His message instead focused on his own person, and his self-presentation as an *avatar* or, in European languages, a divine incarnation. Given that God was incarnate in Meher Baba, logically all religions were also incarnate in him – or, as his followers would write, "Him." During the 1940s, however, Meher Baba took over an American branch of Khan's "Sufi Order,"[33] which became "Sufism Reoriented."[34] It is for this reason that Meher Baba is included in the category of neo-Sufism rather than neo-Hinduism.

Gurdjieff, like Meher Baba, claimed a partly Sufi provenance for his teachings and practice. Despite this, neither teachings nor practice bore much resemblance to Sufism as found in the Muslim world. It is hard to encapsulate his teachings, which focused on the need for, and the means to achieve, a certain variety of self-awareness. In sense, they institutionalized the individual spiritual quest. Practices included some elements probably drawn from Sufism, but rather more elements of which the derivation is not clear. Gurdjieff's self-awareness is not quite the same as self-discovery, but is related to it. It became an important stream within contemporary spirituality, as we will see. Gurdjieff is included in the category of neo-Sufism partly because he himself claimed a Sufi provenance, partly because one of his more important pupils, John Bennett, later became convinced that Gurdjieff was a Sufi,[35] and partly because of the influence he seems to have had over another important neo-Sufi, Idries Shah.

Idries Shah might be seen as close to Sufism in the Muslim world, because his teachings incorporated much of the corpus of classic Sufism. His teachings, however, drew on figures from the Muslim world not regarded there as Sufis, notably the apocryphal comic sage Nasr al-Din Khoja, called "Mullah Nasrudin" by Shah, following Indian rather than scholarly usage. Nasr al-Din is generally regarded in the Muslim world as a wise fool whose tales often make points that are profound, but are not particularly Sufi. Three of Shah's most successful books were devoted to Nasr al-Din as Sufi sage.[36] More importantly, Shah reinterpreted his sources into a form of general spiritual wisdom that resembled Gurdjieff more than anything found in the Muslim world. As has been said, Gurdjieff's pupil Bennett, who joined Shah in 1963–1964, became convinced that Gurdjieff was actually a Sufi. Perhaps it was more the case that Shah was a Gurdjieffian.[37]

Schuon, Inayat Khan, Meher Baba, Gurdjieff and Shah all attracted close followings, the precise sizes of which are unknown, but in most cases were probably in the region of 200–300 persons at any one time.[38] This is a typical size for any organization that depends on close personal contact. Growth beyond this size generally requires the setting up of a formal organizational structure of some sort, which only a few neo-Sufi leaders have done. The major exceptions are Khan's "Sufi Order" (which had a formal organizational structure), Schuon's Maryamiyya (which developed de facto branches in several countries), and Gurdjieff, whose teachings were widely followed after his death. Today, the Gurdjieff Foundation of New York lists 59 affiliated regional groups,[39] and many more are to be found elsewhere. The size of Gurdjieff's following worldwide may now be considerable. Otherwise, perhaps 100,000 people have joined the other neo-Sufi groups mentioned over the years – a relatively small number in comparison to the millions who have read neo-Sufi works.

The extent of the readership of neo-Sufi works

There is no generally accepted system of classification for book sales other than the somewhat vague category of "best-seller." Four more precise categories will be used in this section: blockbusters, major sellers, strong sellers and occasional sellers. Blockbusters will be defined as books on the standard best-seller lists and just off these lists, in Amazon's top 1,000 sales.[40] Examples include Elizabeth Gilbert's *Eat, Pray, Love*, a book in which "a writer's yearlong journey in search of self takes her to Italy, India and Indonesia," which happened to be number one in the *New York Times* non-fiction paperback list when this chapter was being written,[41] Coelho's *The Alchemist* and C.S. Lewis's *Mere Christianity*.[42] These blockbusters may sell in the tens of millions if they remain in the blockbuster category for more than a few months. Coelho's *The Alchemist*, for example, sold 65 million copies worldwide between 1993 and 2005.[43] Books that sell in such numbers are books that "everyone has read"– or almost everyone.

Below blockbusters come major sellers, which will be defined as in Amazon's next top 25,000. At the top of this range come books like Hesse's *Siddhartha, The Essential Rumi* and the *Bhagavad Gita*;[44] in the middle comes Coelho's *Veronika*;[45] and at the bottom end comes Karen Armstrong's *History of God*.[46] Some of these, including Hesse's *Siddartha*, are former blockbusters.

Others are extremely popular books that never, however, achieved blockbuster status. They are not books that "everyone" has read, but they are important books that very many people have read.

The remaining two categories of strong and occasional sellers distinguish between books that are well established or even classics but less widely read, and books that have only limited readerships. Strong sellers will be defined as those between Amazon's top 25,000 and Amazon's top 250,000, and range from Teresa of Avila's *The Way of Perfection* and Edward Said's *Covering Islam* at the top end,[47] to Sayyid Qutb's *Social Justice in Islam* and Ira M. Lapidus's *A History of Islamic Societies* at the bottom end.[48] Strong sellers are less widely read and less influential than blockbusters or major sellers, but are still of real importance. Books defined as occasional sellers are the rest, ranging from books that are established but of interest only to specialized audiences, such as Thomas Merton's classic *Seven Storey Mountain* and Ignaz Goldziher's *Introduction to Islamic Theology and Law,*[49] to works of limited interest such as Constance Padwick's classic work *Muslim Devotions* and *Meister Eckhart: A Modern Translation.*[50]

According to Amazon's data for the US and the UK, the best-selling neo-Sufi authors in both markets are from the Gurdjieff tradition. Gurdjieff's *Beelzebub's Tales to His Grandson* and *In Search of the Miraculous* by Gurdjieff's follower P.I. Ouspensky are both in the major sellers category. Gurdjieff's other main books, *Meetings with Remarkable Men* and *Life Is Real Only Then, When I Am*, only just fall short of this category.[51] No other neo-Sufi group or author sells so well, just as no other neo-Sufi group seems to have such a large following.

To some extent, the sales of Gurdjieff's and Ouspensky's books are a function of the size of their following. Groups such as these generate sales, both directly and indirectly (as recommendations pass through social networks). "The ideal [spiritual] writer," according to the executive editor at the publisher Harper San Francisco, "is somebody who does workshops and retreats and also has something distinct to say."[52] Gurdjieff's popularity must also, however, be a function of his teachings and of his writing style. As has been said, his teachings emphasize self-awareness and are in a sense an institutionalization of the individual spiritual quest. His writing style is also highly original. He does not lecture, but tells intriguing stories. Gurdjieff can be read for entertainment, then, as well as for spiritual content, rather as Rumi can be read for poetic quality as well as for spiritual content.

After Gurdjieff, the next best selling neo-Sufi author is now Shah. Shah's contemporary followers claim that his works have sold "15 million copies in 12 languages."[53] The data to confirm or deny this is not available, but there are three possible reasons to suppose that at one stage Shah may indeed have been in the major sellers or even the blockbuster category. One is that Shah's teachings are in some ways close to Gurdjieff, and so might be expected to share Gurdjieff's appeal. Full investigation of this line of enquiry, however, would require more space than the present chapter allows. A second reason is that Shah, like Gurdjieff, may sometimes be read for entertainment. This is especially true of his three books on Nasr al-Din as Sufi sage.

The third and more easily demonstrated reason for supposing that Shah may once have been a blockbuster is his publishing history. After publishing his first major book, *The Sufis*, with W.H. Allen in 1964, Shah moved to Jonathan Cape, then one of England's biggest publishers, in 1966.[54] He published nearly all of his most important works with Cape, seven books in all, between 1966 and 1973.[55] Four of these seven books went into paperback editions, either with Penguin or with Pan, and five had separate US editions with major US publishers.[56] After 1973, however, Shah began to publish with his own "captive" publisher, Octagon Press.[57] This shift might indicate that he had decided to take control of his own publishing, or it might indicate that Cape was no longer as interested in Shah's new work as it once had been, presumably because of falling sales. The second explanation seems more likely, since only one of the 13 new titles published by Octagon after the end of Shah's relationship with Cape had a paperback edition, and only four have US editions. For comparison, it will be remembered, more than half of the new titles published with Cape had these indicators of significant sales. Even if it was Shah who became dissatisfied with Cape rather than Cape who lost interest in Shah, it might be expected that the distribution networks and marketing power of publishers such as Cape, Penguin and Simon and Schuster would achieve higher sales than Shah's own Octagon Press would.[58] The implication, then, is that Shah's sales in the late 1960s and early 1970s were much higher than they are today.

All the other main neo-Sufi authors fell into the strong sellers category, as is shown in the Appendix, with the exception of Frithjof Schuon, whose works are only occasional sellers (save, perhaps, in France).[59] This is not surprising, as Schuon's work can certainly not be read for entertainment. It is not considered easy even by its enthusiasts. Several of Schuon's followers, however, wrote more popular books, notably Martin Lings, Seyyed Hossein Nasr and Huston Smith, all of whom are at the top end of the strong sellers category.[60] Smith's *The World's Religions* has sold 2,500,000 copies[61] since its first publication in 1958, and currently ranks as a blockbuster, but its first edition was written before Smith discovered Schuon, and its current, revised edition shows only some signs of Schuon's influence.[62]

Shah, then, may once have sold as well as Hermann Hesse or even Paulo Coelho now do. Gurdjieff's own writings, though not in the Coelho or the Rumi category, are within reach of Hesse in popularity, and sell better than Teresa of Avila or Thomas à Kempis.[63] Inayat Khan is widely read, as are some of the authors who followed Frithjof Schuon, if not Schuon himself. Neo-Sufi works, then, do have a significant readership, though it is smaller than the readership of classic Sufi poetry.

As with Sufi poetry, this may be understood in different contexts. Just as Rumi may be read as a fine poet, Gurdjieff and some of Shah's books may be read for entertainment. And just as Rumi's popularity may be understood in terms of the popularity of spiritual works in general, so may the popularity of some neo-Sufis, as will be shown.

Neo-Sufi-inspired novels

During the nineteenth century, Goethe was inspired by Hafiz, as were other lesser literary figures. During the twentieth century, a number of major novelists have been inspired by neo-Sufism. The neo-Sufi-inspired novel is almost a genre in its own right in the West, with no equivalent in the Muslim world, where – as has been said – novel reading is generally far less popular.

"Few books can boast glowing reviews from both Stevie Smith and Ted Hughes on the back cover, and an introduction by Robert Graves," wrote one anonymous diarist on discovering Idries Shah's *The Sufis*.[64] The endorsements were slightly curious (Stevie Smith: "vastness of learning and exposition that calls to our patience – and perhaps to our loss if it calls in vain;"[65] Ted Hughes: "An astonishing book. The Sufis must be the biggest society of sensible men on earth")[66] but the introduction by Robert Graves was clearly enthusiastic. Graves was born in 1895, however, and was already 65 when he first met Idries Shah. Most of his writing was by then already done, and his main role was to add some lustre to Idries Shah's name by association, rather as Gurdjieff gained fame from his association with Katherine Mansfield, or Meher Baba gained fame from his association with the rock guitarist Pete Townshend.

Idries Shah's association with Doris Lessing is more important. Lessing, born in 1919 and known for books such as *The Grass is Singing* (1950) and *The Four-Gated City* (1969), and for her Nobel prize for literature (2007), met Idries Shah early in her writing career. It is generally agreed, both by literary critics and the notes accompanying her Nobel prize,[67] that Shah exercised an important influence over her work from the 1960s onwards. The critics are less sure, however, quite what this influence was, or indeed – quite what Sufism is. "For a non-Sufi to understand what it means to be a Sufi is perhaps impossible," wrote Nancy Shields Hardin, evidently a literature professor and author of the standard article on Lessing's Sufism.[68] Another critic understands Lessing in terms of gnosticism, seeing Shah's Sufism as the possible origin of this, and comparing Lessing's *Briefing for a Descent into Hell* with Hesse's *Damian*.[69]

To go one step further and establish what influence Lessing's novels might have on their readers is probably impossible. Eight readers have left comments on Amazon on *The Four-Gated City*, one of the novels analyzed as "Sufi" by Shields Hardin. Most are unhelpful: "I've read it over 6 times, I would guess, and I keep finding fascinating insights," does not get one very far. Only one comment attempts a summary: "I believe that the common motif ... is her conviction that human evil is primarily caused by a lack of human self-awareness, and is therefore something that can be overcome." This suggests that the reader in question had found Gurdjieff in Lessing, possibly transmitted through Shah, or possibly read in to Lessing from outside. Lessing is a complex writer, with no single message that can easily be extracted.

A further widely read novelist on whom Shah evidently had an impact is Paulo Coelho. Coelho's *Veronika Decides to Die* is categorized by Suroosh Irfani, to whom we will return, as a novel of "surrender and rebirth."[70] The rebirth of the central character, Veronika is preceded by the advice of a Sufi teacher who bases his lesson around "Nasrudin, the great master of the Sufi tradition."[71] As we have seen, Nasr al-Din is not considered a Sufi master in the Muslim world, and is so regarded in the West entirely due to Shah, whose spelling Coelho also follows. Shah, then, must be Coelho's source. Nasrudin not only features in *Veronika*, but also makes periodic appearances on Coelho's blog.[72] A full study of Coelho's work would be required to establish the exact extent of Shah's influence, but it is certainly there. Strangely, given Coelho's vast readership, there is at present almost no critical or scholarly literature on him.

It is somewhat easier to discern about the influence that Coelho's novels might have on their readers than it is to speculate about Lessing's possible influence, because Coelho's message is more explicit. The subtitle of the English translation of his most popular book, *The Alchemist*, is *A Fable About Following Your Dream*, and to follow your dream is the essence of Coelho's message. When speaking to a large audience about his life and work in 2005, Coelho used this phrase more than two dozen times in one hour.[73] It is much the advice that the Sufi teacher gives Veronika: "Allow the real 'I' to reveal itself," he tells the group Veronika has joined. "What is the real 'I'?" asks Veronica. "It's what you are, not what others make of you," replies the teacher.[74] Coelho's message is clear, then. The nature of that message will be discussed below.

Sufism and neo-Sufism in Western spirituality

Sufi poetry, then, is religious, but generally read as spiritual. Neo-Sufi works may be religious or spiritual, but are generally read as spiritual texts, as are neo-Sufi-inspired novels.

"Spiritual," however, is a very general term. Some increased precision can be gained using data from Amazon, which increases sales by making suggestions to its customers. For each individual book, there is a list of other books, headed "Customers Who Bought This Item Also Bought."[75] The basis on which these lists are constructed is not known, as it is regarded by Amazon as commercially sensitive information. The results, however, frequently correspond to what would be expected on some other basis. Buyers of one volume of Rumi frequently buy other volumes of Rumi, or of Hafiz, for example.[76] Given this, "Also Bought" data is of significance, and can be used to trace readership patterns. More precise data derived on a known basis would of course be preferable, but is not available.[77]

According to this data, buyers of Hafiz and Rumi mostly buy Hafiz and Rumi, but they also buy Mary Oliver, Rilke and Kahlil Gibran.[78] Of these links, that with Gibran is strongest.[79] Buyers of Gibran, in turn, buy two other big names in contemporary Western spirituality, Hermann Hesse and Paulo Coelho.[80]

The Pakistani scholar Suroosh Irfani[81] has argued that there are important common themes linking Hesse, Coelho, Hafiz and Rumi. Irfani's argument was prompted by his discovery of a Persian translation of Coelho's *Veronika Decides to Die* in a bookshop in Shiraz, the home city of Hafiz and also the city in which Irfani, as a young man, had first been introduced to Hesse's *Demian*, and thence to *Steppenwolf*. Irfani compared the odyssey of Coelho's Veronika to that of Hesse's Harry Haller, and to the "'ruination' as a prelude to surrender and rebirth [which] runs through the works of Jalaluddin Rumi." This, perhaps, is the most important context in which to understand Western enthusiasm for Rumi and Hafiz, as well as for Coelho and Hesse. Gurdjieff and Shah might well be put in the same context.

This context, however, is distinctively Western, as an analysis of Veronika's surrender and rebirth will illustrate. Although the words of Coelho's Sufi teacher, who tells Veronika to discover her "real 'I,'" might be found in the mouth of Shah or Gurdjieff, they would not be found in the mouth of a Sufi shaikh in the Muslim world. As has been said, Sufism in the Muslim world emphasizes the guided journey rather than the individual search. Sufism in the Muslim world is also interested in the "I," but as the *nafs* or ego. The fundamental objective of Sufism in the Muslim world is to subjugate the ego, not to discover it.

The nature of Veronika's surrender and rebirth is also distinctively Western. One of the most striking aspects of her surrender is that it involves semi-public masturbation,[82] an activity that perhaps fits with the discovery of the ego, but hardly fits with the subjugation of the ego, let alone the cultural norms of the Muslim world or the Sharia. Veronika's rebirth is also Western. Sufis in the Muslim world surrender to God. In the culminating scene in Coelho's book, Veronika answers "I do" when asked whether she believes in God, but only a few lines later she "ask[s] the God she did *not* believe in [my emphasis] to take her at that very moment." She then dies, but is reborn.[83] If there is any god involved in this, it is the "god within her."

Veronika's surrender and rebirth is an extreme example, but does illustrate the distance between certain varieties of Western spirituality and Sufism as found in the Muslim world. Coelho is bought by some people who buy Gibran, and some people who buy Gibran buy Rumi. Some people who buy Rumi buy Shah, and some people who buy Shah buy Gurdjieff.[84] It is not known how many people have Coelho, Gibran, Rumi, Shah and Gurdjieff together on their bookshelves, but anyone who did might be expected to read all of them in a similar, distinctively Western, way.

Conclusions

This chapter has placed the popularity of Sufi and neo-Sufi texts in the context of contemporary Western spirituality, as well as of contemporary Western tastes in poetry. These two contexts are not mutually exclusive, since people interested in surrender and rebirth or seeking to "explore the depth dimensions of the various religious traditions" may also be attracted by fine poetry. These two contexts are, I would argue, a more appropriate way of understanding the popularity of Sufi and neo-Sufi literature in the West than an analysis in terms of, for example, a "revolt against rationality and the crisis of liberalism."[85] Certainly, poetry is not particularly associated with modern industrial democracies, but this does not make appreciation of poetry an espousal of counter-Enlightenment.

One other way of understanding this is in terms of globalization. The nineteenth century was arguably the most dramatic period of globalization, since it was the period during which previously separate regional systems came together for the first time into a single global system. This was one factor in the increased availability in the West of non-Western literature, including Sufi poetry. Globalization also implies "localization," however, as any of today's global businesses know well. A global product must be adapted for local circumstances and tastes. Sufism became a global product in the nineteenth century, and during the twentieth century was localized for Western consumption by the neo-Sufis this chapter has discussed.

Localization for Western consumption may be deliberate, as in the case of Inayat Khan, the religious writer who produced spiritual texts. Whether or not there is deliberate localization, however, localization happens at the point of consumption. Rumi and Hafiz, Gurdjieff and Shah, when not read for their literary qualities or as entertainment, are read for their spiritual content, sometimes by Westerners who are also reading Kahlil Gibran, Paulo Coelho, Hermann Hesse and Mary Oliver.

Appendix

Table 11.1 shows some significant differences between the US and the UK for all groups. In the US, for example, Inayat Khan sells better than his son Vilayat; in the UK it is the other way round. In the US, Meher Baba sometimes sells well (his September 2007 rank was much higher than his October 2007 one), and in the UK he hardly sells at all. These differences correspond with the institutional histories of the groups in question. Inayat Khan founded his "Sufi Order" in Europe (in 1916), but after his death, this split into two main branches and one smaller branch.[88] One, called "The Sufi Order International," was led principally by his son, Vilayat (1916–2004), and was based in Europe, with branches in North America. It is in Europe (or at least in the UK) that Vilayat sells best. Meher Baba sells best in the US, where his following is based. This suggests that the institutional presence of a neo-Sufi order in a particular location may have a significant impact on its book sales in that area. As was noted in the body of this

Table 11.1 Strong sellers in neo-Sufism, 2007[86]

Author	Main title	US rank	UK rank
Idries Shah	*Tales of the Dervishes*	37,000	350,000
	Wisdom of the Idiots	110,000	150,000
Meher Baba	*Discourses*	75,000 in September (300,000 in October)[87]	1,000,000
Inayat Khan	*The Art of Being and Becoming*	145,000	285,000
Vilayat Khan (son of Inayat Khan)	*Awakening*	230,000	33,000

chapter, such a presence generates local sales directly and indirectly. In the cases of Inayat Khan and Meher Baba, an additional factor may be the location of their own publishing houses, and so of sales efforts. Since 1982, Inayat Khan's main publisher has been his Order's subsidiary Omega, based in New York, serving the US market where his books now sell best. Since 1952, Meher Baba has been published by Sufism Reoriented, again in the market where he sells best.[89]

Notes

1 Parts of this chapter were first given as a paper, "European Neo-Sufi Movements in the Immediate Postwar Period," at the annual meeting of the European Association for the Study of Religions, Bremen, September 23–27, 2007.

2 Marcia Z. Nelson, "Islamic Publishing is Poised for Growth," *Publishers' Weekly* November 13, 2000. Online, available at: www.publishersweekly.com/article/CA168805.html.

3 *A Sufi Saint in the Twentieth Century, Shaikh Ahmad al-Alawi: His Spiritual Heritage and Legacy.* Various editions.

4 The term "neo-Sufism" is, confusingly, used by scholars in two very different senses. In Islamic Studies, it refers to a form of Sufism that emerged in the Arab world during the eighteenth century, and was most influential during the nineteenth century. For this variety of neo-Sufism, see O'Fahey (1994) and Sedgwick (2005). In the study of Western Esotericism, it refers to a form of Sufism that emerged in the West during the first decades of the twentieth century, and became influential after World War II. Both forms of Sufism differed significantly from the then norm, but in very different ways. This chapter deals with the Western form; the Islamic form is mentioned only for the sake of clarity, and to illustrate how Sufism has taken different forms in different times and places, in the Muslim world as well as in the West. Ron Geaves prefers to avoid confusion by using the term "universal Sufism" when referring to the Western form (Geaves 2000). However, although universalism is characteristic of many Western neo-Sufis, it is not found in all cases.

5 There are numerous industry sources, from Nielsen Bookscan to the Association of American Publishers. However, their data focuses on new works, not classic ones, and is priced at publishing companies, not academic researchers.

6 Once again, precise market share is not known. There may also be differences between the habits of US and UK readers who shop on Amazon and who shop at other online stores, or offline. Readers born before 1950, for example, are probably generally less likely to shop online.

7 Inayat Khan, for example, is now mostly available online. In 2002, Wahiduddin Richard Shelquist of Longmont, Colorado, started putting the collected works on his website, a task now mostly completed. See wahiduddin.net. Dates from the Internet Archive.

8 Google Trends (www.google.com/trends) reports the origin of Internet searches for selected high-volume search terms. Between 2004 and 2007, the countries from which most searches including "Gurdjieff" came (as a percentage of total searches) were Italy, Chile and Argentina, followed by Mexico. English was sixth in the list of languages in which searches originated.

9 Google Trends shows Argentina beating Indonesia and Turkey, with North America coming next. The margin is so great that there is a possibility that Argentines searching for "Rumi" may be looking for something other than the Sufi poet. There is, for example, a popular nightclub and restaurant of that name in the Belgrano district of Buenos Aires. Although the nightclub/restaurant is named after the poet, an interest in it need not indicate an interest in Sufism! As this problem indicates, data such as this must be used with care, and can be misleading even when used with care.

10 Writers connected to Schuon are known to have been widely read in Iran and Turkey (Sedgwick 2004). Other neo-Sufi writers are also read from time to time in the Muslim world.

11 Where a specific source for data such as this is not given, it has been calculated from Amazon.com and Amazon.co.uk in September and October 2007. The poetry rankings were also checked in June 2007. Collections of poetry by more than one poet, often evidently intended for use in schools, have been ignored. Rumi is often referred to as America's best-selling poet, a view that derives from Marcia Nelson: "Despite the fact that Rumi has been dead for 700 years, he is commonly thought to be America's current bestselling poet" ("Islamic Publishing"). Amazon data suggests that this is an exaggeration.

12 *Der Diwan von Mohammed Schemsed-Din Hafis, Aus dem Persischen zum erstenmal ganz übersetzt*, 2 vols, Stuttgart and Tübingen.

13 An entry for "Hafez, The Works of, with an Account of his Life and Writings. fol. Calcutta, 1791" appears in *a Catalogue of the Library of the Hon. East-India Company* (London, 1845), p. 223. This seems to be the earliest translation into a European language. Another early translation is Harding, West and Hughes, *Persian Lyrics, or Scattered Poems, from the Diwan-l-Hafis: with Paraphrases in Verse and Prose, a Catalogue of the Gazels as Arranged in a Manuscript of the Works of Hafiz, in the Chatham Library at Manchester, and Other Illustrations* (London, 1800).

14 Gosche (1860).

15 Pages 243–550 in the 1819 edition.

16 *Dschelaleddin: Ghaselen* (Stuttgart, 1819). I have not been able to consult this volume, which is mentioned in a number of sources, but does not appear on the standard bibliography at www.rueckert-gesellschaft.de/bibliographie.html. The history of Rumi's translation into European languages is harder to establish than that of Hafiz. He was mentioned by Hammer-Purgstall in 1818 in his *Geschichte der schönen Redekünste Persiens*, which I have been unable to consult. This reference is given by August Tholuck, *Ssufismus sive Theosophia Persarum pantheistica, quam e MSS. Bibliothecæ regiæ Berolinensis persicis, arabicis, turcicis eruit atque illustravit* (Berlin, 1821), p. 2.

17 Leipzig: Weidmann, 1836–1839.

18 *Die Verwandlungen des Abu Seid von Serug oder die Makamen des Hariri* (Stuttgart and Tübingen, 1837). Hariri's *Maqamat* were as popular in the Middle East as they became in Europe, where they were partly translated (into Latin) in 1656, by Golius. D.S. Margoliouth, "Al-Hariri." Margoliouth evidently did not himself much like them: "The reasons for this extraordinary success, which gave rise to countless imitations in Arabic, in Persian, and even in Hebrew and in Syriac, are somewhat difficult to understand and must be accounted for by the decline of literary taste."

19 G.W.F. Hegel (1970) vol. 10, p. 386. For this reference, I am indebted to Cyrus Bina and Mo Vaziri, "On the Dialectic of Rumi's Discourse," revised draft of a paper presented at the Rumi 2000 Conference "Whirling with the Cosmos," October 26–28, 2000, California State University, San Bernardino, CA. Online, available at: http://cda.morris.umn.edu/~binac/Essays/RUMI.FINAL.pdf.

20 Sedgwick (2007).

21 Marcia Z. Nelson, "Gimme That Old-Time Spirituality: Seekers Sift Ancient Traditions for Everyday Help," *Publishers' Weekly* March 22, 2004. Online, available at: www.publishersweekly.com/index.asp?layout=articlePrint&articleID=CA404149.

22 Reprinted on Amazon.com,

23 Robert M. Hamma, quoted in Nelson, "Gimme That Old-Time Spirituality."

24 Both were written within a Christian denominational context, and are being read by readers who were presumably mostly brought up within a Christian denomination al context. They may therefore be being read as religious texts, or as spiritual texts. This is a question that this chapter will not address.

25 Gibran has also been characterized by his editor and biographer, Robin Waterfield, as the "guru of the New Age". Waterfield (1998: back cover).
26 Again, this excludes multi-author collections.
27 Sedgwick (2008).
28 The selection was initially based on factors such as general quantity of references and presence in the catalogs of medium-sized libraries. It was confirmed by the "Also Bought" tests described later in this article. Other groups revealed by this were all most influential after 1990.
29 Newcomers included the Subud movement, M.R. Bawa Muhaiyaddeen and – most importantly – Kabir Helminski.
30 Sedgwick (2008). The following summaries are taken from this chapter.
31 This statement would, of course, be disputed by neo-Sufis.
32 The Maryamiyya and its context is studied in detail in Sedgwick (2004).
33 That led first by Rabia Martin (d. 1947) and then by Ivy Oneita Duce (1895–1981).
34 For this period, see Robbins and Anthony (1972).
35 Sedgwick (2008).
36 *The Exploits of the Incomparable Mulla Nasrudin* (London: Cape, 1966), *The Pleasantries of the Incredible Mulla Nasrudin* (London: Cape, 1968), and *The Subtleties of the Inimitable Mulla Nasrudin* (London: Cape, 1973).
37 This is a provisional judgment. Shah is not dealt with in "European Neo-Sufi Movements," and requires further study.
38 This is my own personal estimate, based more on feeling than on actual data.
39 "Groups affiliated with the Gurdjieff Foundation of New York," www.gurdjieff foundation-newyork.org/affiliate2.html, accessed October 21, 2007.
40 The top 20 books in the *New York Times*' Paperback Nonfiction list for October 28, 2007 were in Amazon's top 1,000. Some books around number 30 in the *New York Times*' list were only in Amazon's top 10,000.
41 *New York Times*' Paperback Nonfiction, October 28, 2007, www.nytimes. com/2007/10/28/books/bestseller/1028bestpapernonfiction.html.
42 These older works are not tracked by standard best-seller lists. *The Alchemist* was at number 120 and number 189 on Amazon.com in September and October 2007, and *Mere Christianity* at number 444 and number 458.
43 Alan Riding, "Brazilian's Missives from a Dream World," *International Herald Tribune* September 3, 2005. The original source of this figure, often quoted, is not clear, but Coelho's publisher HarperCollins gives 85 million as total sales for all books (www.harpercollins.com/authors/1858/Paulo_Coelho/index.aspx), so 65 million for his best-selling book seems reasonable. The book was first published in 1988, but the English translation was published in 1993.
44 Numbers 1,110, 3,705 and 5,296, respectively in October 2007.
45 13,432 in October 2007.
46 25,668 in October and so technically just outside this category, but even so the best available example of the bottom end of this range.
47 Number 33,843 in September 2007 and 45,476 in October.
48 Number 130,174 and 186,020 in October 2007.
49 Number 270,962 and 272,621 in September 2007.
50 Number 1,298,500 and 1,566,090 in September 2007.
51 Numbers 21, 659, 22,735, 54,805 and 37,860, respectively in October 2007.
52 John Loudon, quoted in Nelson, "Gimme that Old-Time Spirituality."
53 http://ishk.net/sufis//shah.html.
54 His first ever book, *Oriental Magic*, was published in 1956 by a somewhat obscure London publisher, Rider, who had also published Inayat Khan.
55 Cape also republished *The Sufis*. This information is taken from bibliographies prepared from the Library of Congress, the British Library and the Bodleian Library.

56   Simon and Schuster and, more often, Dutton.
57   Established in London in 1966–1967. 1967 was the date of its first publication, a reprint of Shah's *Oriental Magic*.
58   Captive presses, however, do serve a function, just as academic presses do: they ensure that works that have small readerships become and remain available.
59   Amazon.fr was not regularly used as a source of data, for reasons given above. That Schuon's *Transcendent Unity of Religions* was Amazon.fr's number 44,003 in September 2007 may nor may not be significant. It was number 320,506 on Amazon.com.
60   Their best-selling books in October 2007 were, in order, *Muhammad* (34,842), *The Garden of Truth* (33,757) and *Islam* (62,376).
61   According to www.hustonsmith.net, which can probably be believed.
62   Sedgwick (2004: 166).
63   Teresa of Avila, *The Way of Perfection*, was at number 33,843, and Thomas a Kempis, *The Imitation of Christ*, was at number 96,801, in October 2007.
64   www.otherlanguages.org/logs/2004m07julylanguagelist.htm.
65   *The Observer*, November 1, 1964, quoted on Amazon.com.
66   According to www.octagonpress.com/titles/books/sufi.htm. I have not been able to consult a copy of the original 1964 edition.
67   Swedish Academy, "Biobibliographical Notes," http://nobelprize.org/nobel_prizes/literature/laureates/2007/bio-bibl.html.
68   "Doris Lessing and the Sufi Way," *Contemporary Literature* 14 (1973), p. 566. Shields Hardin's difficulty probably results mostly from Shah's conception of Sufism, and possibly ultimately reflects the Gurdjieff method.
69   Robert Galbreath (1981: 24).
70   Suroosh Irfani, "Veronica, Rumi and Steppenwolf," *Dawn* [Karachi], February 19, 2002. www.dawn.com/weekly/books/archive/020217/books7.htm.
71   Paulo Coelho (1999: 87).
72   Four in 2007. http://paulocoelhoblog.com, accessed November 3, 2007.
73   Personal observation, Cairo, May 2005.
74   Coelho (1999: 92).
75   Amazon actually makes two types of suggestions. The other – and less useful – type is "recommendations," evidently based on each individual's previous purchases form Amazon. Since individuals commonly only buy some of their books on Amazon, and may also – for example – buy presents for friends and relatives there, these recommendations are sometimes rather strange.
76   Similarly, buyers of Gurdjieff often also buy Ouspensky, and buyers of Ouspensky buy Gurdjieff. See below for these authors.
77   Publishers have carried out studies, one of which is discussed in Elizabeth Puttick (2005: 139–140). This study dealt with the whole Mind-Body-Spirit market however, not the neo-Sufi part of it. Puttick's article is a rare example of an approach to the study of religion that is, I believe, extremely fruitful.
78   Amazon, October 2007.
79   Readers of Gibran buy Rumi, and readers of Rumi and Hafiz buy Gibran, making three links. Mary Oliver and Rilke have mostly one link, and Rilke has that link only in the UK.
80   It is interesting that Google Trends reports most searches for Hesse coming from the German-speaking world (unsurprisingly) and then – again – from Latin America (Chile, Mexico, Argentina). That Coelho is most searched for in Latin America is unsurprising.
81   He teaches in the Graduate Programme in Communication and Cultural Studies at National College of Arts, Lahore, Pakistan.
82   Coelho (1999: 121).
83   Coelho (1999: 186–187).
84   Amazon "Also Bought," September and October 2007.

85 Thomas Lacquer (2006: 112). Lacquer was talking of Western esotericism rather than neo-Sufism, of course.
86 September and October 2007, averaged and rounded.
87 The significant differences between September and October 2007 illustrate the imprecise nature of the data used.
88 The smaller branch was that led by Samuel Lewis (1896–1971) and called Sufi Ruhaniat International. It was based in San Francisco, where its heyday was in the 1960s.
89 Publishing histories are based on an examination of bibliographies compiled from the catalogs of the Library of Congress, the British Library and the Bodleian Library.

References

Coelho, Paul, *Veronika Decides to Die* (London: HarperCollins, 1999).

Galbreath, Robert, "Problematic Gnosis: Hesse, Singer, Lessing, and the Limitations of Modern Gnosticism," *Journal of Religion* 61 (1981).

Geaves, Ron, *Sufis of Britain* (Cardiff: Cardiff University Press, 2000).

Gosche, Richard, "Wissenschaftlicher Jahresbericht für 1857 und 1858," *Zeitschrift der Deutschen morgenländischen Gesellschaft* 14 (1860), p. 137.

Hegel, G.W.F., *Werke in 20 Bänden* (Frankfurt am Main: Suhrkamp, 1970) vol. 10.

Lacquer, Thomas, "Why The Margins Matter: Occultism and the Making of Modernity," *Modern Intellectual History* 3, no. 1 (April 2006).

Lings, Martin, *A Sufi Saint in the Twentieth Century, Shaikh Ahmad al-Alawi: His Spiritual Heritage and Legacy* (Islamic Texts Society, 1993).

Margoliouth, Golius D.S., "Al-Hariri (sometimes Ibn al-Hariri in Yaqut), Abu Muhammad al-Qasim b. Ali b. Muhammad b. Uthman b. al-Hariri al-Basri." *Encyclopaedia of Islam*, second edition (Leiden: Brill).

O'Fahey, R.S., *Enigmatic Saint: Ahmad Ibn Idris and the Idrisi Tradition* (Evanston: Northwestern University Press, 1994).

Puttick, Elizabeth, "The Rise of Mind-Body-Spirit Publishing: Reflecting or Creating Spiritual Trends?" *Journal of Alternative Spiritualities and New Age Studies* 1 (2005).

Robbins, Thomas and Anthony, Dick, "Getting Straight with Meher Baba: A Study of Mysticism, Drug Rehabilitation and Postadolescent Role Conflict," *Journal for the Scientific Study of Religion* 11, no. 2 (June 1972), pp. 122–140.

Sedgwick, Mark, *Against the Modern World: Traditionalism and the Secret Intellectual History of the Twentieth Century* (New York: Oxford University Press, 2004), pp. 249–257.

Sedgwick, Mark, *Saints and Sons: The Making and Remaking of the Rashidi Ahmadi Sufi Order, 1799–2000* (Leiden: Brill, 2005).

Sedgwick, Mark, "Quelques sources du xviii siècle du pluralisme religieux inclusif," in *Etudes d'histoire de l'ésotérisme: mélanges offerts à Jean-Pierre Laurent*, Jean-Pierre Brach and Jérôme Rousse-Lacordaire, eds. (Paris: Editions du Cerf, 2007), pp. 49–65.

Sedgwick, Mark, "European Neo-Sufi Movements in the Interwar Period," in *Islam in Interwar Europe: Networks, Status, Challenges*, Nathalie Clayer and Eric Germain, eds. (London: Hurst, 2008).

Shah, Idries, *The Exploits of the Incomparable Mulla Nasrudin* (London: Cape, 1966).

Shah, Idries, *The Pleasantries of the Incredible Mulla Nasrudin* (London: Cape, 1968).

Shah, Idries, *The Subtleties of the Inimitable Mulla Nasrudin* (London: Cape, 1973).

Waterfield, Robin, *Prophet: The Life and Times of Kahlil Gibran* (London: Allen Lane, 1998).

Glossary

Adab   Ideal behaviour or customary practice used by Sufis to describe the way in which *murids* model themselves on their *shaikh*. It is also used to describe practices unique to the respective *tariqa*.

Adhan   The call to prayer that takes place five times daily, usually from the minaret of the mosque.

Akham al-Tajwid   Making a voiceless break at a Qur'anic word for a brief moment, during which the reader takes a breath with the intention of continuing reading.

Alim   Singular of *ulama*, a learned man, usually used for a religious scholar or graduate of a *madrasa*.

Anashid Diniyya   Measured melodic singing of mystical or devotional poetry.

Aqida   Belief or set of doctrines usually associated with a particular *madhdab* or movement.

Arba'in   Known to Urdu-speaking Muslims as Chehlum, a Shi'a Muslim religious holiday that takes place 40 days after the Day of Ashura, the commemoration of the martyrdom of Husayn bin Ali.

Aurad/Wird(pl)   Repeated recitations of the names and characteristics of Allah, usually unique to a *tariqa*.

Awliya   A 'friend of Allah', usually used for a Sufi or deeply spiritual Muslim who has attained mystical proximity to God.

Baraka   The power to bless given to an *awliya* by Allah. It can be received through physical contact or prayer at a shrine. The tomb or sacred relics may also be endowed with *baraka*.

Batin   The Interior or hidden meaning of the Qur'an.

Baya   Oath of allegiance taken on the hand of a *shaikh* when becoming a *murid*.

Bida   An illegal innovation in religion.

Biraderi   South Asian clan or extended family networks.

Bust   Ritual hand clappers in the Burhaniya *hadra*.

Dawa   Propagation of Islam to both Muslims and non-Muslims.

Dhakirin   Dhikr performers in the Burhaniya *Hadra*.

Dhikr   The remembrance of Allah usually referred to as the continuous and rhythmic repetition of God's names.

Dikra   A form of traditional music found in Egypt and other parts of North Africa.

Din   Revealed religion that constitutes a comprehensive, all-inclusive way of life.

Djafr   A specialist literature concerned with divination, prophecy and astrological prediction named after a major figure in Shi'ite esotericism and purported to be the founder of occult science in Islam.

Du'a   Prayer of supplication which often uses an intercessor or invokes a blessing. Any prayer which is not *salat*.

Dunya   The world; often used by Muslims to indicate being lost in the world; as opposition to a life where one practices the *din*.

Durus   Meetings held to obtain both knowledge and proficiency in the arts and sciences of Islam, usually with a trained leader or Sufi teacher.

Fatwa   Legal opinion concerning an aspect of Islamic law issued by an *alim*.

Fiqh   Jurisprudence; the science of interpreting *shari'a*.

Fitra   Essential human nature or goodness. The natural state of human beings which is in harmony with God's will.

Futuwwa   A Sufi virtue that has some similarities to chivalry and charity. It emphasizes honesty, peacefulness, gentleness, generosity even in poverty, avoidance of complaints and hospitality in life.

Ginan   The devotional songs of the Ishmailis composed in a large variety of languages in which Indian traditional imagery is used side by side with the philosophical vocabulary of the tradition.

Hadith   Report of the sayings or deeds of the Prophet passed on by his Companions. The Hadith collections are second only to the Qur'an as a source of authority.

Hadra   A Sufi circle in which the names of Allah are recited or chanted, usually with rhythmic body movements .

Hakim   Wisdom. Derived from the name of Allah, Al-Hakim, the Wise.

Halal   Permitted or allowed by God.

Harakat   Literally 'motions', it refers to the short vowel marks that appear in Qur'anic Arabic.

Haram   Forbidden by God.

Hijab   The head covering traditionally worn by Muslim women as a symbol of Islamic identity, for modesty or simply for cultural reasons.

Hikmat   Also known as Unani, a medical system developed from the traditions of ancient Egypt and Mesopotamia. When the Mongols invaded Persia and Central Asia, many scholars and physicians of Unani fled to India where it is still practised.

Ibtihalat   A form of Egyptian religious folk music.

Iftar   The daily evening meal which breaks the sawm (fasting) during the Islamic month of Ramadan.

Ihsan   The perfection of character sought by a devout Muslim.

Ijaaza   A form of certification from an *alim* or *shaikh* that confirms that the student is authorized to teach in a particular area of knowledge.

Ijtihad   Technical term in Islamic law that describes the process of making a legal decision by independent interpretation.

Ilahiya   Traditional Ottoman musical praise of Allah still used by Bosnian Muslims and in other parts of East Europe.

Imam   Leader of the community; title given to the founders of the four schools of law; a leader of ritual prayers; an honorific for a religious scholar; used by the Shi'a as a title for the spiritual successors of Ali.

Iman   Faith.

Inshad   A form of religious singing associated with Sufis.

Inshad Dini   Traditional religious hymnody.

Inshallah   By the will of God.

Iqama   The second call to Islamic Prayer, given immediately before the prayer begins.

Islam   Submission to God.

Isnad   The chain of authorities that authenticate the sayings or actions of the Prophet that forms part of a hadith.

Istigfar   Repentance.

Jahilliyah   A state of ignorance or godless society used to describe pre-Islamic Arabia, but also used amongst contemporary Islamic movements to describe the condition of secular western societies.

Jubba   The traditional overcoat worn by scholars and students.

Julus   Processions that take place on the occasion of Muhammad's birthday.

Kaaba   The cube-shaped shrine at Makkah and the spatial focus for all Muslims in prayer; variously believed to have been created by Abraham or Adam for the worship of God.

Khalifa   Arabic term denoting the notion of deputy or successor. Formerly used for the rulers of the Muslim community. During the rapid growth of the community into an empire, the term came to mean imperial sovereignty combining both political and religious authority. It is also used in Sufism to denote authority to teach and initiate conferred on a *murid* by his master. Human beings are also God's *khalifa* or representatives on earth.

Khalwa   Sufi retreats traditionally conducted for 40 days.

Khanqah   A Sufi centre, usually the domicile and teaching location of a Shaikh.

Khatib   Arabic term used to describe a person who delivers the sermon during the Friday prayer.

Khawf   The station associated with the fear of God and one of the stages on the Sufi path.

Kufr   Literally 'hiding the Truth', used to describe a non-Muslim, but carries another meaning; that of a person who refuses to accept the Truth of God.

Kuttab   An Islamic elementary school frequently attached to a mosque or situated above a fountain where boys are instructed on the Qur'an.

La illaha illa'Llah   The first part of the confession of faith (*shahada*), meaning that 'there is no god but God' and the most common form of *dhikr*.

Langar A communal free kitchen often found at a Sufi centre or shrine in South Asia.

Madhdhab The four Muslim schools of law and other schools of thought within Islam.

Madrasa A theological college where Muslims study to become members of the *ulama*.

Majzub A holy fool; someone whose state of divine intoxication renders them unfit for the world.

Maqamat The stages or disciplines through which a Sufi is guided by his or her teacher; a musical term for melodic modes.

Mayatim Funeral gatherings.

Mazar The tomb of a prophet, saint or companion of the Prophet.

Mehdi/Mahdi An apocalyptic saviour figure expected to herald in a final redemption of God's people. Usually associated with Shi'a Muslims but often appearing in Sufi narratives of the end time.

Milad/Mawlid The annual celebration of Muhammad's birthday traditionally observed in most Muslim countries.

Mu'adhdhin The person who traditionally calls Muslims to prayer from the mosque.

Mubtahil A performer of supplicatory prayer.

Mujawwad A melodically Qur'anic recitation.

Munshid A traditional chanter of hymns in Arabic.

Munshidin Ritual singers in the Burhaniya *Hadra*.

Muqaddam An Arabic title, adopted in some Islamic cultures, for an official or a non-religious position in a religious order or movement.

Muqri Qur'an teacher and reciter.

Muraqaba Meditation directed towards the person of the Shaikh.

Murid The followers of a Sufi spiritual leader.

Murshid A Sufi master or teacher.

Mushaf A 'codex' or a collection of written sheets sometimes used to describe the Qur'an as a piece of written material as opposed to its contents.

Nisba Affiliation to a Sufi order or a spiritual affinity to a particular prophet, saint or spiritual state.

Pir See *Shaikh*. Urdu for a Sufi teacher.

Qari Person who recites the Qur'an with the proper rules of recitation.

Qasa'id A form of traditional Sufi poetry placed to music.

Qiraat Literally: 'the readings', one of the seven recognised methods of recitation of the Qur'an.

Quftan A Middle-Eastern style tunic or kaftan.

Qur'an The sacred scripture of Muslims. The final and complete revelation of Allah.

Ramadan The month-long fast from the hours of sunrise to sunset maintained in the month of the same name; the most sacred period for Muslims when the Qur'an was revealed for the first time to Muhammad; one of the five pillars of Islam.

Salaf as-Salih   The pious ancestors usually used to refer to the first three generations of Muslims.

Salawat   Traditional forms of praise to the Prophet.

Sama/Sema   Sufi religious performance consisting of music and rhythmic body movements.

Shahada   The confession of faith: 'there is no god but God; and Muhammad is His messenger'; the first of the five pillars of Islam and the essential requirement to be a Muslim.

Shaikh   The title given to a Sufi teacher.

Shari'a(h)   The principles and application of Muslim law, including religious obligations.

Shaytan   The one who tempts human beings away from the remembrance of God. Can be applied to Iblis, the fallen djinn who refused to pay homage to Adam or to a condition of the soul.

Shi'a   The party of Ali; the second largest group of Muslims. They believe that Ali and his direct descendents are the rightful heirs to Muhammad's religious authority.

Silsila   The chain of authority back to Muhammad that supplies authenticity to a *tariqa*.

Sohbet   Turkish. Preaching or didactic discourse.

Sufi   One who practices *tasawwuf*.

Sufi khulwat   A theosophical term which can be defined as, 'to speak to God secretly'. In Sufi terminology 'khalwat' means by the Shaikh's order and approval to spend time in isolation or retreat.

Sunna   'Custom' as in the traditions of the Prophet and the second source of religious authority for Sunni Muslims.

Sunni   One who follows *sunna*; also used as a title for the numerically dominant group of Muslims who have accepted the caliphate of Abu Bakr.

Taifa   An independent Muslim-ruled principality in Iberia.

Tajwid   Arabic word for elocution, meaning proper pronunciation during recitation, as well as recitation at a moderate speed. It is a set of rules which govern how the Qur'an should be read.

Taqlid   Blind imitation of the *ulama* without self-reflection.

Tariqa   The various organized or collective disciplines for the practice of *tasawwuf*; Sufi orders.

Tasawwuf   The collective title used both for the schools and the science of purification of the self.

Tawashih   Improvised supplications to or praises of Allah or Muhammad.

Tawhid   The central Islamic doctrine of the unity and uniqueness of Allah

Tawhid al-rububiyya   Maintaining oneness of the Lordship of Allah.

Tawhid al-uluhiyya   Maintaining oneness of the worship of Allah.

Tekke   A Turkish Sufi lodge.

Tilawar   A recitation of the Qur'an.

Turath   A heritage or tradition usually applied to cultural norm.

Ulama   A body of religious scholars or Muslim clerics; plural of *alim*.

Umma   The worldwide community of Muslims.

Urs   The celebration commemorating a Sufi saint, usually held on his or her death-day.

Wassalamu Alaykum   'May the peace of God be with you.' Muslim greeting to each other.

Wazifa   A form of personal prayer often consisting of God's names and usually recited after salat.

Zahir   The external or apparent meaning of the Qur'an.

Zawiya   Arabic. A Sufi centre or lodge consisting of a Shaikh and his *murids* or *a khalifa* entrusted to expand the order.

Index

Where indexed terms appear in both Arabic and Turkish within the book, page references in the index will appear next to the Arabic entry